"I....commend you for undertaking the pro~~ject of writing a book about~~ that critical event in my country's history – the mutiny of 1964. Many things have been said and written about the origins of the mutiny, its principal characters and the way it was finally put down. I do welcome any objective research into Tanzania's early history as an independent nation. The book will not only satisfy the curious but also enrich our archives."

HE Benjamin Mkapa (former President of the United Republic of Tanzania)

"An extremely useful addition to the history of the period....it is a very good account of what Tanzania and the British Officers were faced with; [and] an example of how quick military intervention at a modest level, can produce the desired result. The action is in notable contrast to the UN and international reaction to some of today's crises which would not have developed into the bloodbaths they have if resolve had been shown.... I was in Aden in the mid 60s and the Mutiny was widely discussed."

General the Lord Guthrie of Craigiebank, GCB LVO OBE (former Chief of the Defence Staff)

"This is a valuable historical record of a long forgotten army mutiny in Tanzania so soon after independence. Its importance is enhanced by the fact that the two authors write from direct experience, MacRae as a young diplomat in Dar es Salaam and Laurence as a young officer in the intervention force. It is a stimulating and interesting read."

The Rt. Hon. the Lord Luce, GCVO (former Minister for Africa)

"A remarkable reconstruction of a short but important event in the history of Tanzania and East Africa. Solidly researched, the action unfolds with the pace and excitement of a good adventure story."

Sir John Coles, GCMG (former Permanent Under Secretary and Head of HM Diplomatic Service)

"This book describes the action and diplomacy involved in a conspicuously successful British exploit... forty years later, these events may seem to have been only a 'little local difficulty'; but at the time, they were of great significance... the British action enabled Nyerere to reassert his authority as President. Tanzania has (subsequently) enjoyed a political stability and national unity unusual in Africa."

Sir Colin Imray, KBE CMG, former British High Commissioner to Tanzania

"The Dar Mutiny is a masterpiece not only of writing but as a historical work. It reads like a novel, captivating, vivid, graphic, descriptive, and where appropriate, witty. I was impressed by the painstaking research and the utter fairness towards the military and civilians involved. The reflections and epilogue are balanced and sound".

Rémy Gorge, Director, United Nations Peacekeeping Force (Congo) 1962-1964

THE DAR MUTINY OF 1964

AuthorHouse™
1663 Liberty Drive
Bloomington, IN 47403
www.authorhouse.com
Phone: 1-800-839-8640

First published by the Book Guild Ltd. in 2007 in the UK
This edition first published by AuthorHouse 4/2/2010

ISBN: 978-1-4490-9875-9 (sc)
ISBN: 978-1-4490-9876-6 (hc)
ISBN: 978-1-4490-9877-3 (e)

Library of Congress Control Number: 2010903632

Printed in the United States of America
Bloomington, Indiana

This book is printed on acid-free paper.

THE DAR MUTINY OF 1964

And the Armed Intervention that Ended it

Tony Laurence
with
Christopher MacRae

authorHOUSE®

Contents

Foreword

This is a fascinating story by two people who were personally involved, about a little-known episode in the dismantling of the British Empire and our subsequent relations with our erstwhile colonies. Though I was for part of 1964, a Minister in the Foreign Office, I am ashamed to say that I have little personal recollection of the Mutiny and its aftermath. If the armed services had not been so successful in suppressing the mutiny and pacifying Dar, there would certainly have been serious repercussions in the neighbouring countries at a critical moment in the early days of their independence. That the result was so satisfactory, shows once again how the Royal Navy and the Royal Air Force can react quickly, improvise in very difficult circumstances and in the aftermath of a success, behave in such a way as not to alienate the civilian population.

All in all a remarkable story and a very good read.

Lord Carrington, KG, GCMG, CH, MC, PC.

The road
to the north

Bongoya
Island

HMS *Cambrian's* firing position

shallows

⚓ HMS *Centaur's* assault anchorage

Colito
Barracks

The
landing
site

MSASANI
BAY

6°45 S

Oyster
Bay

3

2

Selander Bridge

Miles

1

State House

0

N

The
Stadium

Dar es
Salaam
Harbour

The
Airport

39°15 E

Dar '64 - The Restoration of Order

viii

List of Abbreviations

ADC	Aide de Camp
ASP	Afro-Shirazi Party
CRO	Commonwealth Relations Office
DTG	date/time/group - time of sending message
EACSO	East African Common Services Organisation
FOME	Flag Officer Middle East
GPMG	general purpose machine-gun
HF	high frequency
KAR	King's African Rifles
LZT	Landing Zone Team
MoD	Ministry of Defence
NASA	National Aeronautics and Space Administration
NCO	non-commissioned officer
NUTA	National Union of Tanganyika Workers
Orbat	order of battle
OAU	Organisation of African Unity
PRO	Public Record Office
RSM	Regimental Sergeant Major
SLR	self-loading rifle
TANU	Tanganyika African National Union
TBC	Tanganyika Broadcasting Corporation
TFL	Tanganyika Federation of Labour
TIS	Tanganyika Information Services

TPDF	Tanzania People's Defence Force
UHF	ultra high frequency
UN	United Nations
URMF	United Republic of Tanganyika and Zanzibar
ZNP	Zanzibar Nationalist Party
ZPPP	Zanzibar and Pemba People's Party

Acknowledgements

This story developed as I wrote it. A number of far-sighted people saw clearly that there was much more to be found than I at first realised, guiding and encouraging me. They know who they are. I am deeply grateful for their support.

My wife, Nicola, and our children tolerated my absences and helped me as the story progressed. I met a large number of marines and sailors who served with me in HMS *Centaur*, soldiers who suffered the shock of mutiny, and civilians whose lives were so suddenly thrown into chaos. I spoke with or wrote to over 100. Most are listed in the bibliography. I simply could not have produced this book without them.

Then came the hardest part: the writing, for which I have no professional training. (My previous book had gone through on the the nod from the first publisher I approached, to become a standard textbook. This one would need a lot more effort.) But again a handful of people guided me throughout the rewrites and edits, the clarifications and explanations, until I found Book Guild Publishing, who agreed to take it on. AuthorHouse helped me publish this second edition. I could not have done this all alone.

But I will name one person, who became closely involved. Christopher MacRae came into the project around halfway through and soon began to beef up the 'shoreside' viewpoints, trawling the CRO files in the PRO. He brought style and clarity to the text throughout, and took a major part in drafting the final summing-up chapters.

Prologue
The Single Meeting

One sweltering evening in January 1964, President Nyerere of Tanganyika called his Cabinet together at short notice to give formal thanks to two foreigners. They and their men had restored order in his country after an army mutiny sparked off by the blunderings of his Defence Minister. After a crowded week of tension, doubt and chaos, the five main actors came face to face for the first and only time: a great and humane political leader, an ardent nationalist, a decorated World War II marine, a naval officer and a quiet British diplomat. They knew little of each other. It was the dawn of African independence and the final stages of colonialism. They struggled to make sense of the unforseen challenges they had faced so successfully. Then they separated and went their several ways, some never to meet again. The President was left to try to fathom what had gone wrong, and to re-establish the political authority he had so nearly lost.

Introduction

This book describes an unusual operation undertaken by British troops and sailors in Tanganyika in early 1964 to end the mutiny of the Tanganyika army. The authors were both present during the events, which they witnessed from different angles.

Tony Laurence, then aged 33, was serving as Signal Communications Officer in HMS *Centaur*, the aircraft carrier from which the British intervention was launched. His post involved ship's duties as a seaman officer and head of the communications department. He was also the signals specialist in the task force command, so was well placed to follow and understand what was happening off Dar es Salaam during the dramatic few days of the British military operation.

Christopher MacRae, then 26, was a newly-appointed member of the British High Commission's diplomatic staff in Dar es Salaam, and was a specialist in African politics. He knew many of the civilian actors in this drama, both British and Tanganyikan. At one stage he found himself playing a minor but nevertheless important role at the start of the military operations.

The authors did not meet (or even hear of each other) until some 40 years after the Dar mutiny. To separate their personal views from historic fact in the narrative that follows, their own eyewitness accounts appear as clearly distinguishable comments scattered throughout the book.

3

1

Mutiny at Colito Barracks

The 1st Battalion of the Tanganyikan Rifles mutinied during the night of Sunday 19/20 January 1964. The takeover was planned logically and in some detail. First, the mutineers would take the guardroom. They would seize arms and if possible enlist the guards, before arresting all the duty officers. Then they would take the whole barracks by sounding a general alarm and a fire call. This would bring everybody out onto the parade ground. The junior non-commissioned officers (NCOs) and *askaris* (Swahili for 'soldier') would then be induced to join the mutiny. Officers and senior NCOs would be intercepted on their way in from their quarters. A party would go to the Army Commander's residence to arrest the British Brigadier.

The third goal was to take over the nearby capital, Dar es Salaam. Teams would be made up to do this and transport allocated. Groups of mutineers would first take over from the guards protecting the President, Julius Nyerere, and Vice President Kawawa. Roadblocks would be established at choke points, especially at the bridge in Oyster Bay, on the way into the city, and on the road to the airport. Key buildings would be taken over, including the Telephone Exchange and the Broadcasting Corporation. The army staff officers who were quartered in the city would then be arrested.

To prevent any external intervention, they would then take the Airport and guard against any attack from the sea. A further effort would be made to persuade the 2nd Battalion in Tabora and the independent Company at Nachingwea to join the mutiny; and the police would be made to cooperate or at least remain neutral. Finally there would be a summit negotiation with the President to secure their three aims: a very substantial pay rise for soldiers; the immediate dismissal of all the British officers (to be replaced by Tanganyikan officers chosen by the troops); and assurances of no subsequent victimisation of the mutineers. This would be negotiation under duress.

No copy of such a plan was ever discovered – indeed it is improbable that there was ever a written plan – but it is virtually certain that the mutiny was planned along these lines. In the event, it developed smoothly and in logical sequence, and there would have been no time to improvise during the first few hours of dramatic action. Moreover, all this took place long before the era of mobile phones, or even of personal shortwave radios, and the takeover of the city involved the use of groups of dispersed troops out of direct touch with the ringleaders. As to the mutineers' long-term aims, nothing they did subsequently demonstrated that they intended to take more power than was necessary to improve, as they saw it, their lot. But they certainly demanded the pay rise, the removal of the British officers, and a guarantee against victimisation. These matters were later to be brought up repeatedly in their demands.

Mobilisation for the mutiny began during the evening of Sunday 19 January. The leading plotters, under a Sergeant Ilogi, gathered in an Asian-owned *duka* (provision store) for a final briefing, and dispersed shortly after midnight to begin operations. Their first requirement was to seize arms, all of which were under guard. The plan to do so was simple but effective. The orderly officer of the day was Second Lieutenant Makaranga, a young Israeli-trained officer. At around midnight, he had inspected the sentries on the armouries, transport areas and guardroom. Then he turned in to sleep in the duty officer's room, where the keys of the armouries were kept in a locked box to which he held the key. Soon afterwards, three unarmed soldiers woke him up violently, threatened to strangle him, grabbed the key to the key-box, then forced him, half dressed, to the guardroom where he was pushed into a cell. He was the first officer to be captured.

As they were unlocking the arms in the guardroom, the three soldiers were challenged by a Corporal on duty. He too was quickly overpowered and pushed into the cell along with Makaranga. The three mutineers were then joined by others who rounded up the sentries on watch and the telephone operator, shoving them into the cell too. A regimental policeman happened to call by at the guardroom and was also overcome. The mutineers worked on the minds of the imprisoned men, quickly convincing them that their interest lay in joining the action. By 1 a.m., the cell was empty again: the security arrangements at the barracks had been completely overcome.

But there remained an unforeseen problem: the Duty Field Officer, the senior officer on duty, was nowhere to be found. With him still at large, it would be dangerous to take any action beyond the guardroom which might be detected by an alert observer. So the Field Officer had somehow to be neutralised before the takeover of the barracks was attempted. The only Asian officer in the battalion, Sandhurst-trained Captain Kashmiri, was on field duty that week. He had completed an inspection of the ceremonial guard at State House near the seafront in the city, and had then visited the detachment guarding an arms shipment. Returning to Colito Barracks, he noticed that the main gate and guardhouse areas were in darkness, but that was not unusual. Challenged by the sentry at the gate, he identified himself and drove in. His car was stopped, the door was opened, and he was told to get out. At first he refused. But he was forced out at gunpoint, while threats were shouted about him being 'sent back to Bombay'.[1] With Kashmiri's arrest the first phase of the mutiny had been successfully completed; the more so since the guards had switched sides so easily.

7

The mutineers' next step was to gain control of the whole barracks. It contained about 600 junior officers, NCOs and other ranks, some with their families. The obvious way was to muster them on the parade ground. Shortly after 1 a.m., the general alarm was switched on and a bugler blew a fire call. The soldiers dressed hastily and ran to the parade ground, falling in by companies. While this was happening, pre-briefed groups of mutineers intercepted the British NCOs, diverting them to the cells. Within each company, armed men announced the takeover, arresting anyone who seemed unsympathetic to their aims and dispersing the rest.

The alarms had been heard in the officers' quarters, which lay outside the main camp, up a low hill on the other side of a main road. Some junior Tanganyikan officers at once walked into the barracks from the officers' mess, only to be detained as they arrived. At first, they were imprisoned in the Education Centre; later, they were transferred to the cells. The British officers lived in married quarters further up the hill. On hearing the alarms, they drove down to the barracks in their own cars. It had been planned that they would be captured as they arrived at the main gate, but several cars arrived together, swamping the ambush party. The street lights had been turned off to hide the ambush, but Company Commander Major Leavitt Taylor saw what was happening and just had time to swing round and get away. The mutineers shot at his car but narrowly missed. He got back to his house, intending to protect his family as best he could, but saw a Land Rover drive past to the Brigadier's house and heard battering on the door. Realising he could do nothing useful he stayed put. A foot patrol of five mutineers later came to take him away, ordering his family to stay where they were. On the way back to the barracks the group stopped to argue about whether to shoot their captive. Deciding not to, they searched him carefully and then took him to the guardroom cells to join about 30 other detainees.

The Commanding Officer of the battalion, Lieutenant-Colonel Mans, alone in his quarters, was also woken by the alarm and fire call. Dressing quickly, he reasoned that an attack on the barracks armoury was much more likely than any fire. The senior British NCO, the Regimental Sergeant Major (RSM), had arrived by car and was trying – without success – to telephone the barracks exchange. Suddenly, the Army Commander, Brigadier Douglas, came on the line, asking about the alarms. The two at once agreed that Mans would deal with the problem in the barracks (whatever it might be) while Douglas and his family made for the city.

Mans and the RSM drove straight down to the barracks. But just short of the camp, they were stopped by about ten armed men, and arrested. The Commanding Officer tried to make a break for it, but ran into some barbed wire in the dark and was recaptured. There were cries of 'Shoot him'. But a warrant officer named Kabwegere shouted authoritatively: 'Don't shoot him, he's the Colonel'; and his view prevailed. The two Britons were forced into the already crowded guardroom cell.

The commander of C Company, Major Mike Callaghan, evaded capture. Driving towards the barracks still half asleep, he was shocked to see the driver of the car in front being bundled out at bayonet point. He accelerated away, scattering a group of *askaris* who were approaching his car. Shots rang out. He heard, or felt, two hit the car before he was clear. Reaching the main road, he turned north up the coast and away from the city, lest road blocks had been set up in the more obvious direction. One of his tyres had been shot out, so progress was slow. Fearing pursuit, he turned off the road and hid his car behind some bushes. Then he walked to a house with a telephone line, woke the people inside, and made four crucial phone calls. The first was to Lt. Col. Montgomery, Douglas's deputy, in his quarters in Dar. He then called Major Marciandi, the army's British operational staff officer; the duty Aide de Camp (ADC) of the President and the Commanding Officer of the 2nd Battalion, up-country at Tabora. These were the first warnings that the mutiny had happened.

After making these calls, Callaghan went outside. He could hear a Land Rover moving slowly up the road, presumably looking for him. He hid for some time until it went away, before emerging to drive a further five miles north to a coastal bar/restaurant owned by a friend. Soon he learned that the mutineers had reached the city. Fearing for his wife and children, and seeing nothing else he could usefully do, he asked to be driven back to somewhere near Colito Barracks, where he was dropped off. Then he walked on alone towards a group of mutineers standing beside the main road. They fired a warning shot over his head, but he kept approaching steadily, arms raised. He was arrested and taken to the guardroom to join the other British prisoners.

Earlier on, in the cells, Lt. Col. Mans faced some hard decisions. While dressing, he had armed himself with a pistol and 12 rounds of ammunition – and the mutineers had not searched him. It would be possible, by 'fishing' through the bars of the cell, to get hold of two smoke grenades used for training. There were moments when only a few of the mutineers were close at hand, so the officers could probably escape and retake the guardroom. It might then be possible to take further action to restore order. But there were definite dangers in attempting a breakout. For a start, there were around 90 women and children in the married quarters. Mans had seen troops mutiny twice during World War II and knew how quickly and dangerously shooting might spread. Speaking formally as their CO, he asked his imprisoned fellow officers, both British and Tanganyikan, to think carefully about an attempted breakout and any follow-up action. After reflection, they all realised the hopelessness of their position and recommended that no action be taken. Mans agreed. He ordered that there should be no attempt to escape.

As stragglers were brought in, the cell became very crowded. Some of the mutineers were hostile and aggressive and a sentry kept a machine-gun trained on the door. Other machine-guns covered the window from outside. The prisoners' fate, as well as that of their families in the officers' quarters, lay utterly beyond their control. They could only await events.

After his brief telephone talk with Mans, Brigadier Douglas had quickly dressed, telling his wife and 6-year-old daughter to get up. Listening outside the door, he could hear shouting and a few shots. Then there was silence, followed by the sound of someone apparently addressing the troops. Next came more shooting, getting closer, some of it from groups of mutineers moving up the hill towards the quarters. It was obviously time to go; but Douglas could not risk taking his family out by car since there was only one road – which was sure to be guarded. They must get away on foot. As he left the house by the back door, Douglas was horrified to see his batman looming out of the darkness, carrying a hefty *panga* (as machetes are called in East Africa). The tension lessened when the man explained that had come to protect the family – and he did indeed stick with them faithfully right to the end.

The stumble in the dark through the rough scrub on the hillside was a nightmare, and they fell repeatedly. Eventually the bedraggled group reached the house of Tom and Sheila Unwin, still accompanied by their *panga*-wielding servant. Unwin, an expatriate official from the Ministry of Foreign Affairs, let them in and offered the exhausted adults a stiff vodka. From there, Douglas telephoned Stephen Miles, the British Acting High Commissioner, to describe what had happened and to confirm that a mutiny had broken out. The group were then driven along back roads to Lt. Col. Montgomery's house in town, from which Douglas had his wife and child taken on to the Australian High Commission to seek refuge. There seemed to be no mutineers in the city yet. The two senior officers were soon joined by Major Marciandi and other staff officers, with their families. They made another round of telephone calls. The first was to let Miles know where they now were. He and his deputy, Peter Carter, soon arrived. They were briefed on developments and it was agreed

11

that Carter should take the officers' families to the High Commissioner's official residence for safety, while Miles went back to his office to report to London.

Douglas tried to contact the President and Vice President, only to learn that both men had gone into hiding. After some reflection, he rang Defence Minister Oscar Kambona, to tell him of the mutiny and discuss what to do about it. Douglas reported both at the time and in subsequent records, that the Minister 'sounded surprised and disconcerted to hear my voice'. This phrase was later to have a damaging effect on Kambona's reputation, at least in the eyes of some of the British. It was taken by them to imply that he must have been plotting with the mutineers, and so would have expected Douglas to have been locked up by now. This in turn was taken as evidence of Kambona's involvement in *planning* the mutiny. But objectively, 'evidence' hinging on a surprised reaction to a totally unexpected telephone call in the middle of the night can hardly be regarded as compelling. All accounts at least agree that Kambona and the Brigadier then discussed the wisdom of ordering the 2nd Battalion down from Tabora to quell the mutiny. Douglas's next call was to the Commanding Officer in Tabora.

Now the plotters had the whole barracks under control, they could move on to the third stage of their plan: to take control of the city. State House was their first target. Transport was organised and several squads were given their instructions. There is no record that any Tanganyikan soldier refused to serve the new leadership. Some may well have had their doubts, but by using a mixture of threats and inducements, the mutineers had no difficulty in mustering sufficient manpower for the tasks ahead.

Sergeant Ilogi himself led a strong unit of 25 soldiers to State House – only to face a serious setback. The presidential security staff had already been warned by Major Callaghan of the mutiny at about 2 a.m.. There had followed a brief period of indecision while President Nyerere dressed, called in Vice President

Kawawa, and debated what to do. The murder of the President Sylvanus Olympio of Togo by mutinous soldiers only a year earlier was fresh in their minds. They may have calculated that as the President had not been directly involved in army matters, members of his ministerial team should be in the front line to deal with this crisis. Should the trouble at Colito turn out to be an attempt at a political *coup d'état*, it might be wiser for Nyerere to remain above the fray, perhaps held in reserve to negotiate some compromise. The Tanganyika African National Union (TANU) might not be involved, but could perhaps be mobilised against, or even in some sort of partnership with, a new regime. Many complex factors were involved, yet too few hard facts were known to make rational decisions – and there was very little time to weigh them all up. Reflective by nature, Nyerere needed time to think. The two men's minds were sharply concentrated when they were told that heavy vehicles were approaching. With only minutes to spare, they were shepherded out of a back door by the Chief of Police to seek refuge.

Nyerere eventually reached his holiday beach bungalow on the coast some miles south, where he lay low for two days. His decision was later criticised by some, not least because he had left his family behind. However, most leaders would tend to follow professional security advice in such dire circumstances – as, indeed, did President George W. Bush on 11 September 2001. Some have seen less justification for Nyerere's decision to abandon his family. But he could judge the actions of his own people better than most of his critics: no harm whatever came to his wife and children (unlike those of President Jawawa of Gambia some years later, who were kidnapped during a military uprising while Jawawa was abroad).

The British Police superintendent who had brought his men out of Zanzibar later described how he arrived at Dar's Central Police Station that night and found it deserted.[2] A few policemen were walking about outside, wearing civilian clothes. He tried telephoning various ministries but could get no reply. Finally, he rang

State House to be told by a servant: 'The President has been taken away by Shaidi [the Chief of Police]. What shall we do with the children?' It seemed strange that someone so devoted to his family as Nyerere had not sent them to safety, or even left instructions. Sullivan had no answer to the servant's question. Nyerere later justified his actions by insisting on the need for the Head of State to be kept in reserve as the crisis unfolded.

Meanwhile, at State House, the newly-appointed Head of the Special Branch, Emilio Mzena, assumed the role of Presidential Aide. To gain time, he intercepted the mutineers, and made a number of 'helpful' suggestions. The one which found most favour was to contact Oscar Kambona, but the mutineers did not know where he was to be found. Mzena offered to take them to the Minister's house. But he added that he would have to drive them there himself, and had only a small car. There was further discussion about whether a seat should be left free for Kambona should the mutineers want to take him on with them. Eventually, much later, Ilogi and only two of his fellow mutineers set off with Mzena to meet the Minister. Kambona, already warned, was waiting for them. Anxious to avoid violence or a further search for the President, Kambona managed to convince the mutineers that the next step should be direct discussions between himself, as the Minister responsible for Defence, and the new commanders of the army and the 1st Battalion. It was agreed that a meeting should be held at Colito Barracks: the mutineers were settling for less than their hoped-for discussions with the President.

They set off as dawn began to break over the sea. Before long, Kambona found himself addressing a crowded meeting in the barracks. Responding to complaints about 'colonial conditions under a colonial regime', he promised that there would be immediate remedial action. British officers would be sent home and substantial pay rises would be granted. He offered no resistance to the mutineers' demands – and it is difficult to see how he could have done in the circumstances, surrounded as he was by armed mutineers.

While these negotiations were going on, other mutineers were tightening their grip on the city. Two groups set up roadblocks on the Morogoro and Airport roads, the main arteries leading out of Dar es Salaam. Others took over the Tanganyika Broadcasting House, the Cable and Wireless building, the main Post Office, and the Standard Bank (believed to be holding government financial reserves). Having agreed on its importance, they also took over the Telephone Exchange, though they had not agreed about the need to shut it down. At first, they seemed not to understand how it worked; but by 8 a.m., they had firmer control and only a few calls were being allowed through.

Once they had seized these key installations, the mutineers turned to the police stations. The city's sub-stations were taken without difficulty, and the men on duty sent home. But there was trouble at the main station where a doughty woman officer refused to hand over the keys to the armoury and was badly beaten up for her pains. Next, a group was sent to take over the airport. Sentries were also posted outside foreign embassies. Diplomats arriving at their offices were surprised to be denied access; a Yugoslav diplomat rashly brandished a revolver at some mutineers and was struck with a rifle butt. By dawn, there was no doubt who was controlling Dar es Salaam.

One of the first foreigners to be stopped was John Bridgman, the British manager of the Tanganyikan branch of an insurance company.[3] Dawn was breaking as he drove out to the Airport to catch an early flight to the southern to town of Mbeya on a routine business trip. He was flagged down by armed and uniformed men whose attitude left him in no doubt that they should be taken seriously. Forced out of his car at bayonet point, he saw some soldiers beating up a Goan. Bridgman's captors established that he was no escaping British officer, just a civilian. The tension eased, and he was told to go home: there would be no flights out today. Once free, his first priority was to call at the house of a senior British expatriate. Together, they began spreading the word among the British community that some sort of *coup d'état* was

15

happening, and that civilians should stay at home. Most of the families they warned stocked up with provisions from their local stores while they still could. Some telephoned the British High Commission, thus starting to create the informal network which would keep the High Commission informed of what was going on around the city.

Meanwhile, in Douglas's temporary headquarters, Major Marciandi had been working on the plan agreed with Kambona to get the 2nd Battalion down from Tabora. It could have been involved in the mutiny, but it was of a completely different character and tribal mix, so there seemed a fair chance that it would prove loyal to the Government. At least it was worth a try. Dar airport was still open as far as anybody knew, and East African Airways had three civilian Dakota aircraft available. Clearance to use them was still needed from Nairobi, but was soon granted. However, the plan was frustrated when the flight crews could not reach the airport because of the roadblock. The alternative of trying to get aircraft in from Entebbe or Nairobi was considered, only to be discarded because it would take too long. Then news arrived that Dar airport had been taken by the mutineers, so the first project was abandoned. The possibility of summoning troops from Kenya or Uganda also faded. In any case, they would have been summoned only if the Tanganyika Government had asked for them; and there was no sign yet of such a request. It was difficult to see what else could be done to restore order. In any case, by now Douglas and his group of staff officers faced the even more urgent problem of their own safety.

Each time the British officers placed a telephone call, they had to tell the operator their own number. From the delays and background noise in the central exchange, they had to assume that their calls were being monitored. Their wives and children had already been taken to safety, and at about 4.30 a.m., the staff officers decided they should move on. They split into two groups; and moving from safe house to safe house, they continued their

16

attempts to summon help. At about 6.50 a.m., they were discovered by the mutineers. Most were arrested. But Douglas, Marciandi and the Paymaster, Major Lovell-Butt, escaped. Douglas had to dive through several hedges, tearing his uniform to shreds. Eventually, the trio reached the Acting British High Commissioner's residence, where Mrs. Miles greeted them. She took their arms and locked them away. Douglas's badly scratched back was bathed and clean clothes were found for him. Another officer who had just returned from leave, and a corporal from the headquarters' staff, joined them. The group in the Miles's house also included Sullivan, the former Zanzibar Police superintendent, and his family. There were already about 50 refugees sheltering in the house, mainly women and children, including a new-born baby.

Back in the British High Commission office, Stephen Miles had called in his key staff. Callaghan's early warning, relayed by Montgomery, had given the British diplomatic team a head start over the mutineers.

Christopher MacRae. *On arrival in Dar in February 1963, I had been allocated a flat in the Standard Bank building, only one block away from the office. My wife, Mette, and I were woken at 4 a.m. by a loud pounding on our door. At the same time the phone rang. I was wanted at the High Commission – urgently. Throwing on some clothes, I rushed round to the office through dark, empty streets. Stephen Miles briefed us and allocated tasks. By about 6 a.m. it was clear that we were in for a long and possibly dangerous crisis, so I rang Mette, and asked her to come round at once with our 2-week-old baby (nicknamed Mus) to the office for safety; we might be stuck there for some time. She had stocked up with nappies and baby food by the time I ran to the flat to collect her, and we walked back bearing Mus through the still-deserted streets to the office as it was getting light. They were allocated space in the Military Attaché's office where they were to spend two long days. There had been no time to gather provisions. In the office fridge, Mette found one tin of crab meat, and a bottle of gin – hardly ideal for breast-feeding ...*

To alert London was now the highest priority. The High Commission's communications system was still quite primitive, but luckily a direct telex line had just been installed to the Commonwealth Relations Office (CRO). By 4.45 a.m., the first message was cleared:-

From: British High Commission, Dar es Salaam
To: Commonwealth Relations Office
Copy to: Nairobi (Kenya), Kampala (Uganda), Political Officer Middle East Command Aden, and Washington (CRO please pass to all).
(Priority) EMERGENCY
Brigadier Douglas phoned me at 3.20 a.m. East African time, Monday, to say a mutiny had broken out at Colito Barracks, Dar es Salaam.
Several British Officers detained by rebels.
2 Have phoned Stanley, Nairobi [Deputy at the BHC, Kenya].

London, and the commander of the area's British Forces in Aden, were now alerted.

Notes

1   Nestor, N. and Luanda, E. *The Tanganyika Rifles Mutiny, January 1964*, p. 86.
2   Mans, Rowley: personal papers.
3   Bridgman, John: correspondence with author.

2

Tanganyika – The Peaceful Backwater

Mutinies and coups have all too often threatened the stability of nation states. Only rarely have such events been quickly and successfully reversed by the prompt intervention of foreign force. The mutiny of the Tanganyika Rifles in 1964 was one such case. Tanganyika had been independent for only two years. Although poor, without extensive natural resources, and lacking sufficient qualified administrators to be able to dispense altogether with expatriates, in Julius Nyerere it had an intelligent, humane and incorruptible leader. Suddenly, it faced a threat from its own army, which had mutinied.

This crisis was quickly resolved. It was little noticed by the world's media at the time and since then has been largely ignored by historians. Nevertheless, it proved a defining moment in the development of Tanganyika, shortly to become Tanzania. What follows is the story of the mutiny; how the Government reacted; and how a small British amphibious force responded at once to President Nyerere's request for help, put down the mutiny and quickly handed over control to African peacekeepers. Many lessons are more useful today than ever.

If in late 1963 you had asked experts on East Africa where trouble might be brewing, the last place they would have chosen would have been Tanganyika. It had achieved independence easily, had been spared serious inter-ethnic strife, and was politically calm.

To understand why, it is worth glancing very briefly at the four decades of British rule, as well as the two years following independence.

The treaty of Berlin of 1895 left Germany in uncontested control of the territory they had named Tanganyika. Learning from the Maji-Maji uprising of 1905–7 (in some ways the precursor of the Mau-Mau revolt in Kenya half a century later), the German colonial regime abandoned repressive policies in favour of a more enlightened programme promoting education and economic development. By 1914, there were some 4,000 German settlers. World War I transformed Tanganyika into a minor theatre of fighting between a small German-led force commanded by General Paul von Lettow-Vorbeck, and the British army with support from South Africa and India. Von Lettow's brilliant guerrilla campaign tied down some 160,000 Allied troops in East Africa, but Britain was eventually left in *de facto* control of the territory. In 1922, the League of Nations mandated Tanganyika to the 'British Empire, to be administered in the interests of peace, order and good government ... for the material and moral well-being of its inhabitants'.

In the hierarchy of needs of Britain's far-flung Empire, Tanganyika was not a high priority, being viewed as a territory the British were administering only temporarily. By 1925 the Governor, Donald Cameron, introduced a system of indirect rule, tried and tested in other parts of the Empire including West Africa. Its aim was described as being to 'train the natives that they may stand by themselves ... [and] build on tribal institutions ... suitable to the state of society'. However, the laudable goals of social and economic development were not matched by the necessary investment. For most of the mandate period, Britain was in dire economic straits itself.

By the 1930s, Tanganyikan society had become stratified by race. Europeans (by now mostly British, but including a few German settlers) dominated larger retail business and most other productive parts of the economy. They also administered the country. Asians, who had been encouraged to migrate from British India to provide skilled labour, clerks and accountants, soon controlled most of the local trade and minor retailing. Later, the more successful branched into running and owning coffee and sisal plantations. The indigenous Africans, apart from providing labour for the foreign-run farms and businesses, were left with small-scale agriculture. A few made their way as teachers and into the lower ranks of the civil service. Cameron's successors were apparently less high-minded than he, considering it sounder to 'deflect [African] energies and aspirations ... into the paths of social welfare and away from politics'.

It was inevitable that, sooner or later, a marginalised people would start to seek a new order in which the African majority would take power. The Bukoba Bahaya Union of educated local Africans was formed as early as 1924 in the fertile north-western corner of the country, and was followed by several other local groupings. The cross-tribal Tanganyika African Association sprang up in Dar and Tanga towards the end of the 1920s. However, none of these associations became politically active until after World War II. Large numbers of East African soldiers served with distinction during that war, although there were instances of unrest when the *askaris* were not treated well by their British officers and NCOs. Certainly the veterans returned home much better aware of what was happening in the rest of the world.

After the war, the mandate of the now defunct League of Nations was replaced by a British trusteeship under the new United Nations (UN) which expected the country to make progress towards self-government, and then independence. The British, while accepting these new political obligations, still believed that Tanganyika should not cost them too much, and that for the time being it might yet offer them economic and strategic advantages. In practice, however, the economy remained stagnant. A ten-year development plan was introduced in 1946, Britain hoping for increased supplies of low-cost agricultural products.

21

The colonial Government in Dar es Salaam soon realised that the racially skewed economy and the weak and unrepresentative Native Authorities were never going to work. So they developed policies which considerably influenced the last 15 years of British colonial rule. Efforts were made to bolster large-scale food production to provide job opportunities for the new school-leavers, and at the same time meet British post-war requirements for cheap sources of food. Most of these schemes failed, but at least they encouraged productivity gains. More importantly, the previous methods of compulsion were replaced by incentives and persuasion. The optimistic considered that the foundations of a sound economy were at last being laid. A serious, if belated, attempt was also made to develop both primary and secondary education, so as to encourage greater involvement by the African population in local administration and the cash economy. The new emphasis on education, however, turned out to be too little, too late. At independence – which arrived much sooner that most had expected – there was still a huge shortage of university-educated Africans ready to take over the administration of such a large country.

Another new Government policy was to strengthen local democracy. This proved just as difficult a task. The meagre resources earmarked for it were inevitably controlled from Dar es Salaam and the major provincial capitals, where there tended to be little enthusiasm for any devolution to the local level since neither the British-dominated administration nor the networks of Asian traders and entrepreneurs were keen to relinquish power and influence. In the 1950s an attempt was made to devolve real power to the existing Native Authorities, but the reforms did not work and were never taken too seriously. This failure was attributed by some to the colonial power's 'genteel racism', and by others to the weakness of the existing authorities. Be that as it may, the wind of change was, as Harold Macmillan later remarked, blowing throughout Africa, and time was running out for the British. In July 1954, several long-established ethnic interest groups coalesced to form TANU (Tanganyika Africa National Union). Its moment had come. The British had no effective alternative vehicle to offer the politically ambitious African population, so it was hardly surprising that by 1958 TANU had established 130 branches throughout the country.

The British tried to introduce what they called 'multi-racism'. This involved attempts to promote Africans to positions of real influence, especially within the country's administrative system, with British and Asians 'making way' for them. Many senior British administrators were well disposed to the senior Africans they worked with and supportive of their ambitions, but progress was too slow for many Africans.

By the mid-1950s, the door to independence was unlocked. On the one hand a strongly growing stream of frustrated African nationalists was denied effective political power; on the other, the British were anxious to rid themselves of unprofitable, indeed costly, foreign entanglements in East Africa and elsewhere. In the case of Tanganyika, one man led the campaign to win independence – and got it much sooner than anyone, including himself, had expected: Julius K. Nyerere. Precociously intelligent as a child, Nyerere was the son of Chief Burite of the Zanaki, one of the smallest of Tanganyika's 120 or so tribes. Given special educational opportunities at the Tabora Government School, he went on to Makerere in Uganda, then the only university-level college in East Africa. In 1949 he won a grant to Edinburgh University, where he was influenced by Fabian socialism, which nourished his lifelong ambition to create an African socialist utopia. He returned to Tanganyika in 1954, and before long had assumed the leadership of TANU (Tanganyika African National Union). His political ambitions, and the threat he represented to British rule, soon became obvious to the colonial authorities.

Nyerere first taught at St Francis College, a Roman Catholic secondary school near Dar es Salaam – hence, in part, his later affectionate public nickname of 'Mwalimu' (teacher). By 1955,

23

pressure was being exerted on the school governors to dismiss him as a troublemaking radical. Nyerere resigned to become a full-time politician. He joined a number of well-educated and intelligent colleagues in an energetic political campaign, easily outpacing efforts by the colonial Government to stop TANU's growing influence. At that stage, few nationalists expected the colonial regime to disappear soon: improvements in political representation were the main aim. Nyerere himself said as late as 1956 that he did not expect independence to arrive for another 20 years. TANU officials were as surprised as were the colonial authorities by the eagerness with which even isolated communities around the country rallied to its campaign for *uhuru* (freedom).

TANU's declared aim was to attain and hold power on a simple majority basis, ignoring racial or tribal divisions: one man (or woman), one vote. This appealed immediately to the UN General Assembly and its Trusteeship Council. The British had embraced the principle of multi-racism and attempted to encourage multi-racial local councils to spring up – but with little success since in most areas there were simply not enough Asians or Europeans available to fill the quotas. By then, it was far too late to remodel the state from the bottom up. Attempts to restrict the franchise to those with higher levels of income or education were easily ridiculed by TANU.

By 1958, a new governor, Sir Richard Turnbull, was instructed to prepare the country for early self-rule. A Legislative Council was set up in 1960, elected by 1 million voters, with 50 of the 71 seats being open to candidates of any race. TANU swept to power: they had run unopposed in 58 seats and were defeated in only one of the remainder. Internal self-government was declared on 15 May 1961 and Nyerere was appointed Prime Minister, responsible for all but foreign relations and military affairs. Six months later, on 9 December 1961, Tanganyika became fully independent.

Nyerere's first challenge was over; colonial rule had come to an end swiftly and relatively amicably. Apart from a general preference for socialist solutions, he was a pragmatist who seemed to have no preconceptions about how best to develop a more just social order. He was no dictator; but rather, a courteous, charming and gently humorous philosopher. During the transitional six months before full independence, he gathered his team together to formulate a general strategy, aware that a great deal had to be planned, agreed and legislated for. At a dinner shortly before independence, Nyerere confided frankly to a young Briton that he thought it 'had come two years too soon'.[1] He obviously could not just adopt the administrative, development and welfare policies inherited from the British, whatever merit some of them might have had. Instead he decided, in his own words 'to grope forward'. To a British academic friend he exclaimed, 'What am I to do with this country now?' He sought first to develop a socialist and egalitarian society with minimal income differentials. He saw no place for the British concept of a 'loyal opposition' in national politics. Instead, the country would be run in 'a spirit of *ujamaa* [familyhood]', with unstructured forums working single-mindedly for the common good.

To implement his ideal, Nyerere had inherited a Government machine trained and structured to pursue a completely different, and now rejected, top-down colonial model of development. Nevertheless, his plan was to retain for the immediate future many of the expatriate administrative staff and to rely on them to usher in the new policies. Rural economic development would be achieved by stimulating farming efficiency. TANU would counter any local opposition to expatriates remaining in positions of power. However, these plans soon ran into trouble. The TANU rank and file did not accept continuing expatriate influence, and began to question not only the new national leadership but also the methods being employed to develop an economy which seemed to offer them so little for the foreseeable future. Shaken, Nyerere stood down in January 1962 from the day-to-day leadership of the country, turning over the premiership to Rashidi Kawawa, hoping to be able, as President, to stand back and devise

25

a new approach. On 9 December 1962, Tanganyika became a republic; Nyerere was sworn in as its first President, with Rashidi Kawawa as Vice President. A month later, Nyerere announced that Tanganyika was to become a one-party state.

These constant changes were unsettling for the expatriates still temporarily keeping the administration going behind the scenes. Most were able and decent men seeking to serve those whom they administered; but in the end, this was not their country. So they had also to retain their confidence in the new order because, out of the 3,100 positions identified in 1962 as requiring professional or technical qualifications, only 1,300 were so far held by Africans. Moreover, of the latter, all but 200 were in the lowest grades. True, there were by now many Tanganyikan nationals studying overseas; but some were Asians who might not return. There was as yet no large pool of well educated and trained Africans on which to draw. The key judgement was thus to decide how rapidly to pursue Africanisation – meaning in practice more rapid advancement than would formerly have been thought appropriate. This problem impacted directly on the key department of defence.

Meanwhile, although the power relationship between Tanganyika and Great Britain had completely changed, diplomatic relations with Britain were warm and positive. The Government in London was keen for the newly-independent country to get off to a good start and maintained an important development pro-gramme.

Eighteen months later, this easy relationship was interrupted by a surprising episode. At one of his regular private meetings with President Nyerere, the first British High Commissioner, Sir Neil Pritchard, apparently complained that Tanganyika's frequent attacks in the United Nations Trusteeship Council against British colonial policy were going beyond what might be expected from a friendly Commonwealth country receiving considerable aid from Britain. Pritchard thought that the discussion, if robust, had been perfectly good-natured. Shortly afterwards, he had to fly back to London for a conference. While he was away, the Ministry of Foreign Affairs sent the High Commission a formal note saying that they did not want him to return. It seemed that Nyerere thought that Pritchard had tried to bully him. The CRO in London was taken aback. Never before had a head of mission of a Commonwealth country been declared *persona non grata*. Pritchard never returned to Dar es Salaam, and the newly-arrived Deputy High Commissioner, Stephen Miles, was left in charge until Pritchard's successor could be chosen – a process lasting several months at the best of times, and over which the British Government was unlikely to hurry.

Aged 43 at the time of his promotion, Miles had flown operationally from an aircraft carrier in World War II. He had served in New Zealand, Pakistan, Ghana and Uganda before his posting to Tanganyika in 1963. He was to prove very much the man for the job and would play a decisive role in the coming troubles.

By the end of 1963, all of Britain's former East African territories had become independent: first Tanganyika, then Uganda, Zanzibar and finally Kenya. The British government had encouraged the emerging leaders to build on the existing East African Common Services Organisation (EACSO). The regional armed forces, modest as they were, had been organised on a regional basis as had the railways, shipping and airlines, so some basis for an East African Federation already existed. Regional groupings were in vogue, and Britain had promoted the creation of a Central African Federation. During 1963, therefore, there were a number of discussions to consider this vision, between politicians such as Milton Obote of Uganda, Tom Mboya of Kenya, and the Tanganyikan leadership. In the end, the idea came to nothing; but the human contacts would have an important bearing on what was about to happen.

Note

1 Gurdon, Alan: correspondence with author, April 2000.

3

Fumbles Over Defence

Rarely in times of peace do countries think seriously about their national defence needs. Tanganyika was no exception. No records exist of any forward planning for internal or external defence requirements before independence: indeed there seemed no urgency because a small regional army already existed. Once in power, however, the new Government began to understand why it needed a military force. They saw danger in the relics of colonialism around them, and believed that Portuguese forces threatened Tanganyika's southern borders with Mozambique. There was also serious instability on the border with Burundi, and it might be necessary to play a part in UN operations elsewhere. The need for a small army was clear. However, recent history in Africa showed that all too often 'colonels' overthrew their own governments, sometimes bloodily. An early mutiny had occurred in the Congo. More recently, President Sylvanus Olympio of Togo had been overthrown and murdered by his army. Care would therefore be needed in planning the command structure of the new Tanganyikan army.

Before Independence, the British had run a small but effective infantry force in East Africa known as the King's African Rifles (KAR). It consisted of an administrative headquarters in Nairobi and several battalions. It was mainly British-officered, although recently there had been a few African officers with limited responsibilities. These were known as '*effendis*', men with long experience in the KAR but with low levels of formal education. The KAR battalions were divided between the British East African colonies, based in or near major cities, and generally recruited from local tribes. The 1st/6th Battalion KAR had been stationed near Dar es Salaam, with the 2nd/6th stationed up country in Tabora. The newly-installed Government agreed that, as an interim measure, the Tanganyika-based battalions would be taken over as they existed to form Tanganyika's new defence force. They would be known as the 1st and 2nd Battalion Tanganyika Rifles. Nyerere himself would handle the defence portfolio, assisted by Dr Vadasties Kyaruzi, an able and trust-worthy Permanent Secretary.

Once the transfer of the existing KAR battalions had been accepted, there remained the question of who would run the new force, agree finance, organise establishments, recruitment, training and arms procurement, oversee discipline, decide pay levels and carry out all the other administrative matters hitherto run by the British from Nairobi. The issue was not squarely faced – and this proved a serious oversight. On the evidence, it seems largely a British failure: as the departing colonial power, they understood the need for a clear military management structure, and should at least have drawn attention to it, and suggested ways to achieve it.

Before independence, as an interim measure, Nyerere and his Government asked the British to let their officers remain with their infantry battalions, and to provide a Brigadier and a handful of staff officers and senior technical NCOs to run the new Tanganyikan Defence Force headquarters. The officer appointed as Army Commander in the event remained from Independence Day until the army collapsed two years later.

Brigadier Patrick S. Douglas had been an infantry officer for 30 years and had been decorated for actions during World War II. He had commanded the East African Training Centre of the KAR at Nakuru, in Kenya, in 1954 and 1955. He was formally appointed by Prime Minister Nyerere in December 1961, shortly before independence, to set up and run the Tanganyikan army. It would have been hard to find a better or more suitably qualified officer. Pat Douglas knew how to train and organise a small force of locally recruited troops and was sympathetic to African ambitions.

Things did not go well at first. The British Government decided – over his head – that there should be no contact between the departing British colonial officials and any expatriate servants of the new regime. For several weeks before independence, Douglas was forced to kick his heels, having problems getting even furniture or a telephone. At independence, he took over as Army Commander, and was joined by a small expatriate team of staff officers and NCOs. Starting from scratch they tackled everything from basic provisioning to modernisation of armaments and the supply of practice and live ammunition. They had to devise recruiting terms, military regulations, new uniforms and badges, and training policies. Little of this work was appreciated either by the African troops, the *askaris*, who saw little change apart from delays and stringencies, or by the Government, who were hit with unforeseen costs.

Immediately after independence, nobody formulated the army's role, or the necessary political controls. Nyerere later recalled, rather vaguely, 'It was not the strategy of TANU to infiltrate the army'. His views were summarised in an instruction he gave to the 1st Battalion in 1963, when presenting colours: 'it is your duty to continue the traditions of your predecessors'.

So what might have been appropriate traditions? Most democratic nations maintain their armies for self-defence, or to solve international problems resistant to diplomatic solutions. Their forces may also have to be used internally to bolster the police, in 'aid to civil power'. Since in democracies political power usually alternates, it follows that the army must remain politically neutral, owing allegiance to no one party. This requirement was built into the training, indoctrination and practice of all British-trained officers. However, it ran directly

31

counter to the requirements of a newly-independent African state. The leaders of the emerging African nations had either gained power by force, or more often had taken over with the consent of an outgoing colonial authority. In neither case was the notion of a loyal opposition party recognised. Freedom of speech might be tolerated, but only at an individual level; groups expressing dissent, including trade unions, were likely to be suppressed. Hence the main internal threat to an established government was its own army. It was therefore understandable that many newly-emergent governments in Africa tried to ensure that their forces were tightly integrated into the ruling party.

In Tanganyika, the problem was that the retained British officers had not been instructed to meet this need. They continued to train African officers to their own standards, sometimes at Sandhurst, with Government approval. It is clear with hindsight that either the Tanganyikan Government should have said what they really wanted, or that the British should have been far-sighted enough to work out what was needed. A compromise plan might then have been developed. This issue was to cause much bad feeling between the expatriate officers and the new Government.

In 1962, Brigadier Douglas and his small team controlled an army of two infantry battalions and one training company. They were the only military authority in the country, responsible for actions as diverse as countering border incursions, aiding the civil authorities and guaranteeing internal security. The entire force comprised 65 officers (30 British), 130 Warrant Officers and Sergeants (20 British) and about 1,200 men. By the end of 1963, six Tanganyikan officers had passed through Sandhurst and another eight through Mons, Britain's training school for short service commission officers. Another 11 were long-serving junior officers promoted to Lieutenant from the now discarded *effendi* rank. A further four Tanganyikan cadets were at Sandhurst, and eight at Mons. The force was thus developing slowly but surely into an effective national asset.

In March 1963, however, President Nyerere, who had left things almost entirely to Douglas, decided that he need no longer hold the defence portfolio himself. He appointed Oscar Kambona, a forceful supporter and Secretary General of TANU, as Minister for both Foreign Relations and Defence. Douglas had thus lost his direct contact with the President. At the same time the respected Dr Kyaruzi, Permanent Secretary in the Defence Ministry, was arrested and then replaced by an inexperienced Acting Permanent Secretary, A.J. Nsekela. There were rumours that Kyaruzi had refused to authorise Kambona's use of departmental funds for a political rally. This was, to say the least, unfortunate for the army. Kambona soon added a Parliamentary Secretary (i.e. a junior minister), P.C. Walwa, to his team.

Oscar Salathiel Kambona was to become a key player in the coming troubles. Born in 1928, he was the son of one of the first African Anglican priests in Tanganyika. An intelligent student, he qualified first for secondary education and then won a scholarship to study in England, where he graduated as a teacher, returning to Tabora in 1952. He was by this time a friend of Julius Nyerere. By 1957 he was back in Britain, admitted to the Middle Temple to study as a barrister; but he soon abandoned that career to return home and mastermind TANU's sweeping success in the 1959 election. A popular and charismatic figure, he became one of Nyerere's closest associates, and was Secretary-General of TANU at the time of independence. In early 1964 he was still one of the leading figures in the Government, but there were signs of the disagreements on policy that were later to estrange him from Nyerere.[1]

His actions soon began to fuel the tensions which led to mutiny. By 1964 he was working strongly to reduce British influence. Most British officers thought him not only anti-British but also potentially subversive to the regime. On the other hand, Stephen Miles found him a good Foreign Minister; friendly, courteous, and easy to negotiate with, though he was later to concede that

Kambona was also a hopeless muddler when it came to managing Defence.[2] It is difficult, even now, to be sure about his motivation, which has been variously described as subversive Marxist or pan-African. Now dead, he left little written evidence. However, on balance it seems reasonable to assume that Kambona's difficulties with British officers in 1963/4 arose more from his close empathy with his countrymen, and a reasonable suspicion of any outside influence, including from Britain, than from any intention to destabilise the country for personal ambition or as a Marxist revolutionary.

Nevertheless, his management style was chaotic. For example, he approached Douglas at an official ceremony and told him to double the force, as 'it might be needed to go to South Africa'. Stunned, Douglas asked for a meeting to clarify the requirement, and arrived at the appointed time only to be kept waiting for hours. He then learned that the Finance Minister knew nothing of the proposal, and that there was no prospect of even the most minimal increase in budget.[3] On another occasion, Kambona told a group of senior NCOs, quite untruthfully, that he was unable to get Brigadier Douglas's consent for their promotion. The Minister did not understand the danger of undermining his own subordinates with careless and unjustified comments.

Douglas described his doubts about the management of the army in a confidential letter to Kambona. He saw a weakening of discipline through failure to observe the regulations; under-mining, probably unintended, of the position of both British and Tanganyikan officers; irregularities in the commissioning of officers; and an atmosphere of general uncertainty – of being 'messed about'. Douglas gave a number of examples of these failings.

It was during the second half of 1963 that, after spending two years focusing on internal matters, the Government turned its attention to international challenges. An unspecified fear had developed that departing colonial powers would attempt to 'reenter by the back door' if they were not urgently resisted. It became a priority to act against white domination in southern Africa; and Tanganyika threatened to leave the Commonwealth if Britain did not take a strong line against the white minority government of Ian Smith in Rhodesia. In May 1963 the newly-formed Organisation of African Unity established a permanent Liberation Committee, and its headquarters were established in Dar es Salaam. At a press conference in Washington, Nyerere stoutly defended his country's right to support refugees and politicians from southern Africa using Tanganyika as a base to 'carry the fight forward until the whole of Africa is free'.

It was also during this year that the costs of Government, and particularly Defence, began to bite. An obvious way of making savings was to reduce dependence on expatriates. This accorded with the general need to bring Africans into senior positions. While Dr Kyaruzi was still Permanent Secretary in the Defence Ministry, he and Douglas had developed a plan to speed Africanisation, and had reported it to the President, who had agreed. When Kambona took over and removed Kyaruzi, he began to push hard for the early removal of British officers – but wanted no loss of military effectiveness. This problem was to dominate relations between Kambona and Douglas. The matter was first mooted when the Government ordered an expansion of the army, together with the establishment of a navy and air force. Kambona ordered detailed planning. No finance was ever available to achieve the expansion but Douglas and his staff produced papers laying out how the necessary officers could be recruited, trained and introduced into service. They suggested using British, Kenyan and local training facilities, but none of the proposals from army headquarters were ever agreed by the Minister.

At the same time the British Government tried to encourage the Tanganyikans to take over command of their own forces, with existing British officers and NCOs taken out of the command structure and transferred into a training team. British officers had themselves made a proposal for 'side-by-side' training, under

35

which the British officers and NCOs would be paired with their African counterparts. This would have allowed the British to leave after one year – but it was never agreed. Progress on this urgent and vital matter was lamentably slow, but it is hard to see why it should have been so difficult. The police, the prison service, and to a large extent the civil service, were all being rapidly Africanised. The delay in promoting Tanganyikans in the army would prove very damaging. The evidence suggests that it was the Government, in particular Oscar Kambona, who called the shots and must therefore be held largely responsible.

One of Kambona's well-meaning but muddled initiatives in 1963 proved very damaging. Israel needed support in the UN, and one cheap and effective way of getting it was to provide support, advice and friendship to emerging African nations. Kambona was approached by Israel's Ambassador, and agreed to recommend that in future Tanganyika obtain all its military needs from Israel. This would include providing an Israeli replacement for Brigadier Douglas, training facilities and some small aircraft. Kambona was unable to get this plan agreed by his Government colleagues. Undeterred, he then approached the West Germans, but they rejected the proposal.

Kambona then used his Israeli contacts to launch an initiative which was seriously to undermine the army's morale. He arranged for a group of young TANU activists to be trained in Israel. On return they would be appointed as army officers, introducing party loyalty and political awareness. Brigadier Douglas saw difficulties with the plan. The young men appeared in some cases to be almost illiterate, had shown none of the leadership qualities normally expected of an officer, and had not passed through the recently-agreed army selection procedures. Kambona compromised, admitting that the men's military training in Israel might turn out to be only partially effective – so instead they would be given a three-week infantry tactics course in Colito Barracks before taking up their new posts.

The Israelis found the group hard to cope with, and the subsequent training course at Colito confirmed their unsuitability. They appeared to the Tanganyika Rifles officers to be incompetent and unfit; they showed no initiative and some admitted to having no interest in military matters. An attempt to put them through a hastily-convened Government selection board, under the chairmanship of Vice President Kawawa, was abruptly abandoned when Kambona saw what the outcome would be. Undeterred, he had the group sent for further training at the officers' training wing of the KAR at Nakuru in Kenya. The result was no better: the commanding officer reported that they 'turned my school into a brothel'.[4] Kambona nevertheless persisted in appointing them as officers in the Tanganyika Rifles. The results were disastrous. It was impossible to hide their low standards from the *askaris* and NCOs. The question inevitably arose: if these inexperienced, unsuitable young people could be made officers, why could not experienced, competent NCOs in the existing force be promoted? Morale was inevitably undermined. Brigadier Douglas later wrote that the incident sounded the death knell of the Tanganyikan army as he had known it.

In August 1963 another damaging saga began while Kambona was attending a conference in newly-independent Algeria. Returning to Tanganyika, he announced that he had provided arms and ammunition for an expanded army. Equipment to fit out a brigade would arrive shortly, paid for out of an unexpected windfall from the Government's diamond or cotton holdings. (In public, Kambona claimed the arms were a gift. In fact, they were almost certainly bartered in exchange for high-grade coffee worth some US$250,000 – a substantial sum which would have been enough to re-equip the army properly.) Douglas offered to send his senior operations staff officer, Major Brian Marciandi, to Algeria to survey the consignment. Kambona ruled this out: the arms were already in transit.

When the shipment arrived in Dar es Salaam, Kambona

decreed that no British officers were to be involved with it. The senior African officer in the First Battalion, Sandhurst-trained Captain Alex Nyirenda, was ordered to supervise the unloading. No arrangements had been made to receive the shipment and British officers had to step in to organise transport and cranes.[5] Some of the ammunition was given temporary storage in Colito Barracks, while most of the arms were stored in a government building on the Pugu Road. Lt. Col. Rowley Mans, the Commanding Officer of the 1st Battalion, met the President at a reception and joked that if the ammunition on his parade ground exploded, then Tanganyika would be the first African nation to have men in space.[6] Kambona then told Douglas that some boxes had been marked with a cross and should be set aside, while a small consignment of boxes was to be delivered to his personal office. A group of officers made a thorough survey and reported that the Algerian shipment was mainly outdated junk; World War II rifles of Russian, German, British and Italian origin; a great deal of old ammunition and equipment; a few anti-aircraft guns; and some ambulances in good condition. There were no spares, which alone rendered the shipment useless. The boxes to be put on one side contained hand grenades and rifles. The boxes to be delivered to Kambona's office contained World War II bazookas (hand-held rocket launchers) with a good supply of ammunition. The purpose of these special deliveries was never established.

By this time relations between the Minister and his expatriate senior officers were at a low ebb. Kambona made unnanounced and unofficial visits to Colito Barracks to talk with the junior ranks. Mans, the new commanding officer, found this unacceptable; he could not have junior ranks telling him what the Minister of Defence thought or wanted. He ordered the guard to inform him or the duty officer if any outsider, up to and including the Minister, sought entry to the barracks. Aware that this was a somewhat drastic step, he then spoke to Kambona's deputy, P.C. Walwa, assuring him that he and the Minister would always be welcome if they wished to visit, but it should be by prior arrangement. Kambona was outraged: the new CO of the 1st Battalion was, he claimed, being arrogant and inflexible.

The difficulties within the Defence Department were mirrored in a general rise of tension throughout the nation. Apart from the Mau-Mau uprising, all three former British East African countries had gained independence fairly smoothly and peacefully, and with high hopes. Unlike other parts of the world, some already torn by East–West rivalries, they faced no serious external threats. They could develop a non-aligned, uniquely African future, free from colonial restraints. What dangers there were seemed to be internal. As they gained independence, the people expected material rewards, but it now seemed that the end of British rule had brought little immediate relief from poverty. African intellectuals expected jobs and power; but European, Asian or Arab communities seemed still to control commerce, occupy land and hold senior Government posts. Trade unions demanded a share of power and access to wealth, but the economy was still largely in the hands of foreign companies. The first groups of young men trained in the Soviet Bloc and China were returning, burning for action.

The factor working most favourably for the Tanganyikan people was its Government, the men who had led it since independence. Experienced observers and the western press agreed that the Cabinet was united and sincere in its efforts to put the people first. The mood was of sober integrity, modest dignity and hard work. They would seek outside help when they needed it, but strictly on their terms. They were their own men, determined never again to fall under foreign influence. If they, the decent moderates, consolidated their hold on power, there seemed to be hope for Tanganyika. But there was a challenge they did not foresee.

Within the army there was a stalemate: the Minister was at loggerheads with his senior officers. The result was a collapse of morale in the battalion at Colito. Junior soldiers saw their officers going about their usual tasks: training, planning up-country manoeuvres, and making progress on re-equipment with modern arms. But there was no movement on the crucial matters of pay and conditions, Africanisation or defining the army's role either internally or externally in the anti-colonial environment. The expatriate officers picked up intimations of trouble. They were aware that discipline and morale were being eroded. But they did not appreciate the urgency of the threat to their control over their men. Mistakenly, they believed the most likely threat to be a political move against the Government. In fact it needed only a spark to set off mutiny within the battalion. It came from Zanzibar, only just across the water.

Notes

1   Kambona was a commited Christian. He was married in Westminster Abbey in London, Julius Nyerere giving the bride away.
2   Miles, Stephen: oral evidence.
3   Douglas, Pat: private papers, unpublished account of the mutiny, the source of several other incidents recounted below.
4   Douglas, Pat: papers.
5   A British police officer, Richard Hannington, noticed that the ship was heavily down by the bows; its after-holds were empty. The ship had presumably not sailed from Algeria in this condition, but there was no information about what the holds had contained or where they had been discharged.
6   Mans, Rowley: report of 4 March 1964, private papers.

4

Revolution in Zanzibar

Zanzibar Island lies only 40 miles off the African mainland. But it had long been under Arab influence, especially after the Sultans of Oman extended their sway over the coastal areas of East Africa in the late eighteenth century, making Zanzibar the infamous centre of the regional slave trade and later a prosperous source of spices, especially cloves.

Before independence, this tiny island had been administered for over 60 years by the British, with some Arab junior officials. The Sultan had been left in place and retained titular power. Most of the plantation owners were Arab, while most of their labourers were African. Trade was dominated by Asians. By December 1963, out of a total population of some 260,000, about two thirds were Shirazis (indigenous Africans or mixed Afro-Arabs, some descended from slaves); a sixth were Africans who had arrived fairly recently from the mainland; and a sixth were Arab. There were also some 16,000 Asians and a sprinkling of Europeans, mainly British, most of whom worked for the Zanzibar Government. Racial layering was strengthened by an educational system which encouraged segregation, with teaching mainly in either Arabic or Swahili.

In 1948, economic difficulties had led to a general strike. The British called in police reinforcements from Tanganyika to restore order and strongly advised improvements in the pay and conditions of workers. The significance of the strike was that it

41

gave the Africans a sense of unity for the first time: they had stood together and won. This encouraged political activity, and the Afro-Shirazi Party (ASP) was formed. Successful clove harvests drew in more African labourers from the mainland who by then were influenced by the growing nationalism in their own countries. Although there was some political progress, it was slow – and resisted by most Arabs. The communities grew apart and three main political parties were formed with irreconcilable aims: the ASP, mainly led by 'mainland' Africans; the Zanzibar Nationalist Party (ZNP), the core of which was Arab; and the Pemba People's Party (ZPPP) which provided an alternative for Shirazis who did not care for either of the alternatives.

The exclusion of the majority from both political and economic power was clearly dangerous. Yet when the widely respected Sultan Khalifa died in 1960, his successors did not seek any accommodation with the majority African population. The British were unwilling to get sucked into this question: they had to control any disorder in the short term, but they proposed to grant independence as soon as possible as part of their general policy of retrenchment, and in line with UN demands. The last British Resident of Zanzibar, Sir George Mooring, and President Nyerere both warned that the territory was in no state yet to run its own affairs. But the British were determined to call a general election and to turn the protectorate over to the winners as soon as possible.

The results of the elections held in July 1963 hardly presaged lasting stability. The ASP, whose large majority should have swept them to power, were divided and badly organised. They nevertheless gained 54 per cent of the votes cast. However, anomalies in constituency boundaries resulted in their gaining only 13 seats, against 18 won by the tactical alliance between the ZNP and their junior partners, the ZPPP. The Arabs seemed to have outmanoeuvred the African majority. It was a freak result, but it left most of the Africans unshakeably convinced that the British had handed them over to indefinite Arab domination. The new Government could have acted decisively to counter this suspicion; instead, they reinforced it. Far from making moves towards reconciliation, they treated ASP members as subversives. They even ruled that all Zanzibaris of African origin who sought office must renounce any party affiliation. This was fast turning into one of the least promising situations for Britain to hand over power to a former colonial territory, yet they persisted. Independence was granted on 9 December 1963. With hindsight, the only question was when, and with how much bloodshed, the African majority would react.

Suddenly an unknown 26-year-old Ugandan, John Okello, appeared briefly and violently on the stage of history. An orphan, he had been educated at a mission school and claimed to have fought with the Mau Mau in 1955–7, before working as a labourer in Kenya. He then moved on to Pemba where he found a clerical job which led him into trade unionism. Increasingly an activist, he formed a Revolutionary Council: 300 hard and disciplined Africans, mostly of mainland origin, with the single, simple and narrow aim of seizing power. They studied existing security systems and their weaknesses, and made detailed plans to destroy the Arab community. Their security was effective, and even the ASP leadership knew nothing of their activities – a significant revolutionary achievement, particularly given the size of Zanzibar.

Okello's group had planned to act during independence celebrations, but found conditions difficult because of the great number of visitors and the departing British military and naval presence. The ceremonies themselves only exacerbated African discontent, with Arabs in their national dress openly taking over from the former British rulers. African police officers were discharged, and some joined the revolutionaries, bringing their operational knowledge with them. The new Government had not yet come to any defence agreement with Britain or with anyone else, to provide a foreign security presence or to train and lead a security force. There had been a proposal to recruit Egyptian officers for a Police Mobile Force but it came to nothing, although the very suggestion enraged African opinion. Arabs continued to carry arms openly, as if taunting the majority.

Some hint of the coming trouble reached the African leadership. Sheikh Abeid Karume, leader of the ASP, was no revolutionary, and warned whoever would listen, including at least one British police officer, about his concerns and suspicions. He made a last-minute attempt to form a coalition of moderate Africans and Arabs. It came to nothing, and the last chance had been lost.

When it came, only six weeks after independence, the revolution was brief and bloody. The first phase, the destruction of the existing order, went entirely as Okello had planned. During the evening of 11 January 1964, Karume's party had organised a large fête. Under its cover Okello mustered a force of around 800 armed activists, among whom the coup's leaders moved, detailing squads to primary targets. They acted in the early hours of 12 January and their first targets were the police stations, the broadcasting station, the prison, the post office and the telephone exchange. A crucial battle occurred at the police station at Ziwani where some of the policemen resisted stoutly. Discouraged, many of the attackers deserted, but a well-briefed group, possibly led by a disgruntled former policeman, got into the armoury. The defenders surrendered, and the insurgents acquired their first supply of modern arms. The Sultan's paramilitary force arrived shortly afterwards, but were driven off. At a second police station, one of the senior officers was in league with the attackers and opposition was soon overcome. The broadcasting station had been left undefended, and the British engineers were forced at gunpoint to operate the transmitters for the first of Okello's terrifying broadcasts.

Having organised his revolution, Okello consolidated it with a series of broadcasts demanding the eradication of Arabs and imperialism. He described himself as 'Field Marshal of the

Freedom Fighters' and called on all Africans to take up arms. So violent was his language that many Arabs were terrified into flight or waited hopelessly until they were killed. The broadcasts inflamed the African population who began to pillage Arab and Asian properties. Some Goan children on their way to church were massacred. The Sultan and his family fled to his Government's steamer, anchored off the port.

Around noon on 12 January, a strong force attacked the police station at Malindi, controlling the approaches to Stone Town, the city's centre. The British officer in charge, a tough and resourceful man named Sullivan, held out with European reserve officers and nearly 100 African policemen. They had good radio communications with other East African capitals, and called for help – with no result. Short of ammunition, Sullivan negotiated a safe passage for his men, leading them out for evacuation to Dar es Salaam. With their departure, the Arab regime and administration had lost. Small groups of Arabs held out in the country for some time, but all were eventually overcome and slaughtered.

Okello had planned that no Africans would be killed, but to be safe had arranged for the ASP leaders to be taken out of the country to Dar for a few days. This left the African politicians leaderless and gave him time to consolidate the revolution on his own terms. Having eliminated the Arab leadership, Okello encouraged a general pogrom. The exact death toll has never been established, but is generally put at about 4,000 men, women and children. Most were killed with the utmost brutality. The moderate ASP leadership opposed the massacres, but they were terrified and powerless and could only remain in the background hoping to regain influence later.

News of the revolution spread rapidly. Okello's planning ensured that Europeans were spared. They had no political influence but held key technical positions. Without them there would be no power, telephones, broadcasting or airport operations. So fierce were the sanctions threatened against any revolutionary band which disobeyed orders, that they molested few foreigners. Some communication links therefore remained open and first reports of the violence began to be passed on port control, air traffic and company networks. Okello's broadcasts were soon heard throughout East Africa. Some telephone lines were also still open, and the embassies and high commissions had their own wireless services. The affair was brought dramatically to the world's attention when an Italian photographer chartered an aircraft in Mombasa and flew over Zanzibar to get photographs of the continuing slaughter on the city's beach.

For the British, the problem was clear and urgent. They had nationals in Zanzibar who must be protected. If troops were to be flown in, the airport must be kept open. The Tanganyikan Government was asked to take and hold it, but would not act. The one warship in the area, the small unarmed survey ship HMS *Owen*, was ordered to Zanzibar. A more powerful frigate would follow, bringing a company of British troops. In Aden, HMS *Centaur*, an aircraft carrier on exercises, was ordered to load a strong force of marines. Her flying exercises were postponed and she was brought into harbour on 16 January, but the order was cancelled as the news from Zanzibar improved, and the ship went back to sea.

> Tony Laurence. *Most of us on board hardly noticed this event, which seemed just an unexpected return to harbour. The Executive Officer led a small team of sub-heads of department to make plans to accommodate and feed a large addition to the ship's crew. I only knew about their efforts because I saw all signals in and out of the ship (about 150 a day).*

The USA, in contrast, had 'no special brief', as they later put it, for the Sultan's Government. Their consul, Fritz Picard, had reported growing unrest, but nobody had predicted so violent an insurrection. The American Government saw matters in much the

46

same light as the Tanganyikan one: the rebellion should be contained and directed to a more constructive end. Their most immediate concern was for a civilian National Aeronautics and Space Administration (NASA) satellite tracking station. The majority of Americans on the island were contract employees, who had to be evacuated. This was a time when the security of the western Indian Ocean was left to the British; there were none of the US forces which were to dominate the area by the end of the century. By chance, however, the destroyer USS *Manley* happened to be on a goodwill visit to Mombasa. Picard was instructed to approach the revolutionaries to get permission for the vessel to enter Zanzibar and evacuate the American civilians. This dangerous task took time and courage, but after Karume had been brought back to the island to share power, the destroyer was allowed in.

In Tanganyika the reaction was more complicated. The revolution was viewed as being against colonialism – Arab in this case. TANU was close to the ASP, and there was probably Tanganyikan encouragement for a takeover of power, forcible if necessary, in Karume's favour. Indeed, many have since speculated that Okello's racially-inspired coup pre-empted another one whose instigators were more ideologically motivated. Be that as it may, Okello's revolution was quite different from anything else being considered, and the violence was horrifying. Nyerere explained to British diplomats that he hated the killings, but understood the residue of hatred for the Arabs, which was the reason for, if not the justification of, the violence. His Government decided to bring their forces to readiness, to welcome refugees, but otherwise to wait and see how events unfolded.

In a surprising and unexplained move, Kambona took his Permanent Secretary and Brigadier Douglas to the airport to fly to Zanzibar on 13 January to find out personally what was going on. Before they boarded the aircraft the destination was suddenly changed to Nairobi. They flew there and Douglas waited while Kambona talked with other politicians. Douglas gained the clear impression that Kambona had expected the uprising but had been surprised by the timing.[1] Perhaps he knew about and supported ASP plans to seize power, but not Okello's, which may have pre-empted them. The effect of this trip was that all the top decision-makers at the Defence Ministry were out of contact for the first full day of the revolution – which could possibly have been Kambona's intention.

The 1st Battalion Tanganyika Rifles at Colito had become directly involved. To the British officers, part of their professional duty was to restore civil order and save life. It seemed obvious to them that they should intervene in Zanzibar as quickly as they could. Before flying off, Kambona had instructed them to prepare to do so. Zanzibar was only 20 minutes flying time from Dar, and East African Airways had three Dakotas available. At around 10.30 a.m. on 13 January Lt. Col. Mans ordered Company Commander Major Mike Callaghan to prepare to fly to Zanzibar, in order to take and hold the landing area until reinforced. Arriving at Dar airport, Callaghan, an alert and experienced infantryman, 'invented and prepared a quick demonstration of dismounting from a civilian aircraft on a hostile airfield. It was an action not covered in the training manuals'.[2] As the lead company trained, the remainder of the battalion joined them in readiness for the order to go.

When he arrived at Dar es Salaam airfield, Lt. Col. Mans found no orders awaiting him. The Brigadier was reported to be out of the country. Major Brian Marciandi, the operations staff officer, was in direct radio contact with the British controller at Zanzibar Airport tower and learned that revolutionaries were approaching it. Mans therefore learned that people were being killed and that British lives were at risk in Zanzibar. He wanted to fly his troops in at once. Marciandi understood his concern but insisted that it was out of the question for British officers serving the Tanganyikan Government to initiate any intervention in the affairs of another country; it had to be both a political decision and a Tanganyikan one. His views were reinforced when welcome news came through from Tim Crosthwait, the British High Commissioner in Zanzibar, that Europeans were not being molested.

It was obvious, however, that once the airport had been occupied by insurgents there could be no possibility of airborne intervention. Marciandi therefore made strenuous efforts to seek political authority to act to secure the airfield, but no one seemed available. He managed eventually to extract a home telephone number from a reluctant secretary, and spoke to Vice President Rashidi Kawawa. In some desperation, Marciandi explained the urgency of the situation. He ended by saying, 'Will you authorise us now to fly in and seize Zanzibar airport? If you cannot do so, will you authorise us to hold the aircraft in case we need to use them later?' Without a moment's hesitation and with absolute clarity, Kawawa replied: 'No, you may not send troops to Zanzibar and you may not hold the aircraft.' The revolution in Zanzibar was to be left to run its bloody course.[3]

Mans reluctantly accepted the decision. It was in any case too late because within minutes, the controller in Zanzibar reported that the revolutionaries were close. Shortly afterwards he reported gunfire and shouting in the room below him and said calmly that he was going down. He was not heard on the radio link again. At Dar airport, the battalion settled down to await orders until 9 p.m. that evening when they were ordered back to barracks.

Random killings continued in Zanzibar into a third day before Okello called for an end. He continued to inspire terror. On one occasion, he forced ASP leader Karume, who had returned from the mainland, to kiss his feet. Europeans remained unharmed and on the evening of the 12 January they, particularly the British, were reassured by the arrival of HMS *Owen*. HMS *Rhyl* arrived during the night of 15/16 January, carrying a company of the Staffordshire Regiment. The first outsiders actually to set foot in Zanzibar, on Friday 17 January, were a detachment of 124 men from the Tanganyikan Police Field Force.[4] They were flown in before their Government had accorded any official recognition to the new regime. So urgent was Home Secretary Job Lusinde's belated concern to get the detachment there, that when the airline manager asked for a short delay while he sought permission from his operations manager in Nairobi to carry armed men in civilian aircraft, he was promptly expelled from the country for obstructing the Government.

Okello wrote himself out of history. He flew to Dar es Salaam on 17 January 'suffering from strain'. Returning two days later, he went to Pemba, where he continued viciously to root out Arab and Indian influences. But his time was coming to an end and when a new Government was formed on 24 January, his supporters were outnumbered by moderate ASP members. Karume escorted him to the airport a month later, to visit Uganda, Kenya and Tanganyika, and to be received by their Presidents. He was surprised to be refused re-entry to Zanzibar, and was soon arrested. He then disappeared until he was seen briefly with General Idi Amin in Uganda seven years later.

Centuries of Arab dominance in Zanzibar had been broken, and the islands had been reunited with mainland Africa. The transfer of power to the majority may have been inevitable, but the methods used to effect it were brutal. Of the original Arab population of some 50,000, only about 14,000 remained by the end of the year, seeking reintegration after giving up most of their property and all their privileges. Some 4,000, or perhaps more, had been killed and the remainder had either been forcibly deported (5,000 to Oman alone), or had found refuge elsewhere. The immediate reaction of the neighbouring East African countries was both one of embarrassment about the killings and concern for the stability of their own regimes. One unforeseen and early consequence was the effect on the morale and loyalty of neighbouring East African armies.

Notes

1   Douglas: *op. cit.*
2   Callaghan, Michael: private papers.
3   Marciandi, Brian: oral evidence.
4   All that were available. Their commander, a British expatriate (R. Hannington), was ordered not to accompany them.

5

A Week of Tension

The horrors in Zanzibar alarmed many people in Dar es Salaam. During their short period in power the Tanganyikan Government had taken a certain interest in the affairs of other African nations, but their involvement had been very much at arm's length: support for liberation movements, some brief strengthening of border patrols and many stern statements of principle. Suddenly it had all become more serious: there were reports of carnage only 40 miles over the water. Terrified refugees were arriving and had to be dealt with. Suggestions were even being made that Tanganyikan military or police forces might need to be sent to restore order, risking Tanganyikan lives. Brian Marciandi at army headquarters, an acute and involved observer, later described this period as 'the end of innocence'.

Within the British High Commission, the workload increased dramatically. The killings in Zanzibar had shaken the confidence of the expatriate community. There seemed to be a real possibility of the trouble spreading. Miles and his staff had a busy week keeping up with the fast-moving scene, making what contact they could with Tanganyikan Government Ministers, and exchanging views with their fellow diplomats. They were pleased to see the Tanganyikans sending the armed police force to Zanzibar once the new African leadership seemed to be gaining the upper hand, a move which heralded an end to the killings and a return to public order. Meanwhile, the High Commission staff had no reason to be concerned about Tanganyika's own defence organisation and capabilities. They knew nothing of the state of morale at Colito – it was not their business. Indeed, it would have been improper to be too closely in touch with Douglas and his staff. They were soon to become closely involved, however, whether they liked it or not.

At Colito Barracks, Lt. Col. Rowley Mans had taken over as Commanding Officer of the First Battalion of the Tanganyika Rifles in mid-October 1963. He had found a battalion worn down by constant and often wasteful demands on its time and manpower, and facing serious shortages of equipment. However, although disappointed by the decision not to send his battalion to Zanzibar, he judged that its performance at standby during the crisis showed that the unit was basically sound: it just needed firm leadership – which he would provide. Funding had not yet been authorised for the annual training period up-country, and he set about lobbying for the battalion exercises to be approved. The money was scraped together, and planning began. The workload fell largely on the Adjutant, the battalion staff officer, Captain Lamond, a 31-year-old officer seconded from the Staffordshire Regiment.

Joe Lamond was typical of the type of British officer serving in Tanganyika. He and his family had been in the country for two years. He had been favourably impressed by an early experience after Company exercises up-country when, because of shortages of transport, he had been ordered to march his men back to the coast on foot. The *askaris* were in peak condition and made good progress, marching 125 miles in five days, to arrive one day ahead of schedule. In the bush outside the camp the Company halted while the wives brought out cleaning kit and tables to iron their men's uniforms. The Battalion band played the Company in to a proud ceremonial entry at sunset. The 1st Tanganyika Rifles had seemed a good battalion then, and in early 1964, Captain Lamond was still fully occupied in its routine administration.

Company commander Major Michael Callaghan was another typical British officer, on detachment from his parent regiment, the Yorkshire and Lancashire. He had been seconded to a West African regiment in the 1950s and had been with the Tanganyika Rifles since independence. He enjoyed serving in Africa and got on well with his men, particularly during the endless route marches. He had worked closely with Bill Cook, the previous Commanding Officer, and both liked and admired Rowley Mans, his successor. He thought it was a happy regiment. He faced a challenge when three of the young Israeli-trained officers were appointed to his company, but he set about their development.

Lt. Col. Mans had discussed his concerns about the state of readiness of the battalion with Brigadier Douglas, but had kept his doubts from his own officers. Perhaps his major problem was the absorption of the Israeli-trained officers: whatever their shortcomings, they had all to be retained and given duties, and most of them remained with his battalion. He was also involved with other aspects of the Africanisation of his force. The day after the Zanzibar uprising, a personal message came from Kambona, calling for a list of all officers, Warrant Officers and Sergeants. Mans did not appreciate this procedure, and considered that the request should have been addressed to the army headquarters in Dar, not him. After all, headquarters held all the records, so why were they being bypassed? Despite his doubts, Mans was doing all he could to make the existing system work, and he had insisted already that all his British officers should learn and qualify formally in Swahili at once. He was confident that he understood the battalion well, having served with it for five years during World War II – or at least, its former manifestation as a unit of the King's African Rifles. He detected no hint of unrest at Colito, and was concerned only about political machinations in Dar. Provided he could be left to get on with his job, he concluded that all should be well.

The week of 13–19 January 1964 was busier than usual. It had started with alarm over events in Zanzibar and the airport standby.

Now troops of the First Battalion had to be at short notice for operations. This caused complications. Soldiers do not normally have arms and ammunition in their accommodation. The rules at Colito were that if troops were at two hours' notice or less, then they were issued with their arms. If they were at between two and eight hours' notice, then the arms were kept in the Company stores. If they were at more than eight hours' notice, then everything was returned to the main armoury. Arms were frequently issued and returned during the week, as each company in turn was ordered on standby. Meanwhile, the Algerian arms shipment was still being unloaded down in the harbour. Company Commander Alex Nyirenda was handling this duty, reporting faithfully to Lt. Col. Mans each evening. (Kambona would not have approved of this.)

On 16 January, Brigadier Douglas came out to Colito barracks to tell Mans about a vague warning from Kambona that there might be trouble at Colito that day. Douglas had told Mans to arrange a gathering (a *baraza*, Swahili for a general meeting) of all the men at Colito, adding that he would inspect the barracks and 'walk slowly around and be seen by as many soldiers as possible'. This he did, and 'was greeted by smiles everywhere'.[1] Douglas by now had no links with the Government's security and intelligence services, but was concerned about the President's security which he sensed might be threatened. He needed to be certain of the battalion's readiness to meet any challenge quickly. A raid on the armoury seemed to be the first threat they would face. Mans was instructed to make a plan which would ensure that the arms were kept safe, but that then if necessary the armed battalion could be brought into Dar at short notice to protect the President and Government. A meeting was set up for the following day at which decisions were taken about introducing a simple radio alarm system which would work even if the telephone exchange was closed. This needed equipment from Nairobi, which was ordered – but was not fitted in time.

If it was never possible to identify any specific threat to the stability of the army, there were disturbing straws in the wind and a general feeling that, politically, things were somehow not right. For example, Mans was approached directly (and quite improperly) by the Head of Special Branch who asked if his brother could be recruited into the 1st Battalion. Mans already knew that Special Branch had two people in the camp, notionally working with the Public Works Department. This new request might be sinister, or just about family employment.

In December Mans, supported by Douglas, had tried to get Captains Nyirenda and Kashmiri promoted to Major in preparation for the day when one of them would assume command of the battalion. Kambona had refused, declaring that he was quite satisfied with progress over Africanisation. But almost immediately, in early January, he asked Douglas for a plan to Africanise all posts by the end of the year. However, no Sandhurst-trained officers were to be given any command – Kambona instead favoured 'compliant older officers'. His intentions may have been reasonable, but his undisciplined leadership style made him an awkward boss.

Mans found it increasingly difficult to work with the political leadership. His unease was such that he had asked to be relieved of his command after only two months in the post. However, Douglas persuaded him to stay. Once it had been agreed that the British officers and NCOs would all leave in 12 months, Mans asked to be allowed to announce it to his men at the next of his monthly talks in Swahili. Kambona forbade this, saying that he would make the announcement himself, but in the event he never did. Mans later said that he had announced the general idea of this plan to his men.[2] It is not clear when. If the troops were not told, it would have been very damaging, especially since a recent speech by President Nyerere had warned in general terms against too rapid Africanisation of the country's administration. At the same time, new British appointments had given some in the army the impression that Tanganyikan NCOs might never be promoted.

This mismanagement seems to have tipped a balance, driving a group of about ten long-serving NCOs and other ranks to plan a mutiny. There is no evidence that the plotting was other than an immediate and local reaction to an unhappy, perhaps intolerable, situation.

The plotters were led by Sergeant Francis Hingo Ilogi. Ilogi was an interesting figure, an intelligent activist who, if things had turned out differently, might have served his country well. Aged 27, he had been born in Bukere, near Tabora, and had been well educated to secondary level. Joining the army in 1958, he was at first turned down as an education instructor, being sent instead to Nairobi for six months of signals training. In October 1961 he went absent to enrol in the East African Commercial School in Uganda where he studied book-keeping and accountancy for three months. On return to Colito in December he was arrested pending trial for absence without leave. But a general amnesty followed at the time of independence and after a fortnight under arrest Ilogi rejoined the battalion as an education instructor, his original ambition achieved.

His career prospered for two years. He continued his education, enrolling for an extra-mural course at the University of Dar es Salaam and pursuing a London General Certificate (now roughly equivalent to a GCSE) by post. He also proved an ambitious soldier. During exercises he was attached to the intelligence section. By January 1964, he had become assistant to the Transport Officer as well as battalion education instructor. His duties brought him into close contact the people who mattered in the unit: officers, NCOs and the more intelligent soldiers. The discontent of the *askaris* over their pay was now in the open. He also noticed the burning resentment of the long-serving African ex-*effendis* who now saw no prospect of achieving senior rank, and he was involved in the largely unsuccessful induction programme for the Israeli-trained officer candidates. He saw how things were going wrong — and he also knew the battalion's routine inside out. A promising opportunity beckoned. He gathered a small group of like-minded junior soldiers around him and began to plan.

The Zanzibar revolution had shown how easy it was for an unarmed party first to gain control of arms and then effect a takeover. Much the same could be done at Colito. Ilogi's group plotted exactly when and how they would overcome their officers and seize power in the barracks. During recent battalion training on 'Aid to Civil Power', they had been taught the need, in the event of unrest, to seize key points like the airport, broadcasting station and telephone exchange. They added these targets to their plans. They seem not, however, to have thought much about exactly what they would do after they succeeded.

Meanwhile, in Brigadier Douglas's headquarters, the staff officers were concerned with their own problems: the development of the new army was too slow and expensive. So they forwarded papers to the Tanganyikan Ministry of Defence explaining exactly why, and proposing solutions. They described the difficulties of attracting officer candidates and technical staff of the required standards, and the inevitable shortfall if the force was to be expanded. Proposals to rely on Tanganyikan short-service officers would cause difficulty at a time when better-paid civilian jobs were opening up in commerce and Government. Solutions included economical local training such as a modified Outward Bound School scheme. They recommended that educational requirements be reduced to the minimum standard needed for local service. Training in Britain was expensive, and there would be substantial economies of scale if it were shared with Kenya and Uganda, so they proposed a combined East African Military Training School.

These proposals attracted no Government interest at all. The Defence Ministry did not consider the problem urgent, and in any case the proposals did not address the question of how to tie in TANU's energies and loyalties. The British proposals may even

59

have seemed to Tanganyikans to be trying to perpetuate colonial control, and there was no enthusiasm for collaboration with Kenya and Uganda. Senior leaders such as Nyerere and Kawawa agreed that the army should be maintained at a high standard and they, if not Defence Minister Kambona, were content for the British officers to continue with their existing policies. Kambona may have had a different, though undeclared, aim: to promote like-minded Tanganyikans from the ranks, under TANU guidance. But if so, he signally failed to initiate it. How local officers would be adequately trained to take over was a question which remained unresolved – until the army imploded.

Another worrying development occurred towards the end of 1963. Brigadier Douglas had originally been well briefed on intelligence matters. He saw a weekly bulletin from Special Branch, and was a member of the National Intelligence Committee which met once a month. By the autumn of 1963 he noticed that reports about border incidents seemed no longer to be included in the committee's reviews. Perhaps guerrilla and 'freedom' activity was being dealt with in some other forum? Nevertheless he was disappointed to be told, in mid-November, that he was no longer a member of the Intelligence Committee. The weekly bulletins stopped arriving at the same time. Douglas was left only with such scraps of information as he could pick up informally. This situation was untenable.

Steady though unspectacular progress continued in spite of these political uncertainties. The army was strengthened in 1963 by the addition of mortar and reconnaissance platoons. This considerably increased their effectiveness at an acceptable cost. The addition of one new rifle company to each battalion, together with a signals troop and a simple logistics unit had also been agreed. Both battalions had been re-equipped with modern NATO type SLR rifles, obtained economically from Australia.

As ever, costs had to be pared to a minimum. One result, which concerned everyone, was the low levels of pay for NCOs and other ranks. Senior sergeants were paid less than British officers were giving their houseboys. At 106 shillings a month plus food and accommodation, the average *askari* was paid less than most workers in Tanganyika – although in late 1963 this was comparable with pay levels in the Ugandan and Kenyan armies. Soldiers had free accommodation, but this did not help most married men, only a few of whom had their families in barracks. While low pay may be a problem experienced frequently by Government servants, in this case the scale of the dissatisfaction and the length of time it had existed had begun to reduce the Tanganyikan soldiers' sense of loyalty. Later, Kambona admitted privately to Miles that when the Tanganyikan Government had implemented the recommendations of the Minimum Wages Board in 1962, they had made a mistake by failing at the same time to raise army pay which had fallen behind.[3]

Douglas saw Kambona more often than usual during the weeks before and just after the Zanzibar revolution, not only because of those troubles. The Algerian arms also had to be discussed, especially after Kambona's acceptance that the British officers must become involved in their survey, storage and security. Then there was also an Officers' Selection Board for 20 candidates to be sent for training in Yugoslavia – something the Brigadier had not been told about until the Board met. The meeting was to be chaired by Vice President Kawawa but it proved chaotic: the room was unprepared, and there were no supporting papers or evidence of suitability for the crowd of hopefuls waiting outside. Douglas had no option but to admit that he knew nothing of the Board, or the candidates. Kawawa sent for Kambona, and a heated altercation ensued in front of the Board. The candidates were dismissed and Kawawa was heard to order brusquely that he would tolerate no reduction in the standard of officers.

The incident illustrates the pressures which were then building around the Minister for External Affairs and Defence. His chaotic and misconceived management methods were very damaging, but his growing impatience with what he saw as outdated procedures and 'white man's practices' were not hard to understand. His frustrations were obvious to the British officers, but it was not in their power to address them. They could use only agreed and authorised methods, and go no further than recommending short cuts or alternatives. Policy formulation lay outside their remit.

It was at this time that the Government decided that Brigadier Douglas should leave at the end of the year, to be replaced by an African officer. The Commander Designate was to be promoted to Lieutenant-Colonel immediately, and would be sent on foreign visits for six months to study defence requirements. He would then work for a few months in harness with Douglas before taking over. He was not to be a British-trained officer, and was to be mature. Nominations for command of both battalions were to be made at the same time; neither of these officers was to be British trained either.

The British army staff officers saw serious difficulties with this plan. A few of the older officers in the frame for such promotions, all ex-*effendis*, were competent enough: but most were thought to be unambitious, as Major Marciandi wrote.[4] They carried out orders efficiently, but lacked initiative and energy. If such men were appointed to take over the new army, there would be a real danger of administrative breakdown. Kambona accepted these objections to some extent, and agreed that Sandhurst-trained officers would be appointed as seconds-in-command to the new men. Once that was settled, the army staff reviewed the possibilities and came up with the name of ex-*effendi* Captain William Chacha to become commander. The choice was agreed by Kambona, and the nomination was communicated to the British battalion commanders. But there was an immediate snag: Captain Lamond, Adjutant of the 1st Battalion, who had served on the army headquarters staff, recollected that someone of that name had been court-martialled in Kenya for selling drugs to the Mau-Mau. This was no more than a personal suspicion, but merited investigation. The question remained undecided when it was overtaken by events.

Overshadowing these problems was uncertainty over internal security: was somebody plotting something involving the army? The vague warning from Kambona had presumably been based on intelligence sources. A normally reliable Defence Ministry official had also told Douglas that something serious was brewing, although he did not know what. At the same time, as previously mentioned, Kambona had ordered that bazookas from the Algerian arms shipment were to be delivered to his personal office, giving no reasons.

Douglas found the situation ominous. He and his senior British staff officers saw no threat to themselves or their families, but thought that an attempt might be made to neutralise them during a coup against the nation's leaders. The newly-arrived Lt. Col. Montgomery had been assigned to help with administrative matters, acting also as Deputy Army Commander. Douglas ruled that he himself, Montgomery or Mans (as CO of the 1st Battalion) were never to be in the same place at the same time. It was their first duty to be ready to deploy the army to protect the Government, and one or more of them must always remain free to do so. Another immediate need was to improve communications so as to lessen reliance on the telephone exchange, which might be taken over in a coup. Some requisitioned radios arrived from Nairobi on Friday 17 January 1964, and Douglas instructed his signals officer to install them the following Monday. These discussions were limited to the senior British officers.

At Flagstaff House, his official residence beside the officers' quarters at Colito, Brigadier Douglas thought that he had done all he could in the unsettled week after Zanzibar's revolution. He spent a relaxed Sunday with his family and a few friends at their beach house, some miles north of Dar es Salaam. The following week was to be busy with planning for the important forthcoming visit of Chou En-lai, the Chinese Premier. Douglas later recalled floating in the tepid waters of the Indian Ocean with his pipe in his mouth, his tobacco pouch on a rock beside him, discussing 'Kambona's activities and the odd things going on around us'.[5] Because they were still on alert about Zanzibar, there was a radio-equipped Land Rover and a signaller with them. When it was dark, the guests left and he sent the signaller back to barracks and their children home with their ayah. He and his wife stayed on alone for a while in that peaceful place and then drove home for a good night's sleep before the busy week ahead. Busy it certainly turned out to be – and it started a good deal earlier than usual, because the mutineers were already gathered for their final briefing.

Soon after midnight, the mutiny was launched.

Notes

1 Douglas's report for Kambona on causes of the mutiny, PRO: DO 185/47(239).
2 Account of the crisis to the War Office by Mans, Marston and Montgomery, February 1964, PRO: DO 185/46 (182G).
3 PRO: DO185/46 (91).
4 Marciandi, Brian: private papers: lecture notes for Army Staff College, 1965.
5 Douglas: private papers, unpublished account of mutiny.

6

The Mutiny Spreads

Soon after the mutineers had taken control of Colito Barracks, they called a *baraza*. They had decided that the new-style army would be run not by themselves, but by officers selected by the general acclaim of the soldiers. Those thus chosen would be promoted to a suitable rank and would run the army under the general guidance of the mutineers. Were any of the mutineers to be selected, they would serve in their new role without admitting their part in the mutiny. The *baraza* proved lengthy. The first 'promotion' was easy: Sergeant Hingo Ilogi was chosen to be the new Commander of the 1st Battalion, in place of Lt. Col. Mans, whose rank he assumed. Then Lieutenant Mwita Marwa, a former *effendi*, was promoted to Major; and a number of Warrant Officers, Sergeants and Corporals were promoted to fill other vacancies.

The most contentious issue was the selection of the new Brigadier, in overall command of the army: who would wear the coveted red-banded hat taken from Flagstaff House? An obvious choice was Captain Alex Nyirenda, now locked up in the guardroom cell, along with the other officers. He was one of the three most senior and qualified Tanganyikan officers and could slip easily into the role. However, it counted against him that he was a Nyasa, rather than from one of the main Tanganyikan tribes. Moreover, his detractors described him as a 'white man in a black skin', who hobnobbed and played tennis with the British officers.

It was eventually agreed that he should be released from detention, but should retain only his present Company command, without promotion. A similarly well-qualified officer was Captain Kashmiri. But although born, bred and educated in Tanganyika, he was suspect to the mutineers because of his Asian origin. The third of this Sandhurst-trained trio was Captain Sam Sarakikya, but he was up in Tabora with the 2nd Battalion. Another candidate put forward was Lieutenant William Chacha who had risen through the ranks after long service, but he had little backing. The choice finally fell on Second Lieutenant Elisha Kavana.

Kavana was not well known in the army. He had been a contemporary of Nyirenda at Tabora Secondary School, before graduating from Makerere University in Uganda, with an external B.Sc. degree from London University in physics, chemistry and mathematics. He was therefore regarded as 'brainy', and rather a loner.[1] Moreover, he had not entered the army by the usual route, but had undergone some training in Ethiopia before following a course at Mons in Britain. He had spent some of his brief military service in the army headquarters in Dar, before being transferred to the 1st Battalion. Now he was imprisoned with the other officers. Hastily released, the mutineers presented him with the Brigadier's hat. Kavana seemed surprised and reluctant. He was advised not to make difficulties, but to accept the appointment at once. He did so. Kavana's reactions may have been perfectly genuine, and Lt. Col. Mans, who was observing the scene from behind the bars of his cell, described him in a report written only a few days later as 'looking very scared'. Nevertheless, some people, both Tanganyikan and British, believed at the time that Kavana had been involved in the planning of the coup all along.

Back in the city, Stephen Miles was running into problems. Once he had allocated tasks to his team, he had driven to State House, accompanied by Ronnie Jacobson, one of his First Secretaries, to alert Nyerere. A group of mutineers was guarding the gate, so it was impossible to get in. Instead, they set off to find the Foreign and Defence Minister. On the way to Kambona's office, outside the Ministry they ran into the Minister for Home Affairs, Job Lusinde, and stopped to talk to him.

Meanwhile, the US Embassy had also received early warning of the mutiny. Bob Hennemeyer, a senior American diplomat, was later to claim that Nyirenda had rung him from the barracks to say: 'You should keep your people off the streets.'[2] The US Ambassador immediately activated their system of 'wardens' around the city, to warn US citizens to stay at home. Hennemeyer headed for the Embassy, in the Standard Bank building a block away from the British High Commission, to set this up. He decided to drive via State House. There he spotted the same group of mutineers on guard as Miles had encountered, so did not linger. Driving on, he saw Miles and Jacobson talking to Lusinde by the roadside, so stopped to join them. While they were trying to piece together what was going on, an army Land Rover drove up. The Minister and the three diplomats were arrested and flung unceremoniously into the back of the vehicle. After being driven a few blocks further to the Cable and Wireless building, they were handed over to another group of mutineers and put up against a wall at gunpoint. It seemed that they were suspected of being newly-arrived British officers. Lusinde was obviously not in this category, but kept quiet. Hennemeyer tried to bluff his way out by claiming that he was the US Ambassador, so should be released at once, but unluckily for him, one of the mutineers had recently seen the Ambassador and knew this to be untrue – so the ploy backfired badly. For a while, the situation seemed dire: the mutineers were unruly and some had clearly been drinking, or smoking *bhang* (cannabis). There was talk of it being 'time to kill'. But a sober Corporal managed to exercise some degree of control. Eventually, at about 5.45 a.m., and for no discernible reason, the four detainees were released and went their separate ways.

Christopher MacRae. *I saw Steven Miles often during the course of that day – and indeed throughout the crisis. He*

67

was remarkably cool and unruffled. Even when he came back to the office after having been held at gun-point for over an hour by the mutineers, far from being rattled he related this frightening incident quite light-heartedly, making nothing of the danger he had been in. These qualities of coolness and good humour were to stand him – and us all – in good stead in the days ahead as the crisis unfolded.

Lusinde, in his role as Home Minister and in the absence of both the President and the Vice President, next seems, perhaps at the suggestion of Miles, to have taken the initiative by telephoning Kenya for help. At that point, he was out of touch with Kambona who was probably still on his way back from Colito. While this request was being considered in Nairobi, British troops in Kenya were stood to. Later, however, after Lusinde had at last managed to contact Kambona, the request was withdrawn. This may have been for political reasons, or simply because by then it was known that the mutineers had seized the airport. Whatever the explanation, the Tanganyikan Government had in effect decided to try to solve the crisis on its own.

By mid-morning, Sergeant (now 'Lt. Col.') Ilogi must have realised that his plan was going awry. President Nyerere and Vice President Kawawa had both disappeared. Moreover, Brigadier Douglas and Major Marciandi had eluded capture. Some time after 9.30 a.m., Ilogi set off with a strong search party, accompanied by Kambona and Chief of Police Shaidi – as well as the newly-rehatted Kavana. They ended up at the residence of the Acting British High Commissioner. The driveway was completely blocked by the cars of the many British refugees sheltering within, so the several lorry-loads of mutineers assembled on the road outside. Some of the soldiers, apparently under the instructions of Kavana, surrounded the house. Douglas and his officers had been sent out of sight, hidden in an upstairs bathroom. An improvised school had been set up in the study, to keep the children occupied. It faced the driveway down which the mutineers could be seen all too clearly, so their temporary teacher told the children to lie flat on the floor.

By now, Douglas had decided that he and his officers would have to give themselves up. There could be no question of endangering the lives of the women and children. He had, however, reckoned without Steven Miles's wife, Joy, who proved more than equal to the occasion. She knew Kambona quite well, so marching briskly out to the front gate, she enquired whether she could help him. She told him plainly that it was illegal to allow armed troops onto British High Commission soil, especially since it was now a refuge for a large number of British women and children. When Kambona explained that he was just looking for her husband, she directed him to the High Commission office in town. The whole party soon withdrew.

Kambona later claimed that he was an unwilling accomplice in this episode and was only trying to calm things down. But many British observers felt this was being economical with the truth, as he had seemed so confident and relaxed, and had assured Mrs Miles authoritatively that the British community would come to no harm.

Some, at least, of the mutineer patrols behaved sensibly and responsibly. Colin Baxter ran the Building Deparment at the Dar Technical Institute. The only senior staff member to make it in to work on the Monday, he ventured out in his car on an errand. He was soon stopped and questioned. Once satisfied, the sergeant in charge ordered a corporal to escort him for the rest of the day, to ensure his freedom of movement. But as the morning wore on, the situation deteriorated. Many of the hastily-assembled groups of mutineers patrolling the streets and guarding key points had begun to dissolve into disorder. Minor excesses by the soldiers encouraged unruly civilians to join in. Asian and Arab shops were broken into and looted and what had started as an orderly search for British officers degenerated into general harassment of Arabs,

Asians and white foreigners. The police, faced with unrest led by armed soldiers, but with their headquarters neutralised, and left unsupported by their own mobile force which had been sent to Zanzibar, slipped unobtrusively home. The Tanganyikan Broadcasting Corporation (TBC) (radio — there was no television) went off the air. Rumours spread. The unrest soon led to killings.

At around 10 a.m., Kambona called Miles and asked him to come round to the Foreign Ministry. Miles drove round at once, passing a crowd of unruly mutineers. Kavana was with the Minister. Miles challenged Kambona directly: 'Is this a coup?' Kambona was adamant that this was not so, it was only a matter of 'unrest in the army', and he was getting the soldiers back to their barracks. Europeans had nothing to fear. Asked about the position of British officers, Kambona promised to go out to Colito to get them out of the country safely. This would be his first priority. It was agreed that Peter Carter, Miles's deputy, should accompany the Minister on this mission.

In the city, especially in the Asian and Arab trading quarters, order was collapsing. Two ugly events stand out from this period. In the Asian bazaar, a shot was fired at a soldier. Other troops at once reacted, firing their rifles into the air. Panic and confusion followed, leading to break-ins, looting and arson throughout the quarter. The firing became widespread, with machine-guns joining in. There were numerous casualties. After a while, a small detachment of the Police Field Force began to restore order.

A separate, nastier incident happened in the Arab quarter. A straggler from the mutineers called Kassim went into an Arab store and grabbed a drink. After an argument, the storekeeper fired his shotgun at him, wounding Kassim fatally. Other mutineers, hearing of this, went back to barracks to collect reinforcements. Soon, a heavily-armed group of mutineers attacked the store, using mortars and hand grenades. Then they finished off a large Arab family with sub-machine-guns, by any standards a calculated and vicious over-response to the original shooting.

*

Later in the day, in a second broadcast, Kambona referred to 'a disturbance ... which the Tanganyika Rifles had gone to quell'. He urged the city's inhabitants, especially the Arabs, to 'keep calm and remain indoors ... Those who break the law will face the *askaris*'. Kambona was willing to say anything to avoid upsetting the mutineers over whom he had no control, while doing what he could to keep the lid on the growing violence in the city. In these efforts, he was getting precious little assistance from his fellow ministers.

One junior minister did at least try to help. This was Joseph Nyerere, the lookalike younger brother of the President, who was Junior Minister for Culture and Parliamentary Secretary for the TANU Youth League. He was seen driving around the city, until he was detained and taken to Colito. He was soon released and sent home. When Amir Jamal, the (Asian) Minister for Transport and Communications, heard about the mutiny, he drove his family off to take refuge with a relative, then returned home 'to be available to anyone who wanted me'. Nobody did. It is easy, with the benefit of hindsight to be disparaging about such inertia, but to be fair, the political leadership was new and inexperienced. Moreover, the long-standing administrative structure inherited from the colonial period, which should have been able to support the Ministers in such a crisis, had been largely dismantled.

At about 3.30 p.m., the media gained an insight into what was happening. Two British journalists from the *East Africa Standard*, David Martin and Brandon Grimshaw, were stopped in their car by mutineers wanting to hitch a ride back to barracks.[3] As they were driven towards Colito, the soldiers talked freely about their 'protest demonstration'. They described their poor pay, adding that they did not want any longer to be led by British officers. They complained that they were paid only 106 shillings a month after training, no more than they had received when they were recruited. Even house servants in Dar were paid 150 shillings a month – without being expected to fight for their country. They claimed that the Minister

71

had agreed to all their demands: now they were 'very happy about everything'. When they reached the barracks, the journalists were told that two soldiers had been killed, as well as some civilians. The soldiers were 'very upset about this. We had planned that there should be no fighting and had simply intended to demand in a peaceful manner that our demands should be met'. This could well have been the best description of the origins and development of the mutiny as we are ever likely to get.

At Colito Barracks, the situation in the guardroom cells was still tense. Several British officers had narrowly escaped being shot. In one incident, Lt. Col. Mans was saved only by the intervention of one of the older Tanganyikan officers, Lieutenant Gibagiri. The sight of Kambona and Carter engaged in heated discussions with the mutineers outside the cells came as a relief: perhaps, after all, it might turn out better than the prisoners feared. After a while, British officers were taken out and loaded into army Bedford trucks, along with the few Tanganyikan officers who had been in the cells with them. Many of the mutineers argued that the local officers should be deported along with the British ones, but a Sergeant intervened, freeing Gibagiri and another junior officer. Then Sergeant Ilogi arrived, and insisted that Nyirenda should not be deported either. Eventually, only Kashmiri was left, amidst shouts that he should 'go back to Bombay'. Mans faced up to Kambona and his entourage. The British officers refused to leave, he said, unless the Minister guaranteed the safety of their families who had been abandoned in the officer's quarters. Kambona undertook, in front of Carter, to get them out safely.

The small convoy of trucks left around 10 a.m., first taking the road towards Dar, then cutting through the Asian quarter to the airport road. Things still seemed fairly quiet: the captured officers noticed patrols of soldiers who seemed, so far, to be under control. Some 'covered' the lorries with their rifles as they passed. Kambona had telephoned the airport from Colito to demand that an aircraft should be made ready to fly the party out of the country. There was growing excitement in the terminal while a Fokker Friendship aircraft was found and readied. Once the convoy reached the airport, the (British) Chief Engineer of the TBC, who had argued with the mutineers, was forced to join the British officers. He objected, perhaps too strenuously, and guns were pointed at him. Mans advised him to complain once he was safely out of the country. At one stage, even Kambona had a rifle pressed threateningly into his stomach, and he must have realised how limited was his real control over events. Nevertheless, by about 11 a.m., all the British officers from Colito, together with most of the staff officers, one British and one Asian police inspector, and a BBC engineer were flown out of Dar es Salaam, desperately worried about the families they were leaving behind.

The departure of the British officers seemed to weaken the control the leaders of the mutiny had over the troops. Kambona and Lusinde decided nevertheless to try to get them back to barracks. They toured the city in a Land Rover, escorted by heavily armed men. Arriving at the TBC some time before noon, Kambona ordered radio broadcasting to be resumed. He decided to address the nation, in order to quell the rumours and start to restore order. He announced confidently that there had been a misunderstanding between Tanganyikan soldiers and British officers at Colito Barracks. But he had intervened and the soldiers had returned to barracks. The citizens of the republic were in no danger and should keep calm. Both the soldiers and the police were loyal to the Government and civil servants should resume their duties. Mikidadi Mdoe, the Director of the TBC, who was present during the broadcast, afterwards described the scene as having been very tense. The Minister had acted bravely – but incoherently. Despite his confident tone, Kambona had made some wild promises: 'there will be a big parade tomorrow,' he had told the army, 'and you will all be promoted'.

During the afternoon, Stephen Miles briefed the CRO in London via an open teleprinter conference. He reported reliable figures from the main hospital, listing 14 dead, 20 serious injuries and 100 minor injuries. All the casualties were Tanganyikans, Arabs or Asians; no Europeans had been hurt. The new Commander of the Army had undertaken to have several British nationals released from police stations. However, Miles still judged the situation to be very grave. He considered he would still need help to safeguard British lives. He reported that HMS *Rhyl* had arrived and was anchored offshore. He would confirm to Kambona that the ship was here simply to protect lives and property. Soon afterwards, he reported that Lusinde had asked him to have the warship sail outside territorial waters to avoid trouble with the mutineers who had deployed machine-guns in positions to oppose any landing. In London, the CRO duly passed on the message to the Ministry of Defence; and *Rhyl* promptly moved away out of sight.

Later, Duncan Sandys, the British Secretary of State for Commonwealth Relations and the Colonies, joined in the exchange and it was agreed that Kambona would remain the main channel of communication between the two countries until Nyerere was located. Miles believed that Kambona had had considerable success in persuading the mutineers to return to barracks. Miles and Kambona had agreed that the arrival of foreign troops, even African ones from a neighbouring country, might spark off trouble again and lead to a large loss of life before control could be re-established by the outsiders. Sandys signed off with a personal message of appreciation for the calm and efficient manner in which Miles was dealing with this difficult and dangerous situation. The British Government was now, and would remain, firmly in step with its representative in Dar es Salaam.

Still hidden in the Acting High Commissioner's residence, Brigadier Douglas heard reports about unruly stragglers causing trouble in the town, but also about the action taken by the mutineers to oppose any possible British landing from HMS *Rhyl*. It seemed that although the 1st Battalion's discipline was fraying at the edges, it had not yet disintegrated as a fighting unit.

*

Back in the Colito Barracks' married quarters, the mutineers had
been as good as their – or Kambona's – word. The British wives
had heard nothing except shouting and shooting for over 12 hours.
They had spent their time calming the children and making what
preparations they could to move. Now they were told to get ready
to board transport. At about sunset, some 90 women and children
were loaded aboard three Dakotas for the flight to Nairobi, where
they were reunited with their husbands. At the Colito quarters,
guarded by loyal houseboys and unmolested by the mutineers, the
contents of the families' houses were to remain undisturbed until
British civilian volunteers packed them up, forwarded the
personal belongings, and arranged for the disposal of cars and
pets.

In London, the crisis had already been raised in the House of
Commons, where Sandys described the situation as 'very
obscure'. He knew little more than what Miles had told him. He
added that there were about 20,000 British citizens in Dar es
Salaam, of whom about 5,000 were of UK origin and 15,000 of
Asian origin. He was asked if, in view of the Government's other
very heavy commitments overseas, he could assure the House that
everything possible would be done to safeguard the lives of
British personnel and others in Tanganyika. Also, had the troubles
arisen because of a disagreement between the British officers
and African personnel? Sandys replied that the safety of British
lives was the Government's first obligation. The question of
'commitments elsewhere' did not arise because there were British
troops stationed in Kenya 'only a very, very short flight from Dar
es Salaam. But it is not always wise to rush with troops into
another country, even in a situation of this kind'. The cause of the
crisis, he said, was apparently the slow rate of Africanisation in
the Tanganyika Rifles, and pay levels. Both were issues for the
Tanganyikan Government. But there may have been other causes

and influences about which he was not yet aware, he added. This last point was at once picked up by a Conservative backbencher, Stephen Hastings, who commented that it would be most unusual for a mutiny to take place without outside provocation and that Dar es Salaam had become 'a centre for a build-up of Communist inspired and Afro-Asian subversion'. The Minister was not to be drawn on this issue, which he clearly regarded as a red herring.

By 8.00 p.m. that Monday evening, all was quiet in Dar es Salaam. The mutineers had returned to barracks, leaving behind only groups of guards on duty at State House, and to protect the Algerian arms. No curfew had been announced but everyone stayed at home. Armed police patrolled the wrecked and looted shops. The mutineers had been continuously on the move since the previous evening and badly needed some rest. They had been promised more pay by none other than the Minister of Defence, the British officers had been successful shipped out, they had secured the airport and the *Rhyl* had been withdrawn. They could not have known that 1,000 miles to the north, the force that was to restore order was already assembling.

Notes

1 PRO: DO 185/46 (53), which shows the favourable final report from Mons on Kavana's abilities — a report which 45 Cdo RM was aware of by 23 January (Pennington, personal correspondence).
2 Hennemeyer, Bob: *Robert Hennemeyer in Dar es Salaam, Tanganyika* (61–4) . Stephen Miles's papers.
3 *Tanganyika Standard*, Dar es Salaam, 21 Jan 1964, p. 1.

7

HMS Centaur

In London, the CRO, with information now flowing in steadily from Dar es Salaam, was briefing the Prime Minister, Sir Alec Douglas-Home. 'Situation rooms' set up in the Foreign Office and Ministry of Defence kept in close touch, and were ready to carry out any action ordered by Cabinet Ministers, or propose initiatives themselves. The troubles in Tanganyika and Zanzibar were not the only problems Britain faced that week, but British lives might be at risk in East Africa — and the first duty of the Government was to take whatever steps they could to safeguard them. After making urgent contact with neighbouring Commonwealth countries, it was soon established that President Kenyatta was not at that stage prepared to send Kenyan troops to help restore order in Dar. Instead, he recommended that the British themselves should prepare to evacuate their own citizens if necessary. For the moment that seemed the only option.

The Chief of Defence Staff, Admiral the Earl Mountbatten of Burma[1] was closely involved. A range of options was hurriedly reviewed after teleprinter conferences with local British commanders in Nairobi (East Africa Command) and Aden (the Middle East Command, which was senior). By 12.15 p.m. on 20 January, less than 12 hours after the mutiny began, the Defence Operations Executive in London broadcast an early situation report and issued preliminary instructions to British forces. The frigate HMS *Rhyl* was instructed to leave Zanzibar and sail immediately for Dar es Salaam. Off Aden, the aircraft carrier HMS *Centaur* was told to break off her flying exercises, return to harbour and embark the Royal Marines of 45 Commando, some RAF helicopters and eight army armoured cars. She was then to sail south to the Mombasa area and remain out of sight to be ready for any contingency. This was a quick reaction to a confused and dangerous situation.

Conspiracy theorists were later quick to point out how suspicious it was that a British aircraft carrier was so conveniently at hand. The truth was that *Centaur* was on her way to Singapore for a year of operations in the Far East – and happened to have reached Aden on the way there. After commissioning with a new crew in Portsmouth, the ship and her aircraft had started 'working up' in the English Channel before Christmas. She had then sailed south on the first leg of her passage to Singapore. While passing through the Bay of Biscay, she had been diverted to aid a burning cruise ship, the *Lakonia*. Once this mission was completed, she had reached Aden on 4 January 1964, to begin another period of flying training before an operational readiness inspection in Singapore.

Britain's few remaining aircraft carriers were hard-worked during the early 1960s, and *Centaur* was under pressure to get to the Far East as soon as possible. She was small, relatively slow, lightly armed and could operate only a small number of aircraft. By Cold War standards she was unimpressive, but in the operational environment in which she served, she was highly effective. She could bring force to bear on most remote areas or situations, and was one of the few ace cards Britain still held 'East of Suez'.

The ship's only fighting punch was provided by a squadron of Sea Vixen fighter-bombers. These aircraft could operate by day or night, were equipped with air-to-air radar and weapons, and could also bomb and strafe ground forces. The Sea Vixens were complicated two-seater aircraft and needed a great deal of maintenance in a busy and crowded hangar below the flight deck.

Centaur's second squadron consisted of Wessex anti-submarine helicopters. It was organised and trained to search for and destroy submarines in the event of a major war. However, it was also often used for other duties including moving troops and stores in support of military operations on land. Recently, while deployed ashore in Aden awaiting *Centaur*'s arrival, the squadron had been operating up-country. Yemeni-inspired insurgents had been fighting Federal Government forces in the Radfan district whom the naval helicopters had been supporting. Some of the squadron's helicopters had come under fire. They had only just been released from this task to revert to anti-submarine duties before joining *Centaur*, which involved reinstalling sonar equipment and retraining the aircrew for this role.

There were two other small air contingents on board: a flight of four radar early-warning Gannets (slow, unarmed, turbo-prop aircraft), and two small Whirlwind helicopters of the search and rescue flight. These aircraft, when not on operations, were used as the ship's workhorses, carrying mail, VIPs and vital stores.

Centaur carried only 24 aircraft but was always very crowded and busy. It took time and a lot of work to bring a squadron to full mechanical, electrical and electronic readiness, and then to exercise for a range of possible operations with the aircrews fully briefed. Some pilots were inexperienced and needed to be trained in night flying. *Centaur* had been practising these drills during her second 'work-up' period, off Aden.

Most of the ship's company were new to aircraft carriers, and needed training in their duties. Even the Captain and navigation officers had to learn that air operations in light winds would always be difficult in a small and relatively slow carrier. On board, the range of activities and equipment crowded into the under-deck spaces was bewildering to the newcomer. One Marine afterwards wrote: 'I set myself to learn the way from my cabin, via the loo, to the wardroom and thence to the flight deck — and nothing else at all.' By the end of their time in Aden, however, most of the ship's crew were beginning to make some sense of it all.

An aircraft carrier's duties did not end with air operations: the ship might also be needed in a 'command' role. It had be prepared to provide the services needed to control a task force and to serve as flagship for a seagoing Admiral. This required extensive command, control and communication facilities. In an age when communications systems were far less sophisticated than today, *Centaur* needed over 90 radio operators and signalmen, handling hundreds of messages a day. There were also more colourful aspects of being a potential flagship needing to 'show the flag': the ship also carried a small detachment of Royal Marines with a band which could be guaranteed to put on a fine display during port calls.

The ship itself needed large engineering, electrical and catering crews, with other smaller medical, policing, stores, and hull maintenance (shipwright) departments. A few specialist seamen were needed to manoeuvre the 28,000-tonne ship around the ocean and in and out of port. For more general activities, the whole ship's company was pressed into service. The most onerous tasks were storing and refuelling. An operating aircraft carrier ran out of aviation fuel after a few days, out of ship's fuel after rather longer, and out of victuals and stores in a few weeks. Visits to base would have been impractical, so each aircraft carrier had a dedicated fleet auxiliary tanker and a supply ship to refuel and reprovision it. These ships loitered near the carrier's operating area and a rendezvous would be ordered during breaks in flying operations. While the seamen and engineers coped with refuelling, others grappled with incoming stores, bringing them from the replenishment-at-sea points across the flight deck to the main aircraft lifts, to be stored below. This type of collective activity required much planning and organisation even during routine training operations. The responsibility fell on the ship's Executive Officer, known in the Royal Navy as the Commander, who was also the second-in-command of the ship.

Centaur's Commander, Derek Bazalgette, was intelligent, capable and popular. He had entered the navy from Dartmouth, served during World War II, and had then specialised in gunnery. Appointed to *Centaur* in 1955 as a Lieutenant-Commander, his duties had included acting as Commander's Assistant, the officer responsible for coordinating the ship's interdepartmental routine. His second appointment to the ship, as Executive Officer, brought demanding new challenges. If any one man could be credited with the success of adapting *Centaur* to its new role during the next few days, it was Bazalgette.

The ultimate operational responsibility, however, rested with the Commanding Officer. Captain Steiner had joined the navy in 1935. His full name, Ottokar Harold Mojmir St John Steiner, revealed his Austro-Hungarian ancestry, but he had been brought up entirely in Britain, attending St Paul's school in London before taking the Naval Special Entry examination. A passionate yachtsman, he had joined the navy's sailing association in 1937 and was later to serve as its President, helping to initiate the first round-the-world sailing race. At the start of World War II he was serving in the destroyer which was the first ship to sink a German U-boat, in October 1939. Later he was heavily involved in the Norwegian campaign. Specialising in underwater warfare, he had alternated between command and staff appointments until his selection, as a senior Captain, for command of an anti-submarine cruiser in 1963. However, the cruiser's commission was cancelled when the Ministry of Defence recognised the need for a second aircraft carrier to bolster its Far East forces. *Centaur* was hastily recommissioned, and the cruiser's skeleton staff transferred to bring her back into service. Otto Steiner thus found himself commanding an aircraft carrier, although he had never served in one during his earlier career. His ebullient charm and forcefulness was to prove a great asset in the crisis ahead, but he had never before served in a ship bigger than a cruiser and had no experience at all of air or amphibious operations.

*

The Royal Navy's command and control policy greatly complicated the task of the Captain of an aircraft carrier. Not only did he have to control his own major warship, but also any other ships detailed to support it. Yet the first duty of a Commanding Officer was not to hazard his own ship — so he could rarely delegate even the simplest matter of navigation or collision avoidance to any of the roughly 200 other officers on board, even though perhaps 40 of them were qualified to keep watches on the bridge. If a merchant ship approached closely, the Captain had to be informed. So command had to be exercised from the navigation bridge, a small and crowded 'compass platform' perched above one side of the flight deck. If anyone on board, however senior, urgently wanted to know what was happening, he had to go up to the bridge to see the Captain. Otherwise he had to wait until the ship's daily orders or signal distributions provided the answer.

Until then, there had been no routine operational meetings or briefings aboard *Centaur*. Problems were solved by discussions on the bridge — sometimes between those who happened to be there. But the decisions were not always passed on to other key staff officers – a common shortcoming of the Royal Navy at the time. In an aircraft carrier, those involved in air operations knew what to do and carried out their regular duties smoothy. But once these duties departed from the normal routine, problems might emerge.

Two smaller warships had been allocated to help with *Centaur*'s flying programme. There always had to be a fast escort vessel, ready for long-range search-and-rescue operations. HMS *Cambrian* was a modernised World War II destroyer which had been detached from the Far East fleet to undertake this duty. In addition, the Helicopter Squadron needed to be brought back to full anti-submarine operational standards after its deployment at Aden on the ground support duties. A modern frigate, HMS *Rhyl*, under a senior and experienced Captain, had therefore been detached from the Mediterranean to exercise with the helicopters. The force was needed urgently in Singapore, so the ships sailed from Aden on Friday 10 January, to start their exercises at sea.

The following days were extremely busy, but on 16 January the exercises were interrupted when the ship was unexpectedly ordered back to harbour. Ashore, Captain Steiner was briefed by the Flag Officer Middle East about the possibility of a serious operation. *Centaur* might be needed to embark 650 men of 45 Commando, Royal Marines, to be taken south to deal with trouble in Zanzibar.

45 Commando had been deployed to Aden in 1959 for active internal security duties. An outpost had been set up at Dhala, a small town near the border with the Yemen, and during the next four years the marines maintained a high state of readiness, training, patrolling, and on occasion skirmishing with dissident tribesmen. Individual marines came and went on rotation from the UK. The marines undertook a varied but always demanding range of tasks. When serving with '45' at that time, their duties would have been described as 'mountain/desert low-intensity operations'. The work was hard, conditions spartan and there was a very real risk of injury by gunfire or mines. These routine operations were interrupted temporarily on Thursday 16 January 1964 when the trouble broke out in Zanzibar. The Commando was brought to three hours' notice for a possible move south. An advance planning party was flown out to *Centaur* to investigate how the unit might be embarked, although the notice was soon lengthened to 24 hours. But soon afterwards, 45 Commando was stood down and told to resume its normal Aden routine: it seemed that this had been a false alert. The relief proved short-lived.

When the emergency standby plan was cancelled, *Centaur* resumed her training exercises. Flying continued on Friday and Saturday (17 and 18 January), with another refuelling and a transfer exercise with *Cambrian*, followed by further flying exercises during the next two days. The Aden exercise period was completed at 11.35 a.m. on Monday 20 January. The aircraft carrier had by then achieved the operational standards needed to fly and control both its fixed-wing strike aircraft and the anti-submarine helicopters. The ship had only to make an hour-long call into harbour to load an unserviceable aircraft before sailing to join the British forces in the Far East.

However, this deployment was postponed because, during the harbour call, the situation changed dramatically. *Centaur* was ordered at once to embark 45 Royal Marine Commando with its 24 Land Rovers, its stores, weapons and ammunition, and to take them south to the Mombasa area. She was also to load two large RAF Belvedere helicopters and eight small Ferret armoured cars. Planning for the brief alarm of ten days earlier had concerned only a few people on board. Now everyone was suddenly involved in a dramatic change of role.

On shore in Aden, the marines had been alerted when their commanding officer, Lt. Col. T.M.P. (Paddy) Stevens was summoned to Middle-East Headquarters. There, the Commander-in-Chief, Lieutenant General Charles Harington, ordered 45 Commando to embark immediately in *Centaur*. His orders were terse: 'Get cracking, Paddy.' At this stage, there was no planned operation in mind, nor even a general intention, and the force had no ultimate destination. Stevens had brought his Intelligence Officer with him to the headquarters, and the young Lieutenant Tony Hazeldine called on the Chief of Intelligence for the Middle East Command, a staff officer considerably his senior. The latter had nothing whatever to divulge; no maps or intelligence, nor any up-to-date news of events in progress. He said only that the operation was classified 'secret' and that all would become clear once the Commando was embarked and the CO had opened his orders. He added that up-to-date intelligence would be provided on board, but who would provide it was unclear. Hazeldine soon discovered that his CO had no orders, sealed or otherwise. At first he assumed that the intelligence staff officer had resented having to deal with someone so junior. Later he realised that few people in Aden knew anything much about East Africa or what was going on there – perhaps it had previously seemed quiet and stable in comparison with the simmering tensions of South Yemen. For this unforeseen operation, the Aden Command had acted merely as a postbox for London, passing on the order 'Embark 45 in *Centaur* and send her southwards'. Lt. Col. Stevens later wrote: 'We had been pitched on board a strange ship which was neither designed nor trained for our particular games. There was no precedent for an operational landing from an unconverted strike carrier with its full range of aircraft embarked – indeed it had been described as impossible.'[2] In the best traditions of the Royal Marines, they did it – quickly and for the most part efficiently.

It was a stroke of good fortune that the British military force available in Aden happened to be a Royal Marines Commando. Royal Marines are trained and equipped for infantry work, but with the added dimension that they can be used in amphibious operations. Many of their officers had been trained partly by and with the navy, and a high proportion of the senior NCOs had already served in ships at some time in their career. Indeed there was a small marine detachment already on board *Centaur* as part of the ship's company. Had the military unit available in Aden been a regular army 'line' battalion it would still have been sent off with *Centaur*. But with so much to be done so quickly, it was a huge bonus that they were marines.

An advance party soon arrived on board. Ship's routines were amended. Hangar parties began to clear space for 600 camp beds while crew 'messes' were allocated for more senior ranks. Royal Marine cooks and caterers were integrated into the galley staffs while meal routines were adjusted. Most concerns were administrative and domestic, but there were also real operational problems. The flight deck controllers demonstrated that it was impossible to find space on deck for the vehicles and stores without infringing safety regulations. There were strict limits to the mutual proximity of fuelled aircraft, vehicles with full tanks, and the marine's petrol and ammunition stores. Radiation from the ship's powerful radio and radar transmitters imposed further restrictions. The flight deck crew did the best they could, but only four armoured cars could be loaded, and the marines were told to leave ten of their Land Rovers in Aden. The loading plan completed, the embarkation began at 5.45 p.m. on 20 January.

For the marines, the embarkation had been particularly challenging. Z Company had been out on field firing exercises in the desert, so a vehicle had been sent out to order them back to camp. X Company had been in barracks and were able to begin embarking in the late afternoon. Once on board they could be deployed to load the heavy stores. On the quayside they found a troop of the 16/5th Lancers waiting with their Ferret scout cars. It transpired they were coming too, as were some RAF ground crew for the Belvedere helicopters. Everything was loaded into lighters to be taken out and lifted by the ship's crane up to the flight deck. It would be sorted later once the ship had sailed. Y Company was up-country in Dhala. Although helicopters were soon found to bring them in, there was a snag: the position they were defending was tactically important and no relief had been designated. The Company Commander decided that he could not simply abandon the post. With some reluctance he ordered his second-in-command, Lieutenant Ted Goddard, to remain with a tiny force to hold what the latter later described as 'a fort out of a Beau Geste story'.[3] They agreed that a Colour Sergeant and six Royal Marines should be able to do the job.

Between 5 p.m. and midnight on 20 January, a total of 592 officers and men, 50 tons of stores, petrol and ammunition, four Ferret scout cars and thirteen Land Rovers were embarked aboard *Centaur*. The troops occupied 'C' hangar, the after-end of the ship's main underdeck aircraft stowage area. The hangar's normal occupants, the Sea Vixens of 892 Squadron, were brought up on the aircraft lifts to the open flight deck to be ranged clear of marine stores and there secured for sea. Wire strops had been rigged across the hangar deck, and camp beds were lashed to them, only inches apart. More camp beds were secured across the ship's quarterdeck, a semi-enclosed space allocated for the senior NCOs. The crews of the armoured cars occupied the schoolroom, while the RAF ground crew found space to sleep inside their large Belvedere helicopters on the flight deck.

Corporal Pennington of 'Y' Company, writing later about his experiences,[4] described the hurried return from Dhala and the embarkation.[5] Only recently out from the UK, he had misjudged the power of the sun on the exposed hilltops and had been badly burned. Unable to carry anything on his back, he lost some of his equipment overboard when climbing up to *Centaur* from a ship's boat. Once on board, he found it crowded and confusing – but there were also advantages. The food was excellent: well cooked fresh meat and vegetables from the ship's capacious cold rooms – a far cry from the rigours of Dhala camp. There was even rum for those who chose to draw their tot. (Some, quite improperly, allowed sailors to drink their ration!) The officers did well too, and some, disdaining the wide choice of spirits and wines available from the wardroom bar, and aware that there would probably be little to do for several days, downed welcoming pints of best bitter.

> Tony Laurence. *I must claim credit for this minor triumph because, in my additional and sometimes demanding role as 'wardroom wine caterer', I had organised regular supplies of keg beer to be brought out from the UK by our supply ships.*

Ashore at the headquarters of the Flag Officer, Middle East (FOME), Rear Admiral J. E. Scotland had already taken operational control of HMS *Rhyl* and sent her southwards towards Zanzibar. He now dispatched *Cambrian* independently, leaving

Centaur with only her two replenishment ships. The carrier could make 25 knots to the Mombasa area and then operate for about two days before needing to refuel. Her tanker *Tidesurge* was much slower, so was ordered to sail at once – a rendezvous for refuelling could be arranged later. Both ships were well stocked with victuals and stores, so there was no immediate need to replenish from the stores ship.

Tony Laurence. *This was one of the occasions when the operational planning faltered. To plan the days ahead, Captain Steiner called a meeting of Heads of Department. This included the Engineer and Medical Commanders, but no operational staff officers. So I found out that our replenishment ships had sailed only after they were out of communication range! This lapse was soon remedied after exchanges with the local area radio station in Mauritius; but this early failure of communications, both literally and figuratively, was somewhat unsettling.*

For *Centaur*'s crew, the task of embarking marines, airmen and soldiers was not particularly tricky. They were mostly brought out in ship's boats, then climbed the companion ladders up the side of the ship, and were soon settling in. A bigger problem was the huge pile of Royal Marines' stores waiting in boxes on the quayside. More lighters were found, volunteers called for, and loading began. Work was interrupted for a time when there was a warning of imminent squalls which would make the inner harbour unsafe. The ship's engines were brought to immediate notice while anchor and line-handling parties were called out to allow *Centaur* to move. The ship was just slipping her stern buoy when the squalls died away; the manoeuvre was cancelled and loading continued. The last lighter was cleared soon after midnight. *Centaur* slipped her moorings and manoeuvred out to sea at 1 a.m. on 21 January. Only those sleeping right aft were disturbed by the vibrations as the ship's engines were worked up to nearly full power. It was a bare 24 hours after the mutiny had broken out in Colito.

The speed of this operation was remarkable by any standards. The Government in London had reacted very quickly to the news from Tanganyika. The Royal Marines had immediately abandoned an operational role to board a ship they had never seen before. For her part, *Centaur* had adapted at once to the wholly unrehearsed role of fast transport ship in a little over 12 hours. This was an extraordinary logistical feat. Questions about what the ship would have to do, and how and where its commando force would be deployed, were left for later, as *Centaur* slipped off into the dark.

Notes

1   Strictly 'Admiral of the Fleet' but the rank of Admiral may be more familiar to the reader.
2   Young, David: *Four Five*, p. 306.
3   Conversations with the author. There was a light-hearted sequel. Some days after the Commando had left this tiny detachment was relieved by a company of the Parachute Regiment, after Goddard had agreed that '120 Paratroopers would probably be enough to discharge this responsibility – since they were quite good'. Back in Aden, with no means of rejoining his Commando aboard *Centaur*, Goddard's squad was reinforced by a dribble of marines coming back from leave or from sick parades. With this motley group, he was later sent back to hold his fort, remaining there until the Commando returned weeks later, with tales of African adventures.
4   Pennington, Ivor: correspondence with author.
5   Ibid.

8

Stalemate in Dar

News of the mutinies had affected the whole nation by the morning after the mutiny, Tuesday 21 January. In the West Lake region, 1,000 miles from Dar es Salaam beyond Lake Victoria, John Ainley, the Regional Agricultural Officer, was told by his head clerk that the Government had been toppled. He called on the region's chief of police, who told him that a police radio message had confirmed firing in the capital. On returning to his office, Ainley found that two of his senior African staff had been arrested. Admitted eventually into the office of the Regional Commissioner, he learned that the latter had arrested 'fairly prominent men in the community who were not TANU members', without orders and for no other reason than as a general precaution. Ainley, explaining that his department was crippled, eventually persuaded the Commissioner to relent, and the men were released the following day.

In Dar, it was ominously quiet. Most people stayed at home, waiting for reliable news. The majority of the mutineers stayed in their barracks, with only a few being sent to guard vital points. The airfield and port were closed, as were all businesses and government departments, and there was almost no traffic on the roads. The police appeared to be in control of the town, but as they had fraternised with the soldiers the day before their appearance guaranteed nothing politically. Had there been a coup, perhaps in favour of Kambona? What had driven the soldiers to mutiny and what had they achieved?

91

There was no news about *Mwalimu*, the President. Fearing the worst, his devoted Personal Secretary, Joan Wicken, started burning sensitive papers. We now know that Nyerere was still hiding at his beach hut, some six miles south of the city, shocked into inactivity. Since there was no telephone, he was not in command of his Government nor even in communication with his ministerial team. He did not know what to do, or even whether it was yet safe for him to appear again in public. Meanwhile Oscar Kambona was emerging as the Minister in control, taking decisions without apparently consulting other members of the Government. Yet he had no answer to the key question of how to restore order. He had received offers of help from the British, and had originally expressed some interest; but he and Lusinde, the Home Minister, had soon agreed that the arrival of any outside force, even African, would spark off trouble and could lead to a large loss of life before order could be re-established. Those Ministers with whom Kambona was in contact were arguably the most 'anti-European'; but all agreed to decline even help from Kenya. Their instincts were probably right and their immediate decisions may have prevented a descent into Congo-style chaos. For an inexperienced Government, faced with a wholly unforeseen and serious challenge, they were doing well enough: for the moment the lid was still on, and a potentially explosive situation was not bubbling over.

In Magomeni, few traders were to be seen. The police were restoring order in the litter-strewn streets, guarding the looted shops and particularly the burned outhouse where the soldier and Arab family had died. Police cells were crowded with opportunists who had been caught running off with loot. The British community, advised by the High Commission, was also staying at home and keeping a low profile. Had things taken a turn for the worse, some sort of evacuation from Oyster Bay might have been attempted; but numbers were huge compared with the single Royal Navy frigate *Rhyl*, her armed detachment and the few merchant ships in the area that might have been requisitioned.

Any preparations for, or even warnings about, an evacuation would have become public immediately. The only realistic strategy was to keep heads down – at least until provisions ran out.

Back in London, the Government was now taking the matter very seriously. The 2nd Battalion Scots Guards, normally based in Nairobi, had been exercising in the South Arabian Federation. Their training programme was cut short and they were flown back to Kenya. In answer to questions, the Government could only explain the situation in Tanganyika as 'confused'.

Any hopes that the unrest would be contained in Dar were soon dashed. After Brigadier Douglas had first escaped the mutiny, he had called Lt. Col. Miles Marston, the British commanding officer of the 2nd Battalion up-country in Tabora. Douglas described what he knew about events at Colito, and was told that there was no sign of trouble either among Marston's men, or in town. Douglas's immediate concern was the safety of the President, and he thought it might be possible that Nyerere was on his way to Tabora. In any case, Marston had served in India during unstable times and well understood the importance of keeping the airfields open. Both men agreed that the 2nd Battalion should, as an immediate priority, secure both Tabora airport and the railway station. But the force might also be used to restore order in Dar es Salaam, and the CO was ordered to prepare to bring his men down by road, rail or air. At this early stage, however, it was uncertain whether they, or indeed anyone else, could be relied on. To ensure secure operational control, Douglas told Marston to accept instructions only from him, the Army Commander, personally.

Marston had been in command of the 2nd Battalion in Tabora for only three months. Aged 43, he was from the Argyll and Sutherland Highlanders, and had first been commissioned in 1940. During World War II he had served with the Gurkhas in India, the Middle East, and Italy, and had later attended the Army Staff College at Camberley. A subsequent appointment as Brigade

Major to the 16th Parachute Brigade in the Egyptian canal zone had given him valuable experience. Tabora had seemed a good posting, and he was arranging to be joined by his wife and daughter. He was, however, uneasy about still being in command of African troops, and would have preferred to play some sort of training or support role under a Tanganyikan commanding officer. His doubts had been reinforced by his discovery that the 2nd Battalion lacked military professionalism; they certainly lacked the tactical ability he had come to expect from troops like the Gurkhas or paratroopers. On the other hand, however, they seemed to be in good heart, were very fit and excelled at ceremonial. So he set about improving their field training.

The 2nd Battalion was quite unlike the 1st, down at Dar. It had been allowed, to a large extent, to go its own way over recruitment and basic training. Miles Marston had found his new command conservative, very proud of themselves and their traditions; and happy with their British connections. They had shown a deep regard for their President, although they had barely concealed their contempt for many of the lesser politicians who had visited from Dar. Brigadier Douglas later wrote about an occasion when an old soldier, having been kept on parade for hours for a departure ceremony, had spat as the VIP aircraft took off. Seeing Douglas watching him, the soldier had smiled – the Brigadier was 'one of us' while the politician was not.

Having spoken to Marston, Douglas mentioned the 2nd Battalion when he first briefed Kambona. He reported that Tabora airport and railway station would both be secured and the troops made ready to move down to the coast. Kambona immediately agreed, authorising Douglas to charter civilian aircraft for an airlift. By 4.30 a.m., less than three hours after the mutiny, airline managers at Dar airport were bringing in aircrew for the purpose. But by 7 a.m., however, planning was disrupted by the arrival of mutineers at Douglas's temporary headquarters. He was forced to make a second escape and for a while was again out of contact.

Marston, in Tabora, had by then roused his battalion. Sandhurst-trained Captain Sam Sarakikya, commander of B Company and the senior African officer in the battalion, was ordered to take two of his platoons to safeguard the airport. One of his officers, Lieutenant Musuguri, was sent with the third platoon to guard the railway station. By the time they were deployed, news of the mutiny was being broadcast by Radio Kenya: 'The [Tanganyikan] army has mutinied and the whereabouts of the President and Vice President are unknown'. But there were no transmissions from Radio Tanganyika – the national station was off the air. The news seemed to come as a complete surprise to most of the battalion, and groups gathered to discuss the implications. The telephone service had by now failed almost completely. Although an army radio network linked Dar, Tabora and Nachingwea, the Dar station was now controlled by the mutineers, and Marston suspected that something similar might happen to his isolated Company down at Nachingwea. He therefore ordered that the radio link was neither to be monitored nor used except under his instructions. Unknown to him, his young and inexperienced signal officer permitted, and may even have joined in, radio exchanges with the mutineers at Colito.

Marston himself was kept very busy for the rest of the day. His orders were to prepare to bring his troops to the coast. He waited for news of aircraft availability, but heard nothing from the Brigadier. He investigated rail timings and the possibility of using road transport. He also thought about putting a guard on his battalion's arms and ammunition, but decided that this would be provocative as it might indicate mistrust of his own men. After calling on the Regional Commissioner, who knew nothing whatever about what was happening, he attended a meeting with the regional police, opening with the statement, 'President Nyerere might well be on his way to Tabora; I take it that we all remain absolutely loyal to him'. Everyone present agreed emphatically. For the present he could do no more.

There has been no evidence of plotting in the 2nd Battalion before the mutiny. There is, however, plenty of evidence that the mutineers in Colito pressed their fellow *askaris* in Tabora to join them. Phrases such as 'unless you join us we will break your heads' and 'you will be thrashed' were used. A message, intercepted in Kenya, was logged as 'Our men here striking. Please join us. Police, airport, State House, government store compound, and Tanganyika Broadcasting Corporation captured. Because men do not like Europeans in their army'.[1] The highly charged, emotional and threatening demands, backed by calls for racial solidarity, were enough to persuade a group of disgruntled men in Tabora to start planning their own mutiny.

Kambona was very fully occupied that day. He was parleying with the mutineers, trying to restore order in Dar, and negotiating the evacuation of the British officers. At no stage did he speak to Marston about the plan to fly down the 2nd Battalion, or indeed anything else. Gradually it became apparent that the intervention plan was a non-starter. The mutineers had seized the airport at Dar and there was no further word from the army commander. So the 2nd Battalion spent an unsettled day; soldiers not on operational duty still carried out training.

Early next morning, Tuesday 21 January, Marston decided that in view of the widespread rumours and uncertainty he should address his men. But first he ordered a parade of all officers and NCOs to help him assess the mood and loyalty of the battalion. Some of his British officers were very experienced, Swahili-speaking 'old Africa hands' who would surely know what was going on. Marston also hoped that his talk would be an opportunity to get any potential waverers back on side. A level-headed Tanganyikan Staff Sergeant named John was instructed to translate the CO's speech, sentence by sentence, so that everyone would be quite clear about the message.

Marston began by explaining what he thought had happened in Dar es Salaam. He said that Tabora was a possible refuge for the President and that nobody should be influenced by army malcontents in Colito, or by news of the dismissal of British officers. He reminded the group that he and the British officers were in Tanganyika because the national Government wanted them there to bring the new national army, detached from the old East African KAR, up to scratch. They would leave as soon as the job was done — when Captain Sarakikya would probably be appointed to take command. Government Ministers would soon be coming to Tabora to confirm these points and to affirm their loyalty to the President. Having said his piece, Marston dismissed the meeting.

As the officers left, a burst of firing broke out. They were soon surrounded by armed mutineers: a 'ragbag group of bad characters from the Signals and Motor Transport platoons, some of the Israeli trained "officers", with a few new recruits', as Marston later described them.[2] The officers noticed that the RSM and the senior NCOs had made themselves scarce, and realised that the mutiny had been pre-planned. Marston, his second-in-command, the Adjutant, the Quartermaster, and two British Sergeants were then marched to the guardroom at bayonet point, 'rather aggressively'. Later the Paymaster was brought in to join them. The 2nd Battalion had joined the 1st Battalion in open mutiny only one day later.

The situation was now out of Marston's control, as it probably had been since the day before. His duty to his men was over. But there remained the pressing need to safeguard his British colleagues and their families: no Tanganyikan officers were under arrest. Marston judged that there was a real need to keep everyone calm (and this had also been why Rowley Mans had refused to try to break out of Colito the day before). Keeping the temperature down became the main aim of the detained officers in the guardroom at Tabora.

They started by trying to reassert some of the authority latent in military relationships. Both the prisoners and their guards had to be shown to have respectable, if different, roles. The junior British officer, the Quartermaster, started the process with all the confidence of his Grenadier Guards background. Prisoners in the guardroom were normally ordered to take their boots off. Lieutenant Dobson, a very large man, simply refused, beginning to undermine the mutineers' control. Later the CO, identifying members of the mess staff among the mutineers, and noting the time, asked for his usual gin and tonic, which was forthcoming – on a tray. There was a sharp setback when Company Commander Ian Colley was brought in. Mrs Colley had recently had a baby, and her husband had taken a few days' local leave. Hearing firing, he had remained in his quarters until flushed out by a search party. He was dragged to the guardroom and held down by near hysterical mutineers while rifles were loaded and pointed. Marston was watching through the cell door grill, and thinking that they really might kill Colley, shouted 'Stop it'. There was a brief pause; then the mood seemed to calm down and the danger passed.

As in Dar, the Tabora mutineers sought no political power. They helped themselves to whatever was immediately at hand. The men at the airport had found booty in the terminal, while the soldiers in the city began to loot Indian and Asian shops. However, one man at least kept his head. On his CO's orders, Captain Sarakikya had been calling on the Regional Commissioner, the Hon. Richard Wambura, hoping to learn about the situation in Dar and the Government's views and intentions. While he was there his driver interrupted them to report that troops were rampaging at the airport and were part of his own company. Sarakikya drove there immediately, to find his men shouting, gesticulating and firing blindly, under the influence of drink and drugs. Lieutenant Mwakajana had been shot at by an angry soldier, who missed – only narrowly. Back in the city, the two officers found soldiers looting Arab shops, and brandishing their weapons. They had already killed a trader who had tried to stop them. It seemed that nothing could be done there for the time being.

Returning to the barracks, Sarakikya was confronted by armed mutineers on the gate who tried to arrest him. He faced them down, calling on their sense of duty. At first they would have none of it. Someone fired at him, narrowly missing his head. Shaken, he stood his ground. The situation was saved by a messenger from the wireless office. He was carrying an order from Defence Minister Kambona in Dar es Salaam, instructing Sarakikya to take command of the battalion. The mutineers accepted that, and the disorder in the barracks collapsed as quickly as it had begun. Sarakikya appointed African replacement officers for each Company, deploying them at once to restore order. He led a force which set about stopping the trouble in the city, and within three hours all the rioters had been returned to barracks. It had been a personal *tour de force*.

The outward calm and order, however, did not mean that the battalion had fully returned to duty. The new and inexperienced officers ruled only under licence from the mutineers. All would be well while the pay continued; but there would be no question of the mutineers undertaking any duty they found unpalatable. The 2nd Battalion was neutered and could make no contribution to maintaining national order until the mutineers had been brought to book and discipline restored.

The British officers remained under arrest for the rest of the morning, knowing nothing about what was happening to their families. Sarakikya and the British community pressed for their release and safe passage out of the country. During the afternoon, they were driven to the airport – the CO in his own military Land Rover complete with pennant. The other officers were less fortunate: some were paraded round the camp in open trucks, others assaulted with rifle butts. At the airfield they were closely guarded, gathered onto the tarmac apron near the control tower, in the open. Their families joined them there, Mrs Colley with a baby under 24 hours old. At dusk Sarakikya appeared with the pilot of a South African Airways Dakota which had been chartered to fly them out. The pilot at first refused to take off that evening: the ground was soft and the aircraft would be overloaded. Sarakikya and Marston pressed him strongly to take off immediately – the troops were drinking and out of control and it was essential to leave at once. Gamely, the pilot agreed, but he insisted that all luggage must be left behind. Miles Marston stood behind his seat as the aircraft lifted off at the extreme end of the runway. Once airborne they called Entebbe, only to be told that the airport was closed. Nairobi, where there was a strong RAF detachment, was more accommodating and the party landed there at about 10 p.m. to be welcomed by the men and families of the 2nd Scots Guards.

There was a curious family sequel that night. Mrs Marston, shortly due to fly out to Tabora to join her husband, had been warned of the trouble. She and her young daughters were staying in a remote cottage near the Argylls' regimental depot in Stirling Castle. After a long and anxious day she finally went to bed after bolting the front door securely. She was soon woken by heavy pounding; a reporter wanted to know her reactions to the disastrous news. Could he come in, interview her and have a photograph of her husband? She refused to let him in, and claimed that she had no photograph. He insisted that she must have one. Addressing him through the locked door, she explained firmly that she would neither open it nor broadcast her views on the possible fate of her husband. The exchange became heated. One of the first memories of young Miss Marston, aged 6, was of her mummy kneeling on the hall floor in her nightie, apparently arguing with the letter-box![3]

The restoration of order in the barracks, and even the removal of the rioting soldiers from the streets, had done little to calm the worried inhabitants of Tabora. The news from Dar suggested that the President had lost control, and that there was no functioning government. Trevor Tice, local expatriate Director of the major tobacco firm BAT, was on a regular monthly visit from his base in Dar es Salaam. He was very familiar with Tabora and its leaders. BAT had, some time earlier, employed Sam Sarakikya during his school holidays before he joined the army, and Tice remembered him well. The two met by chance in the street and Sarakikya told him of his concern about the British officers and families held on the tarmac at the airport. Sarakikya strongly advised that all Europeans should keep out of sight. Tice therefore gathered his expatriate employees and their families in a locked room at the back of a hotel. There they remained for two days before they thought it safe to come out. Their fears proved well founded as there had been some unpleasant anti-European outbreaks. Expatriate staff at the prestigious Tabora School, for instance, had been forced to parade in front of their students amidst hostile shouts questioning their attitudes. The threat to civil order in Tabora was indeed serious.

In Dar, Stephen Miles was acutely aware of the plight of the British in Tabora. On Friday 24 January, he sent James Bourn, his First Secretary, with orders to liaise with the community there and give what reassurances he could. James was very much the man for the job. He had served with the Indian Army during World War II as a signals officer, was captured in North Africa but escaped during the chaos of the Italian Armistice and returned to Britain. He had joined the Colonial Office in 1947 and served as a District Officer in Tanganyika from 1953–55, where he learned to speak Swahili fluently. After transfer to the CRO, he had been posted in 1963 to the High Commission staff in Dar as a First Secretary. He had the influence to charter a small aircraft to avoid the restrictions at Dar airport. At Tabora, the airport had been opened again after the mutineers had returned to barracks. At a meeting of about 100 expatriates in the hall of the main hotel, he described the situation in Dar, which was now calmer. He already knew of steps being planned to restore order, but could not disclose them. He could only advise people to stay indoors or to make their way by road to the border.

Next day he walked through the deserted streets of Tabora to call on Richard Wambura, the Regional Commissioner. Wambura

101

appeared bemused by events. He was not sure if Walwa had spoken for the legitimate Government, and had no ideas about what could be done to restore confidence in the region. Bourn returned to his hotel to find an invitation from Sarakikya and the battalion officers to join them for lunch in the officers' mess. In what seemed to him rather bizarre circumstances he exchanged views in a very friendly atmosphere, mostly in Swahili.[4] The 2nd Battalion at least seemed to be behaving itself but the power vacuum in the region continued.

Notes

1 PRO: DO.226/10 (22).
2 Marston, Miles: interview with author, 2000.
3 Mrs Marston: interview with author, 2000.
4 Bourn, James: discussions with author, 2003.

9

No Recovery

During the early afternoon of Tuesday 21 January came dramatic news: President Nyerere had reappeared and was broadcasting to the nation. Speaking in Swahili, he began:

My countrymen. Yesterday a slight crisis occurred here in Dar es Salaam. The causes of this crisis have been explained to you more than once, as has the fact that it ended the same day, yesterday. It is not my aim to repeat the reasons why that crisis occurred.

Firstly, my aim is to dispel your anxiety. There are some people who greatly like to add falsehood to events. In adding falsehoods to yesterday's crisis, fabricators alleged that my whereabouts were unknown, and that there was no more Government. Such inventions could turn a small event into a bigger one than it actually was at the beginning.

Secondly, I want to advise you, my countrymen: do not spread alarmist rumours. Rumour-mongering is no sign of manhood. A man remains calm. I am happy that many people were calm throughout the crisis but there were many many people – Africans and non-Africans, citizens and foreigners – who became alarmists and who started to say and do things which could have created a bigger danger.

Then there were others who were a disgrace to every man

and country, who thought that this crisis was their opportunity to break into houses and plunder other people's property. Perhaps they thought that there was no longer any Government. This, alas, they found out for themselves. It is a pity that a few people, two of our soldiers among them, lost their lives. On your behalf I express the condolences of the whole nation to the families of the deceased. Let us pray to the Almighty that their souls may rest in peace.

Brothers, yesterday was a day of great disgrace to our nation. I thank all the people who helped to stop this disgrace from spreading beyond limits. I hope that our country will not witness any repetition of such a disgrace either tomorrow or the next day.[1]

The broadcast did not reassure everyone. Stephen Miles thought the President sounded 'weak and jaded'. The Chairman of the African Liberation Committee observed that it 'left much unsaid' and was much out of his previous character as *Mwalimu*. There seems little doubt that he was still severely shaken and uncertain about the next steps to take.

In London, the Duke of Devonshire, Minister of State for Commonwealth Relations, reported in the House of Lords that the news from Dar es Salaam was more reassuring, describing events as then known. Lord Alexander of Hillsborough expressed surprise that British intelligence in East Africa had been so ill-informed on two separate occasions (Zanzibar and Tanganyika). The Marquess of Salisbury suggested the events indicated a deep laid conspiracy by eastern bloc powers, and Cuba as well. The Minister replied that it was too early to say what outside influences, if any, had been at work in the recent *coups*.

Soon after 8 a.m. next day, Wednesday 22 January, news came through that the President was making a determined effort to re-establish his authority. In his first public appearance since the mutiny, Nyerere undertook an exhausting, three and a half hour,

70-mile tour around the capital. Accompanied by his wife, the Home Minister and the Coastal Regional Commissioner with his American Press Secretary, George Rockey, he was escorted by only one police car and two outriders. He was dressed casually in a gaily coloured shirt and sandals. Stopping at the burned outhouse in Magomeni, he talked with families who had suffered. He entered several smashed shops, walking over broken glass, and urged the shopkeepers to get their businesses open again as soon as they could. At first serious and tense, the general acclaim gradually made him more relaxed. After a visit to, and an enthusiastic send-off from, TANU headquarters, he smiled and joked confidently with large numbers of workers on industrial and residential building sites. The tour was well received and did much to restore national confidence.

The President's next priority was to try to restore confidence abroad. That evening, Stephen Miles and the American Ambassador were received at State House. Nyerere seemed relaxed and frank, explaining that he intended to deal with his problems by negotiation. He explained that he saw the situation as 'a trade union dispute'. He understood the concerns for foreign lives and welcomed the news that British reinforcements were gathering. Miles noted that although the President professed optimism, he did not say that British forces were not needed or would be unwelcome. The President had not heard that in Uganda, British troops had been asked by Obote to stand by, so Miles briefed him on events there. It transpired that none of the three had any clear idea about what was going on inside Colito Barracks. There had been no new demands and the mutineers had denied any intention to overthrow the government – presumably as long as they got everything they wanted. Nyerere was unwilling, at least to his visitors, to discuss or face up to the longer-term implications of the mutiny.

Later that evening, in a teleprinter discussion with London, Miles reported: 'All safe and well both in the office and the European community. The town is quiet and the soldiers in their barracks. The police are on duty, but had fraternised with the troops on Monday.'

It was also on Wednesday 22 January that the news broke about the mutiny of the last part of the Tanganyikan army in Nachingwea, a town some 260 miles south of Dar es Salaam, inland from the southern port of Lindi and covering the border with Mozambique, then still a Portuguese colony. A company of the 2nd Battalion had very recently been redeployed from Shinyanga in the north-west of the country to provide 'a presence' in the south. The British commander, Major Temple Morris, had long experience of commanding African troops, and was well respected in the battalion. Warned of the trouble at Colito he did what he could to secure the airstrip and the company's own arms and ammunition. Like his commanding officer, Lt. Col. Marston in Tabora, he called at once on the Area Commissioner to discuss what was happening in the capital, and what should be done in Nachingwea. Like Marston, he received neither information nor instructions. Returning to the camp he found the Dar and Tabora ends of his radio link had been taken over by mutineers. After briefing his young officers and NCOs about events, he sent a small detachment to guard the District Commissioner. There was little more that he could do.

The mutiny, when it broke out, was quick and painless. During dinner in the officers' mess a lorry drew up and armed troops disembarked. A Corporal named Mwita spoke firmly but without malice: 'We want to take you to the barracks. Please take the young officer [indicating the only other British officer] with you because he has been a nuisance to us. We will not harm you.'[2] The two were taken first to the guardroom and then to the airfield. Corporal Mwita appropriated Morris's rank insignia and appointed a young Israeli-trained officer in his stead. A flight to Dar was arranged the next day, where, since no one had been briefed to meet them, the two officers made their way to the British High Commission. They were flown out of Tanganyika the same evening.

Major Temple Morris later concluded that the mutiny was fomented by a group of new recruits and their NCOs, all fresh from the Colito training company. The battalion's radio link is also likely to have been a factor. It is not easy to see what Temple Morris could have done to prevent the mutiny in his company, but it marked the end of his career. He soon retired from the army to take up farm management – in Tanzania. His arrest, in his own officers' mess, marked the transition of control in the Tanganyikan army wholly into the hands of African officers, however uncertain the situation might still be.

On Thursday 23 January the President called a press conference in State House. Around 50 correspondents attended and they may have been surprised to be searched as they entered. Nyerere, flanked by Vice President Kawawa and Kambona, began: 'It is my urgent task to restore confidence in Tanganyika as a mature and peaceful country.' He went on to admit that the Government's failure to keep the people informed during the army 'revolt' was a mistake which had aggravated rumours and doubts about the stability of the country and Government: 'It would be foolish to pretend that these events are unimportant … This was a mistake which I fully acknowledge.' He went on to talk about the national five-year development plan due to be launched later in the year – intending, presumably, to give an impression of 'business as usual'. His message was duly reported, but did not deal with fundamental current questions. Few people were convinced that the crisis was all over, or that the Government was securely back in power. Nevertheless, in the city life was returning to normal. Shops were trading briskly, offices were open and tourists were again seen on the streets. East African Airways had resumed its services, except to Zanzibar, and the port was open. On the other hand there were still fears of unrest, and many parents, especially expatriates, kept their children back from school.

From Zanzibar there was both good and bad news. John Okello had returned and was making more vicious threats about hanging, burning and having victims cut up into small pieces before being thrown into the sea, or 'shot by novice marksmen'. But despite this, Karume was now in power and Nyerere formally notified him that, 'The Government of the Republic of Tanganyika has decided to recognise the Government of the People's Republic of Zanzibar'. He ended, 'may our friendship deepen'. Zanzibar still had a long road to recovery, but the worst seemed over.

In Britain, a journalist from the *Daily Telegraph*, John Osman, filed a controversial report on 23 January accusing Kambona of being 'carefully selected and trained in Moscow in every single art of intelligence and subversion'. He went on to describe Kambona as the main Communist agent, not only in Tanganyika but in the whole of East Africa. He had infiltrated the police, prisons and immigration departments with his men, and was doing the same with the armed forces. He had blocked defence agreements between Tanganyika and Britain and had not attended regular intelligence meetings in Nairobi. It was an obvious deduction that he already had all the information he required. This was a devastating attack on a senior politician, and it is unlikely that Osman came to these conclusions without help from someone in the British intelligence community. With the benefit of hindsight, we can now see that while there were elements of truth in some of Osman's story, there were also innocent and justifiable explanations for Kambona's actions, and the main charge, that he was a 'selected and trained' subversive was entirely unsubstantiated.

Next day the *Daily Telegraph* backtracked somewhat with a report from Leslie Beilby, their special correspondent in Nairobi. He started by admitting that Kambona's prestige had been enhanced by his actions during the President's absence. He reported that 'some observers' thought the mutiny had been engineered to enable Kambona to establish himself as the real power in the country. On the other hand, he went on, Kambona had always been reported as being very close to Nyerere and had been one of those who urged him to take up the leadership. He described Kambona as 'ambitious and scheming' and a leading light in the campaign against colonialism. Beilby had done something to set the record straight; but Osman's report had been published first and was the more influential.

In Dar es Salaam, Miles thought Osman's report quite wrong. It reinforced the vague claims by Stephen Hastings MP, during early exchanges in the House of Commons, and led many to suppose that Kambona, with Communist backing, was behind the troubles. In Tanganyika, a British expatriate reporter, Tony Dunn, in trouble with the authorities for his forthright reporting of the mutineers' behaviour on Monday, had been told to leave the country. Despite his personal predicament, he reacted strongly to the *Telegraph* report, writing in a 'reluctant farewell' that he wanted to put it on record that 'All the time I was a political correspondent in Tanganyika, I do not believe I ever met a Tanganyikan Communist. Such talk is nonsense. Rabid nationalists, yes, Communists, no ... The leaders are too proud to exchange one form of colonialism for another.'[3] Kambona later sued the *Telegraph* for libel, and won an apology and damages. Nevertheless, whatever the effects on Kambona's reputation, the reports had seriously undermined Nyerere's efforts to portray his country as suffering only from the effects of minor industrial action.

The general sense of unease was by now shared worldwide. At the UN, the Secretary General, U Thant, admitted concern about developments in East Africa, but expressed cautious optimism that 'with the passage of time there will be stability everywhere'. He went on to explain that 'many countries in Africa are now passing through a phase – a phase similar to that which was passed through by many European countries in the nineteenth century. Stability is lacking in many regions. It will continue to lack for some time to come, but I am optimistic about the future.'

Such trite statements by the leader of the world's principal agency for promoting peace made no contribution to solving

Nyerere's problems. By Thursday evening, whatever was being reported on the ground, and despite U Thant's airy confidence, Nyerere found himself with his mutinous troops having tasted power, his police partly deployed in Zanzibar and his people worried and restless. The anti-colonial rhetoric of the many southern African dissidents exiled in Dar es Salaam hardly helped at this point. In Kenya, President Kenyatta, with a large proportion of his own troops tied down on the border with Somaliland, was more disturbed by the possibility of political instability in Tanganyika than he was by the coup and killings in Zanzibar. Tanganyika was facing an early post-colonial reckoning: the danger of a weakening and eventual disintegration of government control rather than a takeover by some well-organised revolutionary group. At this stage it was far from clear what should be done. But any solution would have to be initiated by Nyerere and his Government – and very soon.

Notes

1   PRO. DO 185/46 (53A).
2   Temple Morris, as quoted in Tanzania People's Defence Force, *op. cit.*, p. 104.
3   Article by Tony Dunn, *Sunday Nation (Dar)*, 26 January 1964, p.1.

10

Centaur's *Passage South*

By daybreak on 21 January, *Centaur* was clear of the land. She was steaming east at 25 knots in a haze which reduced visibility to two miles. Cape Elefante, the northern tip of north-east Somalia, was abeam by 3 p.m. and the ship altered course to the south-east to transit the broad channel between the mainland and the Socotra islands before turning south towards East Africa by 10 p.m. There was almost no traffic in the area. Fuel consumption was high, but the supply tanker had been sent on ahead and there were no worries on that score.

The first day at sea had been intended as a holiday ('Sunday Routine' in naval parlance), but it turned out to be far from relaxed. The flight deck was a jumble of stores, vehicles, ammunition and aircraft. The first priority was to achieve a maximum separation between explosives, inflammables (which included 130 jerricans of petrol), and valuable equipment. Space for the petrol was found in a sponson (a small open space to one side of, and just below, the flight deck). Even there, the well-secured pile of cans remained a serious fire hazard which warranted a permanent sentry. Three operating 'spots' were kept clear at the forward end of *Centaur*'s deck for her Wessex helicopters. The large RAF Belvedere helicopters were kept in two larger 'spots', right aft, where they had first landed. Enough space was even found to provide an exercise track for the marines.

While the Air Department was sorting out the flight deck, other

111

departments tackled their own problems. '815' Squadron had already converted four of their Wessex helicopters from the troop-carrying to the anti-submarine role, reinstalling the complicated winch and sonar gear. Now it had all to be stripped out again. The ship's gunnery department were accustomed to handling air ordnance, but they now found themselves stowing quite different armaments and ammunition for a land force. Everybody soon discovered that the ship was much too small to accommodate the ship's company, the air group and a marine commando with any degree of comfort. People had to queue for everything, including the lavatories – mostly with good humour.

Nobody on board had any clear understanding of what they were being sent to do. The senior officers first had to start planning for operations they had to envisage for themselves. Even if someone told them exactly what was required of them, how would they get the marines off the ship if it were not lying alongside in a port? The overall responsibility lay with Captain Steiner: but busy with navigation and communications with Aden and Whitehall, he delegated 'assault planning' jointly to Commander Randle Kettle, the ship's Commander (Air), and to Lt. Col. Paddy Stevens. Early in the forenoon of 21 January, the first day at sea, these two called a coordinating conference. Some 20 officers crowded into the vacant Admiral's dining room, and a most successful meeting followed which led to the development of procedures which enabled a productive airborne assault to be launched only three days later.

The Royal Marines' CO took charge of the meeting, and quickly imposed a sense of purpose on the heterogeneous group. Stevens had assumed command in July 1963. He was to play an outstanding role in the days ahead. He had just turned 43 and was coming to the peak of his first career. He had joined the Royal Marines during World War II and served in the battleship *King George V* before joining 41 Commando in 1944 in time for the D-Day landings in Normandy.[1] Promoted to command of a

112

company, Stevens later led an attack on a heavily-defended radar station at Douvres-la-Dekivrande, getting his men into it by blowing a hole in the barbed wire. For these operations he was awarded the Military Cross, presented by General Montgomery a month later. Promoted to Captain, he remained with 41 Commando Royal Marines during the breakout from Normandy, the pursuit across France, and then later during the hazardous amphibious assault on Walcheren Island. After being seriously wounded in February 1945, while leading a patrol along the banks of the River Maas, he was repatriated back to Britain.

As with many officers who had achieved early prominence during the war, his career then stagnated for a long time. He had served with 42 Commando in the Mediterranean, and then on the staff of the army's Royal Military Academy at Sandhurst. He passed the Army Staff Course at Camberley and served in various commando and staff posts. Finally, in July 1963, he had been promoted to Lieutenant Colonel and appointed to command 45 Commando in Aden. He found there a tough, capable and experienced unit and was now confident that it would succeed in whatever challenges it might face in East Africa.

Paddy Stevens opened the meeting by explaining that there was a well-established format for controlling the deployment of a military unit: 'getting it to the start line properly prepared and briefed', as Staff College handbooks put it. In this case, however, there was a serious problem: the force had no agreed or designated task. The group had therefore to plan a generalised procedure which would fit a range of possible deployments. Operations in Tanganyika, for example, might include securing the airfield or protecting the main European residential area around Oyster Bay as a prelude for more extensive rescue operations. Then there was a range of possibilities in Zanzibar. There might be one or more landing sites — anywhere ashore within the range of *Centaur*'s helicopters, to rescue British nationals. It might even be necessary to land against opposition.

This would require support from the Commando's own heavy weapons, the ship's strike aircraft or naval guns. All these options could be covered in a general assault plan. But it soon became clear that the main problems would be on board, in the hangars and flight operations rooms. How could a mass of marines, accommodated haphazardly all around the ship, be transformed into well-designed groups of armed troops in tactical formations, with their stores, and then fed quickly and safely into two different types of helicopter at opposite ends of a crowded flight deck, probably in the dark, when the required flight schedules were entirely unknown? A vast amount of detail would have to be agreed and organised – and only two days were left before the force reached the coast of East Africa.

The output of the first day's planning conference was a description of the tasks to be undertaken, and a directive about who was to do what, and how long they had to do it. Work was to be divided between three groups. The first, consisting of the marines' Intelligence Officer, *Centaur*'s Operations Officer, the CO of the navy's helicopter squadron; and *Centaur*'s army Ground Liaison officer would gather all the intelligence available. The task was challenging, since there was very little information on board about East Africa. The second, and largest, group would plan assault operations. It would be chaired by the marines' Second in Command, Major Smith, and would include the commander of his HQ company and the unit Quartermaster. There would also be a strong naval contingent, with Lieutenant Commander (Flying), the Deputy Operations Officer, the Flight Deck Officer, the Deputy Supply Officer and a representative of the naval helicopter squadron. The commander of the RAF helicopters would also join this group. Thirdly, the Signal Officers of both *Centaur* and the Marine Commando were instructed to devise a radio communications plan flexible enough to support any likely operation. Each group had one day in which to prepare an outline plan for consolidation into a general plan from which some 18 individual marine, ship, air, and RAF departments or units would draw up their own orders. Once that was agreed, the meeting dispersed to begin work.

That evening a near-disaster threatened to compromise the expedition on its very first day. Major David Smith still remembers only too clearly how the news broke.[2] He was in his tiny cabin, right aft, working on an outline 'landing table' when the RSM came in to report that, for some reason, the marines' small arms ammunition had not been loaded. Ammunition supply was the RSM's responsibility and now that the stores had all been identified, he was sure that there was no small arms ammunition on board. It must have been mislaid in the rush to embark.

Military commands take a very hard line about the responsibility of Commanding Officers to deliver their force at the right place, on time and ready for action. No excuses are permitted, and no one else can be blamed if they are lost, late or not ready. If the RSM had lost the ammunition and the Commando was unfit for action, then it would be Lt. Col. Stevens who would shoulder the responsibility. Smith went to break the catastrophic news to Stevens. He was long to remember Stevens's stricken face, and his 'going white with anger'. If the problem could not be resolved quickly, he would have to signal Aden and Whitehall that his force was non-operational.

Both officers quickly decided that there was no immediate need to let the news go beyond the ship. Only the most discreet signals would be sent to investigate the possible whereabouts of other supplies. The ship's communications team set about establishing the position of a naval stores ship, the *Bacchus*, which had recently been recovering British arms from Zanzibar. This and other investigations led nowhere and soon it became starkly clear that any remedy must be found on board. *Centaur* herself carried small arms ammunition for her regular landing party, but the latter were armed with old World war II, bolt-action, Lee-Enfield rifles, which fired rounds which did not fit the marine's more recent

115

SLRs. *Centaur's* own Royal Marine detachment was equipped with SLRs, but their stock of ammunition was small. The commando companies held a small reserve of ammunition for their immediate needs, but this was quite insufficient for any serious engagement.

After much head-scratching, a compromise was reached. All the SLR ammunition would be pooled to provide a safe minimum outfit for the two marine Companies which would land first. The third Company, and all the headquarters and supporting troops, would be re-armed with the old World war II rifles which *Centaur* carried. Few of the marines had ever seen, let alone been trained to use, the old-style arms. So a firing range was set up on the flight deck, and half the marines were introduced to the relatively primitive and much less formidable Lee-Enfields.[3]

British commandos had first been put ashore by helicopter during the Suez campaign in 1956. Later, when there was a crisis in Cyprus, naval helicopters were sent to support the troops involved. The Royal Marine Commando then based in Malta was ordered to make recommendations on how troops and helicopters might best work together in future. One of the Commando officers, Major David Smith, was sent to Cyprus to develop standard operational drills. Now he was serving as 45 Commando's second-in-command. Paddy Stevens was fortunate to have a deputy who knew a great deal about helicopter troop-carrying operations.

During Wednesday 22 January, the second day of the passage south, the assault planning group headed by Smith made substantial progress. The system now developed on board was a modification of procedures already in use in the navy's specialised commando carriers. At its core was the concept of a 'Stick' of six or eight men, gathered in their Order of Battle (Orbat) and therefore known as a 'stickorbat'. A list was produced, showing every stick, its relative priority, its serial number and the name of its landing site. Thus ZW3 would

116

Two years after Independence, progress towards Africanization had been slow. Brigadier Douglas and the Tanganyikan Army Headquarters staff officers in late 1963. Photograph courtesy of The Douglas/Marciandi papers.

President Nyerere playing croquet with Stephen and Joy Miles. The British enjoyed good relations with the Tanganyikan Government. Photograph courtesy of Stephen Miles.

HMS *Centaur* fuels an escort in the Indian Ocean.

Photograph courtesy of Arthur Coxon.

The marines' hastily embarked stores are sorted out on Centaur's flight deck while aircrew brief marines about helicopter operations.

Photograph courtesy of Denis Sparrow.

The men of 45 Commando were fitted into any space available on board.
Photograph courtesy of Denis Sparrow.

Paddy Stevens. His incisive planning and leadership kept casualties low.
Photograph courtesy of The Editor, *The Globe and Laurel*.

The letter sent in response to the British insistence that the Tanganyikan Government request for help be confirmed in writing

Courtesy of Stephen Miles.

The hastily scribbled note that Defence Minister Oscar Kambona gave to Brigadier Douglas when briefing him on how to reassure the mutineers. It reads *'I am now the Army Commander   You have seen what happened, and we can all go back to barracks.   You must lay down your arms and put your hands up.   Women and children must remain indoors and not venture out. President Nyerere will speak to on the radio'*.

Courtesy of The Douglas/Marciandi papers.

The guardroom, Colito Barracks, after discipline had been restored. The mast which supported the power cable that deflected the first shot can be seen to the right. Photograph courtesy of W. M. Burns.

A wounded askari is taken to *Centaur's* sickbay.

Photograph courtesy of Denis Sparrow.

The President and Defence Minister Oscar Kambona thank Lieutenant Colonel Carter and the men of 41 Commando, Royal Marines as they are released from their security duties in Dar. Photograph courtesy of Stephen Miles.

Vice President Kawawa thanks Captain Steiner on behalf of President Nyerere. Photograph courtesy of Arthur Coxon.

describe the load of the 3rd Wessex helicopter to take off for the landing site designated 'Z'. Once the stickorbat had been produced, company commanders could allocate individual marines to each stick.

The assault planners first sought the CO's requirements for the landing – who did he want to go in first? Stevens ordered that one Company Group from Z Company would land first, and there should be provision for a support element with heavy weapons. If the landing faced opposition only at the level of a street riot, the support group would not be landed; its troops would go in later as an additional Rifle Company. A 'landing-zone team' (LZT) should go in directly after the first troop had secured the site, even before the remaining troops (platoons) of Z Company. The LZT would control unloading helicopters and direct incoming sticks of troops to their tactical duties. It would also control all helicopter movements in the Assault area. Once Z Company was ashore, the CO would land, accompanied by his tactical headquarters consisting of the unit Intelligence and Signal Officers with the radio operators. The second Company (X), would then land, and so on. Once this outline had been decided, the planners could begin to fill in the detail.

Major David Langley, commanding Z Company, decided which of his three troops would land first. Each troop consisted of about 30 marines, and would have to be broken up into groups of six or eight men. When the names of the first troop had been pencilled in, the next helicopter spaces could be allocated to the LZT. Langley could then nominate his remaining troops and his own headquarters group, all of whom had priority over the following helicopter loads. So slowly, and in order of tactical priority, the stickorbat began to be built up. As it became firm, the second essential stage could be undertaken. Each stick would be described on numbered white cards which established helicopter priority and listed the names of the men in that stick, together with a description and the weight of stores they would carry. Once these cards had been completed they were given a helicopter load number. Every man could then be briefed on his role in loading the helicopters for the assault. For the marines, this would start with them assembling in the ship's hangar.

The problems for *Centaur*'s crew were different. The loading of the helicopters would be controlled by the Lieutenant Commander, Flying, Ken Whittaker, from his flying control position above the flight deck. He knew what helicopters were available; and would order an individual stick to be brought up from the hangar and taken to a 'spot' on deck where a helicopter would be waiting or soon due. Ship's guides were essential to bring sticks forward from the hangar to the flight deck – there could be no question of groups of heavily-laden men finding their own way round the maze of under-deck passages and ladders. Once on deck, the flight deck crew, accustomed to moving about safely when aircraft were operating, would guide the stick safely to the required spot. There, the stick would come under the control of Royal Navy or RAF helicopter aircrew for the flight. Once disembarked ashore, they would come under the control of the LZT which would disband the stick and dispatch the men to their tactical units. The stick method controlled everyone, from the Commanding Officer to the most junior marine: as soon as a stick was formed in the hangar, it would remain in existence, passed from one controller to another, until it was disbanded ashore.

The whole landing process would be controlled by Major David Smith, who would sit with Whittaker overlooking the flight deck. Smith could issue last-minute modifications to stick priority, or authorise remedial action if there was a breakdown, accident or some other unexpected development. As with any operation of this type, last-minute changes or aircraft unserviceability could derail the plan, and it was Smith's job to deal with this. He would, in effect, command operations until Stevens was safely ashore and could resume control.

While the Assault team were at work, *Centaur*'s and 45 Commando's signal officers produced an annex to the general operational plan, described as the 'Complan'. This dealt with the radio communications needed to ensure that the Commando, the ship, its helicopters, and supporting naval ships all acted in unison.

Tony Laurence. *I was in my third naval signals appointment, and had recently joined the ship after two years instructing at the naval signal school, followed by a six-week naval tactical course. I found myself responsible for a big department; separate branches handling radio communications, force tactical control, cryptography, message handling on board, and electronic warfare. Much of the routine work was undertaken by my assistant, the very experienced Lieutenant George Reubens. I had learned to spent a lot of time on the ship's bridge, to keep track of what was going on and pass requirements to the department.*

My opposite number, the Royal Marine's signal officer, 26-year-old Lieutenant Pat Howgill, was in his first staff appointment after 14 months of specialist signals training. For part of this time I had been his signals instructor. There was therefore an immediate rapport when we settled down to produce the joint signal plan. It also helped that we had both attended the same tri-service joint warfare course at Old Sarum in Wiltshire.

In the 1960s, servicemen tended to concentrate on their own service: cooperation with other services was not always a high priority. The tri-service staff at Old Sarum had therefore evolved a dashing style of instruction, highlighting especially the vital role of inter-force communications. Models of ships, land forces and aircraft were laid out on sand tables, and an often complicated communications network was built up, illustrated by coloured battens. By the end of each lecture, students were beginning to grasp the principles, although it was not easy to remember the details. Fortunately, the navy's signal division had recently asked the

119

Amphibious Warfare Centre at Poole to study the communications needed for single battalion amphibious operations. The conclusions had been summarised in an Admiralty signals order (S16), which we held on board. Couched in rather general terms, it proved no more than a guide, but it was a useful start.

The basic communications problems were easy to identify. Once ashore, the CO would normally control his companies from a position close behind the leading one. He would use voice communications on what was then known as very high frequency (VHF). The normal VHF voice equipment was man-portable, but there were also more powerful but heavy, vehicle-borne radio sets. Both types had short ranges, little more than line of sight.

Communications at company level could be provided easily. But the 'rear link' back to the ship posed a greater problem. The Commando might need to operate some distance inland or else the ship might have to put out to sea, moving miles offshore. More powerful, high frequency (HF) equipment was therefore needed; yet all the suitable Commando HF sets were quite large and carried in vehicles. The problem had to be solved somehow or other. So Howgill, and his signaller stripped a set out of a Land Rover. They then found a suitable, though large and heavy, lead-acid battery. With a lot of effort they practised loading it into the back of a helicopter so that it could go ashore to provide a reliable command link. Any number of people on board *Centaur* could then be allocated ship's receivers to monitor what was going on ashore. For example, the ship's gunnery officer could also be provided with effective communications to the supporting ships, in case things began to go wrong ashore and naval gun support was needed.

Some of the other technical details were even more complicated. One example was air traffic control. Even in action conditions, aircraft near a carrier or military airfield were always marshalled by air traffic controllers. Their job was exactly the same as those needed at a civilian airfield. If there was to be an assault landing, then an air traffic controller would be sent to the site to marshal the helicopters locally. This precaution, neglected in many subsequent operations (including the failed attempt by US forces in 1980 to rescue hostages in Iran), was as vital during emergency operations as it was for routine peacetime flying. There might also be a need to control helicopters carrying out missions further inland. So a 'traffic control net (shore)' was therefore created.

Once the list of radio networks had been drawn up, each net had to be given a name and frequency. The signal officers then handed the proposed 'complan' on to the Commando headquarters office. It was approved and incorporated in the overall plan – and in the event was to work well.

Assembling adequate intelligence was another priority. The Royal Marine charged with that responsibility was Lieutenant Tony Hazeldine. Aged 28, he was serving on a six-month extension to his second tour as 45 Commando's Intelligence Officer. Also responsible for weapon training and the Commando's snipers, he was one of the three unit officers with no direct subordinates, since he had only planning and other staff duties. A keen Arabist, and destined to make a further career in that field, he was a resourceful and talented young officer who could be relied on to master any brief quickly. His opposite number was the ship's Operations Officer, Lt. Cdr. Willie Heathcote, but he also acted as a personal staff officer to both Captain Steiner and Commander (Air) Kettle, so had little time to spare for intelligence-gathering or analysis. There was also, however, a small army unit on board: the 67th Carrier-Borne Ground Liaison Section, led by Grenadier Guards Major Gavin Anderson. His duties included advising the ship's command and air departments on shore targeting, and he was therefore the custodian of the ship's shore intelligence and land maps. A quick search of his safe confirmed that there was almost nothing on board *Centaur* about Tanganyika or Zanzibar!

Fortunately, the Major's assistant, Captain 'Jimmy' James of the Coldstream Guards was an adventurer who had travelled extensively in East Africa, and had kept his own fairly up-to-date and usable maps.

The intelligence team soon began to piece the story together. British Land Forces, Kenya, had sent a series of signals during the day of the mutiny, starting at 5.40 a.m., and then reporting the progress of the mutiny and Brigadier Douglas's escape. During the next day there were further descriptions of the unrest in Dar and of the looting, together with a report of the mutiny at Tabora, and threats to the up-country diamond mines and to major sugar estates at Arusha. The team listened diligently to the BBC, and searched for other sources. Some of their information was inaccurate or false (such as a reported possibility that the broadcast attributed to Dr Nyerere on 22 January was made not by him but by his brother who might be privy to a coup), but none of the errors were operationally significant.

Once the ship was well south, a helicopter flew the intelligence team to Mombasa to meet the local RN liaison officer and also staff officers from British Land Forces, Kenya, who had come down from Nairobi. They brought recent air photographs, some good maps, and much useful background information. By the third day (23 January), the intelligence team had a clear and reasonably accurate description of the Tanganyikan army before the mutiny, and a fair knowledge of the personalities of its post-mutiny commanders. They knew exactly what weapons the mutineers were likely to deploy, should a landing be ordered, and were warned about the Algerian arms shipment. They had also identified potential landing sites which looked likely to give access to possible targets. What they did not have, however, was any vital, up-to-date intelligence about what was actually happening in Colito Barracks or even Dar es Salaam. Any operation would have to be launched into the blue unless someone with good local knowledge could be brought out to brief the force. This was worrying, and the need was duly reported to Aden and London.

After *Centaur* set sail, the Royal Marines' training was at first rather general. Fitness routines, small-arms firing and briefings about helicopter loading and the political situation ashore, were the main staples. As staff officers in the three teams finished their work, the results were made available in the form of specific assault intentions, communication plans and detailed intelligence summaries. Individual marines began to grasp the shape of possible future operations and their part in them; what might be done, how, and in broadly what order. An outline of an unspecified future operation had begun to take shape.

At least one man on board could make very specific preparations for his unusual role in forthcoming events, whatever they might be. Lt. Cdr. Graham Holt, always known as 'Brutus', had entered the navy to undertake educational duties, but had transferred to naval air to fly operationally as a pilot in Korea. This led in due course to his appointment as *Centaur*'s Senior Air Traffic Control Officer. When the need for a forward helicopter controller became clear, his was the obvious name: an operationally experienced officer who was used to close control of aircraft in difficult circumstances. Later he admitted that there was another reason for the choice. Captain Steiner's style was, justifiably, to keep both his ship's and air operations closely under his own control. Some delegation was inevitable, but he kept it to a practical minimum. While Stevens seemed an excellent CO of the Commando, once the troops had landed they would inevitably deploy, perhaps over a wide area. Small formations of Royal Marines, under relatively inexperienced officers, might then run into trouble and call for fire support, and this might in turn involve *Centaur*, her helicopters, strike aircraft with their cannon and bombs, and the fire of supporting ships. If significant numbers of civilians were hurt, Steiner could easily become involved in an incident with international repercussions.

He sent for Brutus Holt, and told him plainly: 'I have selected you because you flew armed aircraft in Korea. You know what 20mm cannons can do to people. All requests for fire support from the marines ashore will either be routed through you personally, or you will know about them. You are to act as my adviser as to the justification for the requests. If you are in any doubt, say so.'[4] Otto Steiner had done more than provide a helicopter controller for the landing party; he had inserted his own Naval Liaison Officer. It is unlikely that he told Paddy Stevens that he had done so.

Entering enthusiastically into his new role, Holt collected a battle smock and personal weapons (a Sterling sub-machine-gun and a revolver). He arranged to have firing practice from the flight deck into the sea, and soon regarded himself as an 'honorary commando'. This ambition was thwarted when he realised that the A43 portable radio needed to communicate with naval aircraft on ultra-high frequency (UHF) was heavy and bulky. The marine officers had operators to carry and work their radios; he had to do his own communicating, lugging his radio set around as best he could. This, as he afterwards realised, was to cause him to lose face with the young marines, who tended to view him as the heavily-loaded, unfit old man panting along behind – an image which clashed with his new role as 'Naval Counsellor to the Land Force'.

By Wednesday 22 January, the second day of the passage south, the daily operations meeting concluded that, whatever the eventual task might turn out to be, a workable plan now existed to launch an assault from the ship. Stevens and Kettle ordered a full dress rehearsal. It confirmed that *Centaur* had indeed developed her role from 'fast transport ship' to assault carrier. A stickorbat was ready, white cards had been issued, stick guides briefed, helicopter loading drills agreed, and control and communication procedures established. Paddy Stevens was later to report 'We could have landed earlier [than Day 3], but not without undue risks of confusion'. It was an achievement which many could look back on with justified satisfaction. Under Paddy Stevens' incisive and intelligent leadership, matters had progressed very fast.

It had even been possible to devise a plan for the ship to launch its fixed-wing aircraft while the Commando was still on board, although with great difficulty. Stores and vehicles would have to be moved down by one elevator while aircraft were brought up on the other. The helicopters would take off and hover while the fixed-wing aircraft were launched and recovered. This ingenious plan was called 'Sardine Stations'. Luckily, events moved on before such a hazardous operation could be attempted!

Individual marines still had a lot to learn. Before *Centaur* set sail, few had any knowledge of East Africa, or even knew where Zanzibar or Dar es Salaam were. Informal briefings were gradually replaced by detailed, typewritten intelligence and operational briefs, concentrating on the possibility of operations around Dar es Salaam. It is clear that Paddy Stevens had by this time concluded that the protection of British nationals in Dar es Salaam, and possibly the countering of the mutineers, were the two most likely tasks he would be called on to undertake. There was a brief flurry of concern about Zanzibar, and for a few hours men were brought to readiness. One Company was even ordered to prime their hand-grenades so that they were ready to land. But the focus soon shifted back to Tanganyika.

At first light on Thursday 23 January, *Centaur* sighted her tanker, the Royal Fleet Auxiliary *Tidesurge*, and refuelled between 7.00 and 9.20 a.m. Then the vessels parted, *Centaur* pressing on at 25 knots while the tanker followed. At this point it was suggested that two Gannet airborne early warning aircraft might be flown off to the British airbase at Nairobi. The aircraft would be unlikely to be of any use in the coming operations and space was at a premium. On the other hand it would add to complications if they had to be recovered after a change of plan, and it would greatly aggravate 849B flight's maintenance problems. So it was decided to shelve the idea for the moment. *Centaur* did, however, launch

125

two helicopters at 4.45 p.m. to fly to Mombasa. They returned at 8 p.m., intercepting the ship over 80 miles south-west of their launch point. Lt. Col. Stevens and his Intelligence Officer emerged, bringing useful information after their intelligence briefings ashore. Willie Heathcote, the ship's operations officer, had picked up nothing of interest to the ship's operations, but at a more pedestrian level, he did bring out plenty of fresh fruit. The wind had risen, so the ship had to slow down until the helicopter's rotors were folded. It had been a useful sortie.

Centaur arrived 'on station' early on Friday 24 January to await further orders. She reduced speed to a comfortable 12 knots to patrol an area south and east of Zanzibar, directly off Dar es Salaam, but out of sight of both. *Rhyl* and *Owen* had been released from 'guard ship' duties, and *Cambrian* had taken over, steaming regularly between points which might in principle allow radio communication with the beleaguered British High Commissions in Dar and Zanzibar, while also remaining out of sight of land. *Centaur* sent a helicopter to collect *Cambrian*'s CO, David Hankinson; and he and Otto Steiner reviewed their vague role as the 'South Zanzibar channel force'. Ships' staff officers had the slightly cynical impression that the incoming signals from London had more to do with preparing answers for possible Parliamentary questions than briefing them on forthcoming requirements. To be fair, there *was* no immediate role; the force was as ready as possible and could only wait on developments ashore.

During the afternoon it became clear that the Americans were in a similar position. Their station guard ship, the destroyer USS *Manley*, was patrolling in the same area, steaming at a very economical 2 knots. *Centaur* and *Manley* carried out some simple helicopter and communications exercises, and planned more advanced ones for the next day. If the Americans were better briefed than the British they were not letting on; but they clearly had better communications with their diplomats ashore.

*

The action started earlier than expected. By early evening on 24 January the Royal Marines all seemed to have disappeared to sleep early. Their absence from the wardroom, ship's messes and the flight deck was striking. They seemed to have sensed that 'tomorrow would be the day'. Few on board heard the ship start to pick up speed at around 11.45 p.m. Shortly afterwards there was a quiet announcement on the ship's broadcast system: 'darken ship'. This order mainly involved electricians turning off upper-deck lighting, and was quickly achieved. Below decks no one was affected, but experienced sailors could now feel the vibrations of the ship increasing its speed to 22 knots. *Centaur* was on her way somewhere.

The Ministry of Defence (MoD) Operations Centre in London, a recent innovation of Admiral Mountbatten's, had released a high priority, secret signal at 8.29 p.m. GMT. Mountbatten remains a controversial figure and many have doubted his judgement, but he could be an incisive and clear-sighted operational leader. The wording of the signal suggested his personal presence in the Operational Centre:

242029 Cosmic Secret 42
MOD to Commander Middle East
Information to RN Flag Officer, Middle East
    Commander British Land Forces, Kenya
    High Commission Dar es Salaam
    Centaur

From Chief of Defence Staff. Ministers have agreed to meet the request of President Nyerere to intervene to maintain law and order and quell the mutiny in the Tanganyikan army. Troops when landed are to be under the command of Brigadier Douglas, Commander of Tanganyikan Army and the political direction of the Acting High Commissioner. You should act accordingly. Speed is essential and it is important to make early contact with Brig. Douglas.

On the bridge, Otto Steiner and his staff quickly picked out the salient points. Obviously *Centaur* had to get close to Dar es Salaam. That part was easy: Dar was not far away. The problem lay with the last sentence. How was the ship to make early contact with Brigadier Douglas? Indeed the signal was alarmingly vague about how to achieve this. *Centaur* might at least have expected an order to send a helicopter somewhere, at a given time, to pick up Douglas. Nor could they contact the British High Commission. The officers on *Centaur*'s bridge were not to know that the MoD in London had exactly the same problem: they had no effective way of contacting the High Commission in Dar other than during the regular radio schedules, or via intermittent commercial telex link-ups. In fact, the British Government's decision to authorise an intervention was not known to Stephen Miles ashore until much later.

While Captain Steiner was trying to interpret his instructions, a strange message was brought up from the bridge radio room. It was written in longhand, just as it had been received by one of *Centaur*'s operators. It had no date or time group and followed no known military procedure. It bore a strange originator's radio callsign, possibly American. Even stranger was its plain language text, which read: 'To *Centaur*. Please send taxi for VIP to flashing light at beach in front of State House.'[5]

The proposed pick-up point was immediately obvious. State House was shown on the Dar es Salaam Approach chart and the position described was just to the north of the main channel into the harbour and should be easy enough to find. *Centaur* could be brought in along the normal approach route to a position some two miles off the beach. She could then send in her fastest motor boat. Once there, the boat's crew would have found out for themselves about any off-lying reefs and the state of surf on the beach. There appeared to be no jetty or pier heads at the location, but the chart might be out of date. Much more worrying were the security problems. Was the message genuine? Who had sent it? Would the boat party have to land to search for the VIP? And who was he: Douglas or someone quite different? Captain Steiner decided to send in his second-in-command, Commander Derek Bazalgette.

On the bridge, the plan was confirmed. The ship would come in towards the shore and slow down for the boat to be lowered. A few of the ship's landing party would go in with the boat's normal crew. They would be armed, including with a light machine-gun. Derek Bazalgette would lead the expedition, and the boat would be navigated by Lieutenant John Cunningham, the ship's Second Navigation Officer. He was a keen sailing man, so if anybody could find their way in to a strange beach in the dark, he could.

At 1.02 a.m. on Saturday 25 January, the ship stopped and the boat was lowered. It headed inshore, showing no lights. Conditions were calm and *Centaur* was left to drift until the boat returned. With time on his hands, Captain Steiner turned to planning the next steps. Obviously, if the Brigadier returned with the boat, he would know what needed to be done ashore. A lot of people would be involved. Despite the hour, for the first time in the short but so far eventful commission, Otto Steiner called a full staff conference for all key operational marine, naval and air department heads and Staff Officers. Messengers were sent round to wake those concerned – no easy task because officer's cabins were spread about the ship, on different decks. While that happened, the small party on the bridge watched out for signs of trouble, or the return of the boat.

Notes

1   Stevens had been among the first troops onto Sword Beach in the Normandy landings on 6 June 1944. In the teeth of fierce fire, he found himself in a situation described in the unit diary as appearing 'a shambles, littered with dead and wounded, some bobbing in the shallows in their Mae Wests [lifejackets], and burned-out tanks. Flail tanks and bulldozers were working while mortar bombs and shellfire

crashed down fairly regularly'. Stevens recalled 'standing up, vaguely thinking it might calm people' when the commandos were pinned down by machine-gun fire. The marines were able to break through to their objective, Lion-sur-Mer; but bitter street fighting slowed the advance. The unit was unable to call for naval gunfire support because their radio equipment was damaged and their signalmen were wounded. Stevens and his men were separated from their Company by two German armoured cars: he destroyed the first with a hand-grenade, forcing the crew of the other to flee. On that first day, the Commando suffered 125 killed or wounded out of their strength of about 450. The commander of the Royal Marines embarked in *Centaur* was thus a battle-hardened veteran of opposed amphibian landings.

2   Smith, David: conversations with author, 1999.

3   Subsequent investigations were unofficial and internal to the Commando — no Board of Inquiry followed. It turned out that all military ammunition in Aden was held in a central depot. A force ordered for action was entitled to draw an agreed 'outfit'. It consisted of small arms ammunition, mortar bombs, grenades, pyrotechnics and demolition explosives and was drawn in bulk. On completion of operations, unused explosives were collected and returned in bulk to the command depot. These transactions were conducted by the unit RSM, who reported partly to the unit's Adjutant and partly to the CO himself. 45 Commando had drawn ammunition for the earlier proposed embarkation in *Centaur* – which had not taken place. This consignment had been returned to the depot when the operation was cancelled. It had still not been broken down into its constituent parts when the requirement suddenly arose again late on the actual day of embarkation. What went wrong is not clear. But Marine Keith Brettell of X Company later recalled that he was part of the working party sent to collect the ammunition. The armoury, in Aden's Crater district, was deep underground and the lighting was poor. Ammunition boxes were loaded onto a manually-operated conveyor belt and then taken to the surface by a lift. By the time it was ready for loading onto lorries it was dark. Nobody was checking box identification at each stage of these movements. As a result it was not until the following day that the RSM discovered that he had been issued with blank (practice) ammunition. Questions about the mishap were never asked officially, or if they were, the result of the investigations was not made public.

4   Holt, G.J.: Correspondence with author, July 2003.

5   The original message was never logged as a formal communication or signal and was lost. A telegram to the CRO was drafted in the High

Commission, and dispatched at around 3 a.m., asking *Centaur* to 'send launch to pick up Douglas and Marciandi at President's pier on starboard side of harbour entrance, close to ferry'. This message arrived too late to be of any use. (PRO DO 226/10 (83)).

11

The Decisive Request

By Friday 24 January, four days after the initial mutiny, the unrest at Colito was worsening. Discipline had broken down completely, and soldiers refused to wear uniform. The new officers had adopted the insignia of their ranks, but nobody took any notice of their orders: by now, rank meant pay level and little else. The selections for promotion, agreed by popular acclaim on the day of the mutiny, had favoured the old guard of discontented senior NCOs and warrant officers, many of whom had encouraged, and perhaps even conceived, the mutiny but then had played little part in executing it. The work had been done and the risks taken by junior NCOs or soldiers – none of whom had been promoted. They were still armed, and were sullen and resentful. During a meeting on Wednesday 22 January, 'Brigadier' Kavana, 'Lt. Col.' Sarakikya (who had flown down from Tabora), and Kambona had formally approved the selections the mutineers had made on Monday, although they could offer no increase in the number of promotions. They hoped that the large pay rise, due to come through on Friday, would calm the unrest.

News from Colito was overshadowed by a much more general problem: the attitude of the trade unions. The Tanganyikan Federation of Labour (TFL) had once been an integral part of TANU, now the ruling party. After independence, however, when the TANU Government became the biggest employer of labour, they enacted union legislation curbing the right to strike. Going even further, they tried to bring the TFL under state control. By 1963, relations were at a low ebb. Nyerere's declaration, in his speech of 7 January 1964, that there should be an end to discrimination against non-Africans in recruitment, training and promotion in the civil service, had caused the TFL great concern. Whether trade union activists had already made serious contact with the mutineers or not – and there is no conclusive evidence that they had – the very possibility of such an alliance must have seemed to the Government a threat which would grow with every passing day. In both the Belgian Congo and Dahomey it had been combinations of armies and trade unions which had overthrown the legitimate Government. In a later interview, Nyerere said, 'The mutiny put the fear of God into our heads. This fear made us round up leaders in the labour movement.'

Meanwhile the Tanganyikan public, their confidence already shaken by the bloody revolution in Zanzibar and the unrest in their own army in both Dar and Tabora, heard of further troubles by the end of the week. On 23 January, there had been an outbreak of indiscipline in the Ugandan army. The Prime Minister, Milton Obote, had immediately requested British help. In a quick reaction, two companies of the Staffordshire Regiment and a company of Scots Guards, all based in Kenya, had been sent in to help stabilise the situation. They secured the airfield at Entebbe and key points in Kampala before a detachment re-established control at Jinja barracks where the trouble had started.

Next day Kenyan army soldiers at Lanet, some 80 miles north of Nairobi, defied authority and attempted to seize the armoury. President Jomo Kenyatta also asked at once for British help. Gunners of the 3rd Regiment, Royal Horse Artillery, acting as infantry, entered the barracks and disarmed the mutineers. The remaining British forces in Kenya had been stretched, but had been able to respond rapidly to the requests of both Obote and Kenyatta, and order had been restored. Neither Obote nor

134

Kenyatta (especially the latter who had spent years fighting for independence and had been imprisoned for years by the British) could be accused of being 'stooges'.

The rapid spread of disruption in East Africa inevitably suggested to some that there must be some controlling influence directing the unrest. How otherwise would three incidents of mutiny plus the revolution in Zanzibar have occurred in such quick succession? Some commentators concluded that this surely pointed to subversion at an international level; and the obvious culprit was 'International Communism'. Russians and Chinese and their followers from Eastern Europe or Cuba, had perhaps set up a sinister network, pulling strings to replace the new nationalist Governments with as yet unidentified puppet regimes. Such fears were aired in both the House of Commons and the House of Lords.

The *Daily Telegraph* in London claimed on 22 January that Kambona had held a meeting with the Chinese Ambassador Ho Ying. Next day, it carried an article under the headline: 'Moscow's boss in East Africa, Kambona runs forces in Tanganyika'. This was definitely not the view of those on the ground. When Stephen Miles and the US Ambassador William Leonhart called jointly on Nyerere on 23 January, the President referred to the stories that there had been an attempted coup by Kambona against him, commenting that 'Poor Oscar had always been unlucky in that people were always saying he was trying to oust the President'. Nyerere added that Kambona had broken down and wept when the allegations had been reported to him earlier that day. This may explain the tone of a personal handwritten message which Kambona asked Miles to send to Sandys on 23 January which read: 'Events in Tanganyika during the last few days, I regret to say, have not been as harmonious and straightforward as we in the Government would have wished. You will appreciate that at the moment I do not wish to write a long and involved letter, but I would just like to take this opportunity of saying to you quite simply, "Thank you for your help". Oscar S. Kambona. P.S. Although our reputation has gone down, we are determined to build up the lost reputation in Africa and overseas. I hope you will help us in doing so as you have in the past.'[1]

Meanwhile, in Tanganyika, the unease was widespread by the end of the week and Nyerere's attempts to restore confidence had been seriously undermined. The special correspondent of *The Times* in Dar es Salaam wrote on 24 January: 'In spite of the much calmer atmosphere in Dar es Salaam following President Nyerere's press conference and University address yesterday, Ministers remain deeply conscious of the dangerous situation in which they now find themselves. Tension will remain.' The article finished, 'Subversive and youth wing elements are, however, still active and further developments must be expected.'

A new and threatening problem emerged on 22 January when a serious coup attempt was detected at Morogoro, a small town some 90 miles inland from Dar. After independence, a handful of trade union leaders had so strongly opposed Nyerere's refusal to countenance calls for the instant Africanisation of all administrative posts that they had brought the working of the TFL to a standstill. One, Victor Mkello, the Secretary General, had been placed in preventive detention; another, Christopher Tumbo, former Tanganyikan High Commissioner in London, was in exile in Kenya. Both were now free, and had apparently formed a group of black power activists, planning how they could make use of the mutiny to unseat Nyerere's Government. More moderate politicians, such as Harun Lugusha, not themselves extremists but frustrated and ambitious politicians, declared themselves ready to accept high office in a Mkello-Tumbo regime.[2] News of the plotting reached Government Ministers the following day.

What relations the plotters had with the mutineers, if any, is unclear. The fact that the mutineers turned against their newly-elected officers on the same day that the plotters established contact with Colito may have been coincidence. However, it seems likely that Nyerere became convinced that there was a link, real or potential, between the two. This was a decisive factor in changing the President's perception of the gravity of the situation.

The army, small and disorganised though it was, now had the country by the throat – and it was not even clear who controlled the mutineers at Colito. The Tanganyikan Government, seriously weakened, faced two crucial decisions. The first was straight-forward: should the mutineers be brought back under control and order be restored, if necessary by force? If the answer was yes, the second question was far more awkward: who should be asked to take the action this would require? Restoring order clearly had to start at Colito, but who could overcome the well-armed mutineers? The 2nd Battalion at Tabora had gone the way of the 1st, so was now part of the problem. No other armed forces existed. Most of the police were unarmed and powerless (and were indeed believed to be likely to join the mutineers in demanding immediate and financially crippling pay rises) and their elite force had been sent to Zanzibar. The Government still enjoyed massive goodwill within TANU ranks, but this could not be mobilised quickly or as an effective military counterweight to the mutineers. If order was to be restored, then external help must be summoned – but from where? Kenya and Uganda had been ruled out because of their own military unrest. Nigeria and Ghana were potentially friendly but Tanganyika had no close rapport with them and in any case they would face insurmountable logistical problems in providing help quickly. The USA was not an option, given Tanganyika's non-aligned position in the Cold War. In 1964, the notion of UN peacekeeping forces being mobilised quickly and effectively was still a distant dream. The only realistic possibility therefore was to call back the British since no other nation had forces readily to hand. But to turn, so soon after gaining independence, to the ex-colonial power seemed unthinkable. Tanganyika, the proud centre of anti-colonial activity in central and southern Africa, would be exposed to accusations that Africans were not capable of running their own

137

affairs. Nyerere must have realised that the political damage would be profound. But there was no obvious way to avoid it, since negotiation with the mutineers had been tried and had failed.

During his joint call on the President with the US Ambassador on the morning of Wednesday 22 January, Stephen Miles had mentioned that British warships were standing by in case of need and that Douglas and four other British officers were still in hiding in Dar. Nyerere asked for the officers to be kept where they were for the time being.

On Thursday 23 January, Miles called on Nyerere again, this time accompanied only by Peter Carter, his deputy.[3] He described what had happened in Uganda earlier in the day, and Obote's reaction to the unrest at Jinja. He then passed on a message from Douglas, who regarded himself still to be the President's military adviser, saying that he felt Nyerere could clear up the trouble in Tanganyika without bloodshed by seeking similar assistance from Britain (e.g. from the ships off Dar). If he did not do so, he would never regain control of the army, which would always be a source of trouble and discontent. Miles reported to London that Nyerere had 'listened thoughtfully and without comment'.[4]

Next morning (Friday 24 January), Miles and Carter called on Kambona and Lusinde together, repeating the information they had given Nyerere the night before about Obote's request for British troops. Kambona had assured them that the Tanganyika Government 'had not closed their minds to the possibility of asking for outside assistance to restore their own situation. But this was a matter for the President as Commander-in-Chief'. When Miles and Carter then went on to see Nyerere again, he said he still wanted to give the new army officers a chance of gaining control over their men. If this did not work, he would have to think again, and he had not ruled out the possibility of asking for help. Miles pointed out that this was not an industrial strike but an army mutiny, punishable by death, and warned him of the possible snowball effect on the police and dockers. Miles reported that by now Nyerere was clearly very worried and beginning to appreciate the danger of giving in to all the soldiers' demands. This warning was later portrayed as 'undue pressure from the British'.[5]

Nyerere did not respond immediately, although his concern was clearly growing. He reviewed the situation with Kawawa, Kambona and Lusinde during the afternoon of Friday 24 January. They concluded that it was no longer possible to continue with the uncertainties of the past few days. Help was needed and Tanganyika had run out of options. Nyerere and his inner group of Ministers decided they had to ask for military assistance, and only the British could provide it quickly enough.

By mid-week, the newly-installed telex link from the High Commission to London was working well. Miles was thus able to report within an hour his exchanges with the President, including the possibility of a request for help. For much of the time, the Secretary of State for Commonwealth Relations, Duncan Sandys, was in direct touch. Miles found him sound, supportive and decisive. On the British side, if any request for help were made, it would be reviewed quickly: the Government was ready to make an early decision. They recognised, however, that there could be substantial political as well as operational dangers. What if Nyerere asked informally for help, an intervention occurred, but Tanganyika later claimed that the response had been too much, too bloody or too early? Sandys passed on to Miles the British Government's insistence that any request from Nyerere must be put in writing before it would be considered.

The mutiny had caught the High Commission staff by surprise, but they had reacted quickly. Having ensured their families' safety by bringing most into the Miles's house or the High Commission office, they set to answering the queries pouring in from the British community. Staff from other embassies also looked to the British to tell them what was happening, and Miles was widely regarded as the diplomat most closely in touch with the Government. For several days, many foreign diplomats and British families came into the High Commission for news, and the waiting room sometimes became very crowded.

> Christopher MacRae. *From time to time, my wife had to burst through the group of ambassadors and senior diplomats from the office where she was quartered, bearing our baby's dirty nappies – since the only lavatory where they could be disposed of was off the public waiting room! She found the juxtaposition of basic domestic needs and high political drama comically surreal.*

Outside in the streets, mutineers had wandered around during the first two days, some crazily. Robert Bullivant, the High Commission's communications operator, ventured out one evening to the nearby New Africa hotel for a meal and a drink. The proprietor, an Alsatian expatriate, was alone, and welcomed him. Soon afterwards Oscar Kambona came in, with a handful of his staff. He greeted the two expatriates politely, but went on to search through the bars of the public rooms. He was clearly looking for somebody, but left without finding him. The incident was typical of a number of instances of Government confusion noted at the time. Even Kambona, at first the man of action, seemed to have lost his way. But by Friday, things had calmed down and High Commission families had started to go home.

Nyerere meanwhile had delivered the Hammarskjold Memorial Lecture at Dar University College on Thursday 23 January, before a crowded audience, as though nothing was wrong. His theme was 'the courage of reconciliation'. In his best philosophical vein, he discussed the balance of freedom and order, rights and obligations, within and between different societies.

At around 2.45 p.m. local time on Friday 24 January (11.45 GMT in Britain), the President summoned Stephen Miles to State

House. Nyerere came straight to the point. He and Kambona had reached the conclusion that it was impossible to allow the ringleader of the revolt, Sergeant Hingo, 'who had appointed himself Colonel of the 1st Battalion' to get away with it. They realised that he was now achieving dangerous popularity with the soldiers. Nyerere had accepted Kambona's advice that Hingo and the other ringleaders should be rounded up and dealt with. He realised that this could only be done with British military help. Nyerere clearly understood that this would involve a full-scale military operation.[6] Would British troops restore order immediately? Miles replied that he was confident it could be done and he would pass the request on to London immediately. The President had made a courageous decision. But he added that the British Government would definitely need the request to be put in writing before they could respond. Nyerere seemed unenthusiastic about this proviso, but eventually said that 'it could be arranged' and that Kambona would bring round a letter later. Since this discussion was taking place in State House, Nyerere could have dictated a letter on the spot had he wanted to; perhaps he preferred to give himself time to consider how best to reduce his exposure to future criticism.

About two hours later, a short, handwritten letter, marked top secret and addressed to Miles personally, was brought round to the High Commissioner's residence by Kambona and Finance Minister Paul Bomani: '*I am directed by the President of the Republic of Tanganyika to approach the British government with a request for military assistance in order to enable us to maintain law and order in the country.*' It was signed by R.N. Kawawa, the Vice President. Why Nyerere did not sign it himself is a matter of speculation. It may simply have been because Kawawa officially chaired the ministerial Defence Committee; but some suggest that Nyerere may have wanted to avoid putting his name to a document which could later be used against him. Having delivered the letter, Kambona told Miles that his Government wanted only British forces to be used (i.e. not forces coming from

141

Kenya or Uganda) and that he hoped the operation could be mounted that night.

The request was passed on at once to London. Miles then summoned Brigadier Douglas and Major Marciandi, who were still hidden upstairs. Kambona and Bomani joined them to talk through this entirely new situation. Kambona confirmed that Douglas remained the Commander of the Tanganyika Rifles. The Ministers agreed with Douglas's proposal to land British troops on Colito Barracks. They realised that the troops might have to use force, and that this could lead to casualties both among the mutineers and perhaps also to the many civilians in the barracks. However, while accepting this, they passed on the President's personal wish that casualties be kept to a minimum. Douglas reassured them that if the British moved quickly, there should be no time for resistance to develop.

In the circumstances, only one person had the local knowledge and experience necessary to lead this operation at such short notice: Douglas himself. So it was vital to get him out to *Centaur* at once to direct the marines. Furthermore, once ashore with the landing party, he could address the mutineers to reassure them that nobody wanted to harm them – and that the British were only there at the President's request. Kambona quickly wrote out a message in Swahili for Douglas to use, and coached him on how to deliver it.

Stephen Miles's first priority was now to get Douglas and Marciandi out to *Centaur*. A former sailor himself, Miles quickly abandoned any idea of sending Douglas out to sea in a tug to search for the British warships: it would take too long, and the tug might be spotted by the mutineers. A better way would be to make covert contact with *Centaur*, now presumably somewhere quite close offshore, and ask her to send a boat in to collect Douglas. Miles delegated the job to a junior member of his team who happened also to have been in the navy.

Christopher MacRae. *Stephen Miles told me to get Douglas*

142

and Marciandi out at once to Centaur, *any way I could. He had reported Nyerere's request to London but had not yet received any response. If the operation was to take place by first light next morning, which was what the Tanganyikan ministers were hoping, no time could be lost. Stephen left it to me to work out how to do this job, but mentioned that the US Embassy had offered to help over ship/shore communications if necessary. There seemed to be three potential ways of contacting* Centaur, *which I knew to be not very far away somewhere over the horizon. The first was to set up a link via London, but our telex line was busy, and any messages would have to go via the CRO to the Admiralty and then back to* Centaur, *which seemed too lengthy. The second was to try the Harbour Master's coastal control net, but this seemed too insecure. The last was to see if the Americans really did have the means to contact a British warship direct – which seemed the best bet.*

Next, I had to think where Centaur *should be asked to send a boat to shore under cover of darkness. I sailed regularly in races organised by the Dar Sailing Club, so had some general idea of the coastline. But the Commodore of the club, who was the Chief Justice, had much more detailed knowledge – and happened to live close to the beach near State House where Nyerere lived. So I sounded him out, explaining what was afoot. He confirmed that a suitable place for such a rendezvous was near the harbour mouth, in front of State House. He also agreed that Douglas and Marciandi could wait in his house for the boat to arrive.*

Now I had the outline of a plan. But would I be able to get in touch with Centaur? *I went round to the US Embassy and explained the problem to the Ambassador, William Leonhart. He agreed at once. His radio operator told me that he was maintaining regular contact with the USS* Manley *on a circuit which* Centaur *might also be manning. All he needed to know was* Centaur's *callsign. My heart sank: I had not the slightest idea what it might be! Dredging my memory of my National Service years spent mostly in another aircraft carrier, I managed to come up with the international callsign for 'Any British warship'. That should do:* Centaur *and* Cambrian *were probably the only British warships within range, so would surely respond.*

'OK. We'll try that,' said the operator, and started tapping the callsign in morse. He kept on repeating it for what seemed an eternity – but may have been only the time for Centaur's *team to retune a transmitter. At last, there was a response. 'What is your message?' asked the operator. I was caught short by this: in the rush of events I had failed to write out any text, so had to make it up on the spot. The message would have to be passed en clair, and might be intercepted. It seemed vital to disguise our intentions so I worked out a brief message I hoped would hide what was afoot from anyone other than* Centaur's *crew: 'Please send taxi for VIP to flashing light in front of State House'.*

I learned later that a radio ham who was also an expatriate newspaper reporter had monitored the transmission and had experienced no difficulty whatever in working out what was happening! To his credit he kept the news to himself, but he did go to the foreshore at dawn to see if my message had achieved anything.

Next I had to get Douglas and Marciandi down to the Judge's house, and then on to the beach. At the High Commission office I ran into my fellow diplomat, friend and sailing partner, the Australian 1st Secretary, Tony Dingle. On an impulse I asked him to come with me to provide moral support during the night's activities and he agreed without hesitation. Once Douglas and Marciandi had been safely transferred to the Chief Justice's house, Tony and I went, slightly apprehensively, down to the beach near the harbour mouth. By then it was getting on for midnight and very dark. Nothing much seemed to be happening, and there was no sign of ships or boats offshore. We took it in turns to flash a torch out to sea. Time passed very slowly. Suddenly a truck stopped behind us, and we could hear booted passengers, presumably soldiers, jumping off. We could hear military orders being shouted, and thought we had been rumbled. I was very nervous. Tony agreed we should stop flashing the torch, keep quite still lying flat in the sand and hope for the best. It was a tense moment. Only slowly did it dawn on us that this was simply a routine change of guard for State House behind us. The troops going off watch climbed into the lorry, and drove away – to our immense relief.

Some time after 1 a.m. we heard engines getting closer. Soon afterwards a smartly-painted motor boat loomed out of the darkness, manned by sailors in white uniforms. Commander Bazalgette, who was in charge, introduced himself. Leaving Tony Dingle to explain the situation, I rushed back to collect Douglas and Marciandi. They waded out to the boat, were hauled aboard, and the boat disappeared into the darkness. Much relieved, we returned to the High Commission office where I found some cold beer in a fridge. By then, there seemed no point in going to bed, so Tony and I sat up chatting for the rest of the night, before going up to the roof terrace at daybreak to see if anything was happening.

The urgent and improvised operation to restore order in Tanganyika was still on track. The right people were assembled somewhere offshore to plan the action.

At the Acting High Commissioner's house, people in the know had also gathered, waiting for the sound of guns or helicopters. Dawn broke; it started to grow light, but all was still quiet. Then, suddenly, from the north, the direction of Colito Barracks, came the crashing sound of heavy gunfire.

145

Notes

1   PRO: DO 185/46 (83).
2   Listowel, Judith: *The Making of Tanganyika.*
3   The frequency of Miles's contacts with the President during the week left the British exposed to accusations that they had exercised improper influence. British diplomats undoubtedly saw more of the President, and other key Ministers, than those of other nations, but this was inevitable. There were still a considerable, though lessening, number of British expatriates serving the former colonies in East Africa. A high proportion of foreign aid came from Britain, and the British had armed forces immediately to hand when no other nation did. Miles had also formed a good relationship with the President. The allegations of interference, when they came, were explicit, as we shall see. The President was himself, much later, to comment adversely, while Stephen Miles himself strongly denies any such undue pressure. There were no taped recordings of these meetings, and memories fade. But there is one reliable body of evidence. Immediately after each meeting, Miles reported to London. Copies of his messages can be found in the British National Archives. In view of the later allegations, we take care to refer to these records where there might be any doubt about what exactly was said or agreed by Miles or Nyerere.
4   PRO: DO 185/46 (99)" DO 226/10 (78A).
5   PRO: DO 185/46 (99)" DO 226/10 (78A).
6   *Ibid.*

12

Assault at Colito

Brigadier Douglas and Major Marciandi arrived on board *Centaur* at 2 a.m. They had been surprised at the length of the boat trip, but the ship was lying nearly three miles offshore. They were taken to the bridge to meet Captain Steiner and Lt. Col. Stevens and were shown the signal from London ordering *Centaur* to take action, and appointing Douglas as commander once the 'troops were ashore'. There was no time to lose. The subordinate commanders and staff officers were already assembled in a small operations office. Into it were crowded the ship's second-in-command Derek Bazalgette, who had brought them out to the ship, and Commander (Air) 'Randy' Kettle, with the CO of his helicopter squadron, Lt. Cdr. Bob Bluett. Also present were four other ship's staff officers, responsible for operations, navigation, gunnery and signals. Stevens had eight Royal Marine officers: his deputy, Major David Smith and four company commanders, together with his adjutant, intelligence and signals officers. It was hot and crowded.

The Brigadier, although designated to command the proposed action, started at a slight disadvantage: his troops had mutinied. He was also dressed informally in borrowed clothes and as he and Marciandi had waded out to their boat, their trousers were dripping onto the deck. In any case Captain Steiner was in command while the force remained at sea, and Lt. Col. Stevens would be responsible for handling his own marines once they

147

were ashore. The Commando had also, of course, already prepared outline plans for a helicopter-borne landing. The Brigadier therefore had no immediate authority; he would command only once the force was ashore. He did, however, have vital local knowledge. He understood exactly what the force had to do to restore order. He also knew the mutineers had been given a pay rise, and as they had been paid that very evening would probably be celebrating as the British forces hovered offshore. His news that there was plenty of small arms ammunition in the barracks armoury, of the type left behind in Aden, would also greatly interest the Royal Marines.

The meeting was between three virtually independent commanders, each with his own responsibilities. No minutes or records were kept. Many of the officers who attended would subsequently remember exchanges, opinions, suggestions or comments that others had missed or forgotten. But, in short time, a detailed action plan was agreed and put immediately into effect. There was no recourse to higher authority, and indeed all orders were issued orally since there was no time to write them down.

Tony Laurence. *This was one of the more exciting moments in my life. I had never been involved in anything remotely as serious. It was the first time Captain Steiner had ever called an operational staff conference, and was to prove the last that I attended during my time in HMS* Centaur. *I was riveted, and thought I could recall everything of moment that occurred. It was only when I started to write this book that I learned that others present had different recollections of the detail of what was discussed. We all confirmed, however, the principal factors considered, and the action plan that emerged.*

The three men first agreed to land the Commando in the Colito area at dawn, in only four hours' time, before any word of the British presence got out. They also agreed that the overriding

148

imperative, politically and in human terms, was to keep casualties to a minimum. This could only be achieved if the mutineers were given no time to react.

This decision led to the next question: where to land? Even helicopters could not land anywhere, especially if they had to operate in assault waves, and there were very few feasible sites. The Brigadier suggested Colito Hill, near the officer's mess. This overlooked the camp, and from there it would be easy to deny access to the town. But there was an insoluble problem: there was no space large or level enough. The playing field immediately adjoining the barracks offered plenty of room: could that be used?

At first Lt. Col. Stevens was uneasy about landing there. It was closely overlooked by some of the barracks buildings which might contain armed men. This ran directly against current military thinking on helicopter landings. 'Going straight down the chimney' was to be avoided unless the attackers had over-whelming strength and detailed intelligence – which this force did not. The principle espoused by the US Marine Corps was 'hit 'em where they ain't'. This suggested a landing on the only other obvious site, a plantation to the south, out of small arms range of the barracks, from which the force would then approach on foot.

Brigadier Douglas agreed the dangers of his playing field option. The 1st Battalion Tanganyika Rifles had been a first-class unit. The men were equipped with Australian-made SLR rifles of the same type as the marines, and they had at least eight modern general purpose machine-guns (GPMGs). If they did begin to fight there could be a bloodbath, and Douglas knew that there were hundreds of women and children in the barracks. He wanted to allow the mutineers, for the time being out of control and undisciplined, no time to react. He was convinced that the element of surprise would give the marines time to win control bloodlessly. It was very unlikely that the ship had been seen or the force's presence even suspected. So he argued that the first landings should be made while the mutineers were still asleep. If there was then a lot of noise, the mutineers could be kept disorientated.

149

Stevens was persuaded. He accepted the risks inherent in landing right next to the barracks, but stipulated that if any resistance developed, follow-up waves of troops would be landed further away, under the protection of the first group; there were simply not enough helicopters to lose a single one. The marines would then need to be tactically aggressive to keep the mutineers off balance. So the three commanders agreed that the initial landing at least would be made on the playing field.

Brigadier Douglas warned that the guardhouse might be manned by relatively alert mutineers. He offered to land with the first marines, carrying a loudhailer to address the mutineers in Swahili, using the reassurances written by Kambona which he had mastered that evening. This offer was accepted. He was closely questioned by Major David Langley, commanding the lead Company, on points of immediate concern to the first wave, particularly flight approach hazards, but he could give few detailed answers on helicopter operations.

The discussion turned to the ship's launch point for the operation. Captain Steiner had his navigator, Lt. Cdr. Charles Le Mesurier, explain the proposed anchorage. It was inshore of outlying reefs, in a tide-swept channel with a depth of 7 fathoms (42ft). This was only just enough water for the ship, which was drawing 29ft. Mangrove-lined mud flats and coral reefs surrounded the proposed anchorage on three sides. If the ship anchored in the centre of the channel, there would be room to swing without going aground, only one and a half miles away from the barracks' beach club. Douglas wondered if it was right to bring the ship in so close: it would be well within range of the 1st Battalion's mortars if things went wrong, and the mortar platoon were very good. Captain Steiner explained firmly that the safety of the entire operation depended on a brisk initial success. If the Royal Marines were to land on the barracks, he was prepared to take the risk of anchoring within mortar range of the beach.

Tony Laurence. *Charles Le Mesurier, the ship's navigation*

officer, had seen a good many Commanding Officers handling their ships. He had unstinted praise for what he described as Captain Steiner's 'skill and courage'. I also spent a lot of time on the bridge, and at first had not been impressed. Steiner adopted a hesitant tone when manoeuvring, interspersing his helm and engine orders with a muttered dialogue along the lines '... shall we? ... No, not yet ... What do you think, Pilot? ... I wonder, yes – Half Ahead Port ...' This style gave an impression of indecisiveness. It was only after he had completed a manoeuvre that it became clear that the Captain had achieved it quickly, surely, and with a minimum of engine orders. He was, in fact, a very fine seaman, as his choice of anchorage had just confirmed.

Once the outlines of the plan had been agreed, Stevens took over to give his orders. He was dealing with matters of life and death. The naval officers sat quietly listening, for the first time in most of their lives, to other people being sent into action. What had so far seemed a rather discursive meeting became a taut *order group*. Paddy Stevens began by stating his aim: to seize and hold the initiative. He continued, 'We land at first light, Z Company leading. The key to this operation is the guardhouse. David – you are to take it immediately, even if you have to write off a section getting it.'

By saying this so bluntly he gave the Company Commander a clear directive about how strongly he was to press home his attack. Should there be active resistance, then Langley should push on his leading platoon until they had sustained 25 per cent casualties, perhaps six or eight of his Royal Marines wounded, a few even killed. If that happened the CO would think again, and call in naval gunfire or air strikes. This would in turn lead to massive casualties among the mutineers, probably including civilians. In a few words he had laid all this down for Langley, and accepted responsibility in advance.

151

Stevens continued with the tasks for the follow-up waves. The younger naval officers, particularly those not involved in air operations, were stunned: nothing in their peacetime careers had prepared them for this. But Paddy Stevens was right, as events were soon to show. The meeting broke up and the Company and Helicopter Commanders hurried off to prepare their men for the coming assault.

Meanwhile, after recovering her boat at 2.06 a.m., *Centaur* had got under way and stood out to sea. Captain Steiner left the operations room with his Operations Officer Willie Heathcote. Then he remembered that they had planned no role for the escorting destroyer, HMS *Cambrian*. *Centaur* had only a light anti-aircraft armament, but *Cambrian* had three 4.5in guns which would be devastating against shore targets. They would also make a huge noise. Time was very short. Both ships were stopped, and Commander David Hankinson, *Cambrian*'s commanding officer, was ordered on board the carrier. He came over in the darkness in his ship's motor whaler. Someone remembered that *Centaur* was now short of .303 rifles and ammunition, having turned over most of her stocks to the marines. *Cambrian* was ordered to transfer all her rifles and ammunition, and they were brought over as the COs conferred.

Steiner brought in his senior commanders and both Douglas and Stevens to his second operational meeting. It was a very brief council of war. Hankinson was asked simply if he could lay down a 'diversionary bombardment' with his main armament. The shells should burst in the air about 1,000yds north of Colito Barracks. Sisal was grown in this area, which would be deserted at that time. The air bursts should be noisy but harm nobody. Hankinson, a gunnery specialist, explained the hazards in this plan. They included the extreme range and the lack of any 'forward observer' with communications to direct the fire. The ship would have to be navigated very carefully, and the guns fired blind. Even a small error could lead to loss of life. However, he

152

thought it could be done if everyone was very careful. *Centaur's* own gunnery specialist, Lt. Cdr. Alec Simpson, would act as radio link between the landing force and the destroyer. If things went wrong, *Cambrian's* guns could be stopped, although a few salvoes would still be in the air. After this diversionary firing, the guns would be kept ready to support the marines in case there was serious resistance. The plan agreed, Hankinson went up to *Centaur's* bridge to order *Cambrian's* crew to action stations by radio. It seemed to him 'the quickest way of getting them all up and about at an ungodly hour'.

As he returned through the tropical night to his darkened ship, Hankinson had time to think about the considerable risks involved in the responsibility he had undertaken.[1] His career in the Royal Navy had gone well, and after early promotion he was now commanding a fleet destroyer at the age of only 35. But he had just agreed to fire a live bombardment, at the maximum range of his guns, with no warning, in peacetime, into an independent foreign country; and close to a crowded barracks that was not shown on his navigational chart. As a specialist gunnery officer, he knew the lethal consequences of any inaccuracy in fire control. He would need quickly to develop an effective system to air-burst the ship's high-explosive shells accurately just to one side of the barracks. His briefing had been short, and he had gained an impression that his Commander had been making up the plans as he went along. It seemed that no senior Area Commander, nor any directive from London, had authorised Hankinson to fire his main armament into African territory, so he would be taking far greater risks that he had ever done before in his 18 years of naval service. More importantly, could this act be justified afterwards to the outside world?

But he realised that the marines crowded into the small aircraft carrier he had just left were taking even greater risks. They would be landing an advance guard from a handful of converted helicopters right beside 600 infantrymen who had mutinied. Nobody seemed to know whether they would be alert, or how hard and effectively they would fight. The marines' commanding officer had been quite clear: to succeed, he needed the shock and noise of heavy gunfire when his men first landed. And the naval guns must remain ready to keep on firing until he got enough men and weapons ashore. The British troops were only risking the operation because they knew the destroyer would support them in this way, so Hankinson soon reassured himself that he had been right to accept the responsibility. He had agreed to open fire and militarily it would be right to do so. Moreover, it was the Tanganyikan President himself who had asked the British to put an end to the mutiny by first light next morning. By the time the boat had come alongside HMS *Cambrian*, Hankinson had put all doubts to the back of his mind, keen only to get on with the challenge ahead.

On board his ship he found his gunnery and navigation officers 'tearing their hair out' about the navigational charts of the area. They did not show Colito Barracks or the sisal plantation, having scarcely been updated since the 1920s. The locations were pencilled in. A firing run was plotted in waters that would be deep enough for the destroyer. From there, fire would be directed onto the latitude and longitude of the target which would be at the extreme range of 12,000yds. The trajectory would pass over an inhabited island. Hankinson thought briefly about aiming more than 1,000yds wide of Colito, but decided that the shock effect would be unduly diminished. The destroyer crew continued their preparations as the ships closed in towards the land again.

Centaur ordered *Cambrian* to act independently, before turning south-west for her run into Msasani Bay. Both ships were still darkened and the approach made by radar. *Centaur*'s starboard anchor was let go at 5.48 a.m., in a relatively deep nine-fathom hole surrounded by shallow water. The vessel lay awkwardly cross-wind, complicating the helicopter launch. Both engines were worked to turn her round the anchor, but the water was so shallow that the normal propeller flows were reflected off the sea bottom. It took several tense minutes to bring her head to wind – only six minutes before the time scheduled for the start of helicopter engines.

The order '45 Commando to assault stations' had been piped over the ship's broadcast system soon after 2 a.m. Few of the 2,500 men on board had heard that order before. The marines knew what to do; they had been practising for three days. They realised that preparations for any landing were likely to take place at night, with the ship darkened. It was awkward in the crowded main hangar, where they had to stow bedding and other unwanted equipment before packing operational kit for the assault. Personal ammunition and 24-hour ration packs were issued next. There was time for quick briefings at the lowest levels (sections) before the job of forming landing sticks began.

While the troops worked on their preparations, Paddy Stevens held his final 'O' Group meeting in *Centaur*'s large wardroom. It was attended by all the commando officers, and several of the senior NCOs. Stevens went over the intelligence and the plan agreed with Brigadier Douglas, whom he introduced. He also explained that there would be a naval presence ashore.

Steiner had been keen to have a representative ashore, and it was all the more important to have a Forward Air Controller if the landing site might have to be altered. Senior Air Traffic Controller 'Brutus' Holt had drawn the ammunition for his sub-machine gun from sleepy ship's armourers, and now felt very adventurous. He had been greatly impressed by Paddy Stevens' briefing.[2]

By around 5 a.m. the stickorbat (in full, '*Centaur* Plan 1 Helicopter Detailed Landing Table') was coming to life. The initial landing force would consist of four eight-man Wessex sticks drawn from Z Company, together with the Company Commander, plus Brigadier Douglas, Major Marciandi and the naval Forward Air Controller. The two RAF Belvedere helicopters would follow, each bringing in 12 or 13 men, together with the first supporting weapons. These six helicopters would form the first wave and would return immediately for the follow-

155

up waves. It was now clear that the flight times would be much shorter than planned as *Centaur* would be so close inshore. The follow-up sticks would therefore have to be very handy to the flight deck if there were to be no delays. This took a lot of organising, and a great deal of help from the naval teams.

The ship's Air Department was considerably disrupted by all these activities. The removal of the marines' camp beds had freed up the hangar deck and aircraft could now be repositioned, using the ship's lift. But a number of sailors had been requisitioned as stick guides, much had to be done, and there was a feeling of tension. Inevitably, clashes happened. The towing of an unwanted Gannet radar picket aircraft through a troop of marines, already formed up for action, led to a very heated exchange: the naval tractor operator wisely left the aircraft where it was until the marines had left.[3]

The commandos were called forward at 5.15 a.m., and began to move towards the flight deck. There was a last-minute flurry of adjustments. One started when Stevens, thinking beyond the immediate takeover at the barracks, directed that his personal vehicle be landed early in the follow-up waves. The stickorbat was duly amended. It was then realised that the CO's driver had only just joined the unit, and was too young for action. His predecessor, Marine Cook, now in the transport section, was ordered to take over again as the Colonel's driver.[4] But in his transport job, he had been re-armed with an old rifle. His original SLR was reissued but now he had the wrong ammunition. By this time the Land Rover was on deck and scheduled to be lifted off in an early Belvedere load, so Cook took up his readiness position with no personal ammunition at all. He did not bother anyone with his problem, but a senior NCO had noticed. Marine Cook saw his ammunition brought on deck – just after he had been lifted off the ship.

The assault waves were ready for action by 5.45 a.m. This was only ten hours after the confidential signal ordering the operation had been encrypted in Whitehall, and under four hours since

Douglas and Marciandi had stepped on board. It was only just in time: dawn would soon break. It was overcast, and there would be some mist over higher ground. Otherwise, conditions were perfect.

Shortly before 6.00 a.m. the order was given to start helicopter engines. The operation at once hit its first snag. The engines of neither of the RAF Belvederes would start. Onlookers saw crewmen insert a starter cartridge underneath the fuselages and everyone then stood back – there was a muffled bang and some smoke; briefly the rotors jerked round but then stopped. The loaded naval helicopters were by now airborne, and circling offshore.

Tony Laurence. *I was on the bridge, monitoring the commando rear link radio channel, intending to keep track of events ashore. The delay was agonising. Daylight comes quickly in the tropics. People ashore had evidently seen the ship, and I could see cars gathering along a track behind the beach. Would one of them contain someone who would alert the barracks, and how much time would that take? Beside me, Captain Steiner was talking urgently to Commander (Air) asking how long we could delay before the operation was fatally compromised. Somebody suggested, rather gloomily, that 'it would only take a couple of machine-guns on the shoreline'.*

In the main commando headquarters, still sited in the assault operations room, Lieutenant Ewan Sale, the Assistant Adjutant, who had served in trials with naval helicopters in Cyprus, knew that their aircraft would give no problems. But would the RAF helicopters (which the marines had only limited respect for) now foul up the assault? Out to sea, David Hankinson had brought HMS *Cambrian* onto a firing run which would give steady conditions and an accurate position. The course inclined towards

157

the shore. If he did not get the order to fire at the scheduled time he would run into shallow water. He asked Alec Simpson, an old gunnery colleague, who was on *Centaur*'s upper bridge, about the delay. The ship's Flight Deck Control Officer wondered aloud whether it was time simply to ditch the offending helicopters into the sea to give space for more naval helicopters to be ranged. This upset (and perhaps motivated) the RAF ground crew who redoubled their efforts to start their reluctant aircraft.

Eventually a Belvedere engine did start. The first big helicopter engaged its rotors and took off. Soon the first wave was headed inland. The whole flight, from ship to barracks, took only five minutes. After the reef, a thin white beach with a fringe of palms, and then coarse grassland and neat settlements, with scattered shrubs and eucalyptus trees. There was a small plantation works with a chimney. The five helicopters flew low, swinging south to run in upwind towards the barracks. It was, by D-Day standards, a very tiny assault.

Lieutenant Commander Bob Bluett, CO of 815 Squadron, touched down at 6.20 a.m., to drop his stick of eight men. The remaining three Royal Navy Wessex helicopters followed closely, then the RAF Belvedere. Within six minutes, 46 men were ashore. Dust enveloped the landing ground. One marine, Corporal Ivor Pennington, recalls listening to the pilot talking to his helicopter Marshall. Soon after land replaced sea in the restricted view out of a small window, the marshall took his earphones off and signalled a 'countdown' with his fingers. As 'zero' approached, a klaxon sounded and the marshall began to push them out of the aircraft. Ivor thought he fell seven feet. As the last man jumped, the helicopter 'certainly did not hang about'. Grabbing his radio operator, he headed for some long grass beside the playing field. Seeing no officers or senior NCOs, his group went to ground. They were immediately attacked by red ants.

By now it was light, but the landing came as a complete surprise to all at Colito. The site was entirely exposed, so the two leading troops ran for cover in the grass or in monsoon ditches

158

running beside the pitch. They had been ordered to fire wide of the buildings to heighten the noise. Holt had landed with the first wave, lugging his heavy radio. He joined in the firing enthusiastically, but only for one shot – his sub-machine-gun immediately jammed. A neighbouring marine rolled over and inspected it. Holt had the wrong ammunition. The marine handed him a magazine of his own, and ordered him to use it only for personal protection. This reminded Holt of his real mission, which was to control the helicopters. The second wave was approaching, but so much dust had been stirred up that their pilots could not see if the helicopters of the first wave had cleared the landing zone. Holt could see that they had, and called in the follow-up group. He could now, working with the ship's air controllers, establish a 'racetrack' with the helicopters working continuously. Later he complained about his ammunition problem but got no sympathy from the marines; it was up to each man to check his own ammunition, and Brutus was considered lucky to be beside 'probably the only marine in Z Company kind-hearted enough to give up some of his own ammunition to a complete stranger, and a naval one as well'!

At the landing site, Company Commander Major Langley assigned his Seven Troop, under Lieutenant Ian Martin, to use the cover of the ditches and move in a left flanking direction towards the guardroom, armoury and the main gate. This would stop vehicles leaving the camp and secure the ammunition. Nine Troop, under Second Lieutenant Steven Weall, was dispatched to the east to cover the landing site. Steven had only joined the Commando two weeks before, straight from his officer's initial training course. He had hardly expected to be leading marines into action quite so soon. Langley, with his company headquarters, followed Seven Troop closely. With them were Brigadier Douglas, carrying his megaphone, and his staff officer Major Marciandi. There was some sporadic fire, at first only from the Royal Marines.

159

*

Offshore, David Hankinson had run out of sea room, and had turned his ship back onto another firing course. Slightly later than planned, *Cambrian*'s 4.5in guns fired their first salvo, then kept up a continuous bombardment. By prearrangement, Z Company added to their small arms fire by launching rocket projectiles near to, but clear of, the camp buildings. Together with the noise of the helicopter engines and rotors, there was a deafening din, as had been intended.

Stevens and his personal staff officers, forming advanced headquarters, came in with the second wave of helicopters. His signal officer helped the 'rear link operator' manhandle their heavy radio set out of the helicopter and into a position under a small tree. While the operator set watch with *Centaur*, Lieutenant Howgill moved about to discover what was going on. He found himself hurled to the ground in a rugby tackle by his operator. The explanation lacked respect, especially when he was referred to as a 'fucking idiot'. Only then did he realise that hostile fire was being aimed at them.

Stevens was content with developments so far. He was particularly pleased about the noise level and confusion. *Cambrian*'s firepower was accurate and effective. But as with many military achievements, this was not because the engagement was flawless; rather it was a story of difficulties overcome.

Cambrian's three guns were being fired under central control at an intended sixteen rounds a minute from each mounting. The Captain had ordered that 60 rounds of high explosive were to be provided for each gun. The type of fuse to fit into the shell had posed a problem. The ship had a supply of proximity fuses which were intended to explode if the shell approached anything solid. This would have seemed the right fuse to use, exploding the shells just before they struck the ground. But proximity fuses were often unreliable, and might allow the shell to land unexploded. They might also pass close to a helicopter – and prove only *too* reliable. A safer alternative was to use 'time-mechanical' fuses. These could be set individually, by hand, to explode after a given time. If they hit anything solid before the time was up they would also explode, but only after a slight delay to allow the shell to penetrate. This seemed the best solution for the 'bombardment as distraction' role. But it was complicated. The time of flight could only be set after someone had first read the firing range off a gunnery calculator, entered distance/time of flight tables for the constantly changing distances, and then passed a figure to each gun crew, by phone. The fuses then had to be set – by hand. A number of gunnery experts had been very busy setting up this ad hoc procedure since the Captain returned from *Centaur*.

Don Macdonald was *Cambrian*'s senior gunnery Petty Officer, or 'GI' (gunnery instructor). He moved continually round the mountings to confirm that the procedures were working. Almost immediately 'A', the forward gun, stopped. The Captain of the gun thought that they had simply loaded an incorrectly-set fuse. If so, the shell might explode anywhere — over a village, or near a helicopter. The solution was to clear the suspect shell by firing it safely. Macdonald ordered the gun to be depressed to the horizontal and then fired locally. The shell should land only a short distance from the ship. It did. But the sea was calm and the shell ricocheted off like a pebble in a series of bounces. It exploded shortly before skipping onto the beach and into the palm trees – harmlessly as it turned out. All this happened under disapproving eyes on the bridge, where the Captain in particular was seen not to be amused.

Moving aft, Macdonald found that 'B' gun had also stopped firing. A nut from the gun shield had been shaken loose. By very bad luck it had lodged between the breech and the gun cradle. This stopped the gun running out after firing, and interrupted the firing circuits. The gunnery ordnance artificer quickly made up a temporary lead to short-circuit the firing gear. As the gun fired, he deftly extracted the bolt before his fingers were trapped by the run-out.

161

There were adventures right aft as well. The firing circuits of 'Y' gun failed, but there was a drill for this. The Captain of the gun, Petty Officer Bruford, had a 'local' firing push. His duty, in the event of circuit failure, and in 'surface fire', was to push this every time the gunfire gong sounded. Mistakenly, he followed 'anti-aircraft fire' procedure, which was to keep his firing push depressed continuously. The gun therefore fired again as soon as it was loaded. The gun's crew were most proficient: they were soon achieving 28 rounds per minute, double the planned rate of fire! The paint on the barrel began to melt. Don Macdonald arrived in some haste and set things right.

There was a sequel. A few weeks later the sailors learned that the British had been accused of killing 2,000 Africans when 'their battleships had bombarded Dar'. This wholly erroneous accusation will be explained later, but lower-deck humour was not to be deflected by political correctness. The small ship was proud to become a battleship, and a shoe polish tin was made up as an outsize medal and presented to the gun Captain who was renamed 'Broadsides Bruford – the Butcher of Dar'.

Meanwhile a serious problem had developed ashore: Major Langley's group had run into resistance. As they approached the guardroom at the barracks entrance they came under scattered fire. They returned it, but not heavily. Douglas, with his loudhailer, tried to reassure the occupants by shouting the message from President Nyerere translated into Swahili by Kambona, they should stop firing and come out. But there was no response, and firing continued spasmodically. Major Langley, in local command, said that he could not hold back much longer: he had only two sections on the ground and they would be heavily outnumbered once the mutineers were fully aroused. Douglas gave the men in the guardhouse two minutes before repeating the warning, with a countdown. There was still no response, and firing continued. The new Tanganyikan RSM, appointed by the mutineers, had started to make his way to the guardroom, but the firing unsettled him and he later admitted to running away instead.

Major Langley, who was right forward with Brigadier Douglas and Major Marciandi, and like them was in real personal danger, ordered a 3.5in rocket projectile to be fired into the guardroom. It was a long, low, single storey building with a pitched roof. The first missile was aimed above the main door. Fired by Marine Priest, it was accurate enough, but by some incredible mischance hit a power line little larger than a telephone wire. It bounced directly back, and exploded very close to the shaken officers. A second missile was fired, hitting the roof, and killing one of the occupants outright. Six other mutineers were wounded and later flown out to *Centaur* for treatment. Two died later. The uninjured occupants rushed outside in some terror. The first – and last – organised resistance, such as it was, had been overcome.

An exchange between Marine Priest and his Company Commander typified the relationships between officers and men in a well-run unit. Major Langley, his ears still ringing, petulantly asked why the first shot had been a mistake, nearly killing him. Priest replied: 'What makes you think it was a mistake, Sir?'

Tony Laurence. *All these events were reported, as they occurred, by Stevens's radio operator. The sound of firing could be heard between his short and clear sentences, which we were logging carefully. I later sent copies to the signal officers of the schools involved in amphibious warfare training.*

Z Company quickly occupied the nearby part of the barracks, securing the magazine and armoury. A piece of open ground was earmarked for casualty evacuation and as a collection point for the mutineers. By 7.00 a.m., Y and Z Companies were beginning to land, along with the Commando tactical headquarters. All three commando Companies and their fighting equipment were ashore 80 minutes after Bob Bluett first touched his helicopter down. The landing on Colito Barracks was over. The next step was to restore order.

Tom Binley, from March in Cambridgeshire, was serving in Z Company. He remembers ducking clear of a helicopter and being ordered to head for some distant buildings. There was still some firing going on. To their left lay a fence marking the boundary with the main public road. It was already lined with spectators. This struck him as odd; should people be watching a war as if it were a football match? His section cleared some barrack rooms and then the canteen. It was deserted and there were no officers or senior NCOs in sight. The marines decided that some minor pillage would be in order: pushing past the cash till, they helped themselves to deliciously cool Fantas.

Colonel Stevens ordered that the first task was to collect up the mutineers in the Barracks area. They were in a more chaotic state than foreseen. Some were still ranging about fully armed and had to be taken seriously. Others had moved into barrack rooms and appeared to have brought their extended families with them – they would present more of a welfare than a military problem. Y Company, under Captain Gavin Hamilton-Meikle, was ordered to block off all exits to Dar es Salaam and to cover the high ground to the west to prevent any interference. They also had to supply a mobile reserve. Allocated helicopters, they flew low around the camp, cutting off *askaris* who were trying to get away, roping down to accept their surrender. X Company, under Major Mike Banks, were ordered to cover the northern approaches, on the side of the camp furthest away from Dar.

The planning was orderly enough, but on the ground things were lively. Marine Brown of Nine Troop has described his thoughts in the history of 45 Commando. Of Nigerian descent, he was the only black marine in Z Company. The obvious panic and fear shown by so many *askaris* upset him deeply. A number of surrendered mutineers could not understand why someone so obviously of African origin could stand guard over them with a rifle. They spoke to him in Swahili which he did not understand. In another incident, a pilot of 815 Squadron reported being fired on by a machine-gun as he left the camp area. Another troop took cover on hearing fire, but found it was not directed at them. These incidents have never been fully explained. The Marines themselves did once open fire, though. A car, driven by an understandably panicky European, ran through a marine block on the main road passing the camp. A marine fired a burst alongside it. The car stopped and the shaken driver was cautioned. This may have been the source of the reports of automatic gunfire.

The sound of *Cambrian*'s guns had been clearly heard in Dar. Spectators began to arrive, and had to be kept clear of the main gate to the barracks. An enterprising reporter from *Paris Match* secured an interview with Brigadier Douglas. Shortly afterwards, Douglas was horrified to see a High Commissioner from another African country under arrest, sitting on the ground with his hands on his head. He was quickly released and was offered profuse apologies. The Ambassador cheerfully admitted that he had been too pushy and so this did not become a diplomatic incident.

The mutineers' initial reaction appeared to the marines to be unconcerned with disciplinary or political matters. It seemed more a matter of self-preservation. Some thought the white troops had come to loot their possessions and rape their women. Once this fear passed, they quickly saw the advantage of cooperation. Many had been deeply ashamed of what had happened, in particular the looting and misbehaviour in the city. A large number of women and children seemed, unlike their menfolk, only too pleased to see the British soldiers, and applauded the Brigadier. (At least, he thought, *somebody* liked him!) A few civilians staying in the camp were sent on their way. As things settled down, Alex Nyirenda presented himself to Major Langley. Six years earlier, when he had been a Commonwealth Officer cadet on a pre-Sandhurst course at Mons, Langley had been his instructor and commander. He seemed to Langley 'a delightful man caught up in an awful mess' and was at once set to work helping search the camp and rounding up the stragglers. Apart from the men killed and wounded in the guardroom, there were no further casualties. At that stage about 250 men had been captured. There was no sign of a politician. Several Government Ministers had known that the action was to take place, and must have heard that it was over, but nobody arrived to show interest or speak to Douglas. It was, perhaps, a missed opportunity to demonstrate leadership.

Douglas managed to get through to the British High Commission by telephone and spoke to Stephen Miles, whose responsibility it was to decide what should happen next. The British had been requested to provide 'military assistance in order to enable us to maintain law and order in the country'. It was obvious to both men that the marines must move, initially, to the British High Commission to assess the next move. They would then disarm any mutineers left in the city. Miles would drive out to meet Douglas at the Selander bridge on the approach road. The marines were instructed to commandeer transport for the move.

Stevens's feeling at this point was that if the Royal Marines had had more intelligence and time to plan the operation, then the assault might have been carried out more quickly and effectively. He particularly regretted the guardroom casualties. He also thought that the number of mutineers who escaped could have been reduced. The main problem had been the absence of any indication about how seriously the mutineers would resist. They had hardly been raw innocents, having killed a number of people in the days following the mutiny. However, he later concluded that the simple, forthright approach adopted had been right in the circumstances. On the available evidence, it is hard to disagree.

Two other aspects of the operation were unusual. The first was that, apart from the pre-planned stickorbat, there were no written orders at all. Every instruction, including tri-service ones, had been passed on from man to man. The second was that after the initial MOD instruction, there had been no further reference back to London for approval of the plans, including the use of

166

Cambrian's main armament in support. The relatively junior officers commanding the force had simply used their discretion. No Minister, General or Admiral was asked for approval. This may never have happened again.

Z Company, having led the assault, were instructed to remain in the camp to restore order. There was a great deal to do. It took a further three days to round up the rest of the mutineers, collect the arms and ammunition and get the administration of the camp going again. Another 150 stragglers were recovered on the first day. It was believed that all but about ten *askaris* were eventually found, but some of the battalion might have been away at the time of the mutiny, and the exact numbers were never known. During this period, one of the patrols was fired on, but suffered no casualties. One brave, or perhaps reckless, British civilian, with little regard for his own safety, brought in a fully-armed *askari*, festooned with ammunition and grenades. Fortunately, despite his menacing appearance, he surrendered quietly.

Marine Ray Lavery, from Arbroath, was a Z Company cook.[5] He recalls acting as personal escort for Nyirenda. Later he went out on 'welfare patrols'. This involved bringing in families left without support. He dealt with a great number of children and pregnant women, and got on very well with them. Two *askaris* had been assigned to him to help with the language and transport problems. Towards the end of the period he managed to get a few hours leave to visit a local British settler who was a retired Royal Navy Petty Officer. It was as though the marines had been granted an unofficial freedom of the city: beer was free. He remembers how relieved the European community seemed to be about the restoration of order after days of chaos and cruelty.

The mutineers were screened and 26 were arrested and transferred to the city. Major Langley, in conjunction with Nyirenda, restored military discipline and order. He addressed first the whole battalion and then the officers separately, through an interpreter, laying down the standards of discipline, smartness and cleanliness he required. Having arrived as a conqueror, he quickly found himself transformed into an administrator and counsellor. Action was taken immediately to clear up the filth: in the six days since the mutiny, an indescribable mess had accumulated. Major Langley reported that Nyirenda cooperated very closely with the British. In view of the *askaris'* strong wish to be rid of British officers this was not a popular stance. His commission was terminated soon after the British left.

On 28 January, three days after the landing, Brigadier Douglas, by then back as Army Commander, was instructed by Kambona that the battalion was to be disbanded. The *askaris* of '1TR' who had not been arrested were to be sent home in disgrace. They were not allowed to go home by train lest they be recognised and hailed as heroes. Douglas thought this mass dismissal unfair. There had been no investigation or trial; and many soldiers had not taken part in the mutiny. Furthermore, the 2nd Battalion, up-country, had also mutinied, yet there had been no arrests and they were not to be disbanded. However, his objections were overruled, perhaps understandably in the circumstances, and it was ordered that the discharge was to take place immediately. With great difficulty, and with the help of the British High Commission, enough buses were collected to carry out this operation.

Langley ordered his marines to cordon the barracks when the announcement was made to the battalion, but there was no trouble. The President arrived himself to give the orders. He described, passionately, how disappointed everyone in the country had been at their betrayal. Some of the mutineers showed remorse and all seemed relieved that they had not been treated more drastically. Nevertheless, it was a sad end to what had been a good battalion with a long record of service. It was also, for Tanganyika, an expensive loss of a trained infantry unit which would have to be replaced. Z Company organised the dispersal. As the ex-*askaris* left the camp, many waved and applauded the marines. Brigadier Douglas later commended David Langley and his men for the intelligent and humane way they had tackled a thankless task.

Notes

1   Hankinson, David: correspondence with author, November 2004.
2   Holt, G.J.: correspondence with author, 2000.
3   Pennington, Ivor: correspondence with author, 2000.
4   Cook, J.L.: correspondence with author, 2000.
5   Lavery, R.: correspondence with author, 1999.

13

Restoring Order in Dar es Salaam

At 9.15 on Saturday 25 January, Stephen Miles, who had not yet
heard from Brigadier Douglas, sent an immediate, plain language,
telegram to the CRO in London. It read:

> Tanganyika Mutiny. Mock bombardment from warships
> commenced at 06.25 hours, Saturday 25th January. Heli-
> copters observed at 06.45 hours. In answer to enquiries we
> have replied as follows: the Government of Tanganyika
> approached the British Government with a request for military
> assistance to enable them to maintain law and order in the
> country. The British Government has immediately responded
> to this request and British troops have now landed in
> Tanganyika. The city is quiet. People are remaining indoors.

Shortly afterwards, Douglas telephoned him from Colito and
described what had happened. What should he do next, he asked?
Miles agreed that the British troops should come into Dar es
Salaam. He at once sent another message to London: 'Tanganyika
Operation. Landing completely successful. All over very quickly
with minimum of fighting. Situation at Colito Barracks well under
control.'[1]

While Douglas was speaking to Miles, Stevens reviewed progress
in the barrack area. His three rifle companies and his own

advanced headquarters were ashore. The big RAF helicopters were bringing in the marines' Land Rovers. The Commando Support Company was still in *Centaur*, as were his second-in-command, David Smith and the main HQ staff. The army scout cars would not be available for some time because they were too heavy to be carried by helicopter and would have to be put ashore by lighter. Well aware of the vital need to retain the initiative over a shadowy opposition, he had diverted some of his scarce helicopter resources to reconnoitre the town and airfield. They had reported no signs of military activity except for a few armed men at the main airport.

Meanwhile, several civilians had arrived at the barracks confirming the helicopter reports – there was indeed an armed group at the airport. They were reported to be holding hostages and might help the ringleaders of the mutiny, who were missing, try to escape up-country or abroad. So the next priority was to gain control of the airport, a task allocated to X Company.

Shortly before 10 a.m, several refuelled Wessex helicopters took off with Major Mike Banks and as many of his company as could be squeezed in. Major Banks was an adventurous and charismatic figure. He had been awarded the Polar Medal in 1956, and had led expeditions to the Himalayas in 1958, and to Alaska only a year before. He later wrote several books of exploration. He 'thought vertically', as he explained it, and was in his element commanding a helicopter-borne sortie. As his force approached the airport, Banks decided to 'storm it in a very warlike way'. The lead helicopter landed immediately in front of the control tower. It carried a Sergeant and six marines, with instructions to stop all air movements, and was rather loosely under the command of Brutus Holt, who was still carrying his heavy radio. The commandos sprinted up to the visual control position. Holt followed more sedately, to find the British Airport Controller pinned against the wall at gunpoint, telling the marines '*Nothing* will move on this airfield until I say so! So relax.' Holt noticed the Controller's shirt, which had tell-tale holes for shoulder boards; it was soon established that he was an ex-naval Aircraft Control Officer. There were no other signs of trouble, so the marines did indeed relax.

In the main building, Banks learned that three armed men had left the airfield as the helicopters approached. They had attempted to coerce the airport staff into getting them a helicopter or light aircraft, but had chosen the wrong person to bully. Their victim, an engineer with no flying qualifications, had eventually persuaded them that he was incapable of flying them out, but it had been a frightening experience. A troop of marines was sent down the road to Dar to search for the missing mutineers.

The suspects were never found, while the Broadcasting Station was found to be running normally under its usual management. The arms dump was deserted, and a guard was left to secure it. The airport was now secure, but a potentially embarrassing incident followed. Holt joined his squad in the crowded passenger terminal to enjoy a soft drink. A marine Corporal joined them, putting his rifle down on the tiled floor rather carelessly. The weapon fired and a bullet lodged in the ceiling. People's reactions varied. Some threw themselves to the floor, while others shouted and gesticulated. Holt noticed one boy still munching his lunch, but obviously wishing he had such a fine weapon. Meanwhile, the marines, who knew what a grave view was taken of an 'accidental discharge of a weapon', placed bets on whether the Corporal would only lose his stripes, or face time in the 'cooler' as well. Only slowly did it dawn on them that Holt was not a Royal Marines officer, so would not report the incident!

While the airport was being occupied, the marines back at the barracks commandeered Tanganyika Rifles' transport to augment their own vehicles for the drive into the city. At around 10 a.m., Paddy Stevens ordered Y Company to lead out. The Company was commanded by Captain Gavin Hamilton-Meikle. With no knowledge of what lay ahead, the Company set off cautiously towards town. The leading troop was followed by the Company Commander, followed by Douglas and Marciandi. They advanced 'tactically,' with scouts and lead units covering one other, but it soon became clear that this was unnecessary: Asians, Europeans and a sizeable number of Africans lined the road into town, applauding and smiling. Their welcome was as unexpected as it was tumultuous. What had started off as a probing advance soon became a triumphal march.

Knowing that the marines were coming, Miles had driven out to Selander bridge to meet the force, taking Christopher MacRae with him. The two sat on the parapet of the bridge for some time. There was little traffic and no sign of the approaching marines. Well aware of the pressures on the High Commission, Miles decided that he should return to his office.

Christopher MacRae. *I was left alone by the roadside feeling exposed and slightly uncomfortable. Eventually the leading marines appeared. I introduced myself; then Pat Douglas arrived. 'Show of force?' he asked. 'Show of force.' I agreed. To save time, I guided the troops into the city in my own little car, along with Tom Unwin who had just turned up on his motor scooter, sharing the warm welcome. We noticed one European waving particularly enthusiastically and recognised him as the man we thought of as the 'spook' from the Soviet Embassy. Grinning widely, the Russian gave a cheery 'thumbs up' sign, apparently as glad as anyone else to see order restored. I could not help wondering if his enthusiasm would be shared by his superiors in the Kremlin.*

After a stop at the British High Commission and a brief talk with Miles, Douglas and Stevens decided to base themselves in the Tanganyika Army Headquarters. The building was near the British High Commission and other government buildings. There was still no sign of any Government Minister. Hamilton-Meikle was instructed to send out patrols to search for deserters in the town, and eight were soon recaptured. The landing force had taken control of the nation's capital city and it was not yet noon.

While Y Company settled into their new quarters, Douglas and Stevens went back to review priorities with Miles. Their discussions were short, but eventful. With Dar es Salaam under control, the focus of concern had shifted up-country. Miles had up-to-date information from Jim Bourn, his man in Tabora. The 2nd Battalion's British officers, and their families, had been treated more harshly than those of the 1st Battalion, as had some European civilians, and the security situation in the town was still uncertain. The unnatural calm might not last and troops should be sent there at once.

Before he had left Colito at about 10 a.m., Stevens had requested *Centaur* to send ashore the Support Company commanded by Captain J.E.J. Lloyd, and the last marine force. Stevens had also asked for the Ferret scout cars, a detachment of *Centaur* seamen, and the ship's regular Royal Marines detachment which numbered 28. Weighing anchor at 11.28 a.m., the ship quickly re-anchored near the Dar harbour approach, and two miles north north-east of State House. A lighter was soon secured alongside. Throughout the early afternoon, the landings continued by helicopter, lighter and the ship's own boats. Major David Smith, also went ashore at this point with main head-quarters. Stevens delegated command of the Dar es Salaam area to Smith, while he himself concentrated on the move inland.

During the morning of the landings, there were no announce-ments whatever on the radio about what was happening. Many people had heard the noise at dawn, and some had seen British troops come into town. But others knew nothing at all until rumours began to circulate. Joy Skinner, whose journalist husband happened to be away, lived in an isolated house not far from Colito, near the sea. She was woken by the sound of shells whistling through the air nearby. Her cook declared it was the Devil. But when Joy saw an aircraft carrier apparently at the foot of her garden, she concluded there must be a more rational explanation and decided not to worry.

Barry Parton was a representative of Brooke Bond, the tea producers. He had been working in Tanganyika for five months, after doing military service in Kenya, and lived in Oyster Bay. Woken by gunfire, he walked to the sea front and dimly made out a destroyer firing inshore. Driving further round the coast he saw *Centaur* at anchor, with her helicopters operating over the sisal plantations. Sensing that order would soon be restored, he went to his office, close to army headquarters. African soldiers let him through roadblocks, which they had not done during the previous days. Gradually all his staff came in to work. At about 11.00 a.m. he heard rifle fire and saw some bullets hit the road, raising dust. Then *askaris* appeared, throwing off their equipment and weapons before running on. A marine Corporal, evidently unschooled in political correctness, asked him, 'Have you seen any black buggers, sir?' Nevertheless, he thought the marines seemed very efficient. Later he saw armoured cars heading out to the suburbs. His African staff had been very upset during the mutiny and were now glad that it was over, but they seemed genuinely frightened by the prospect of recolonisation. Many Europeans gathered in hotels to celebrate the end of the mutiny while they tried to find out what was going on. Then people's attention turned to restocking their larders.

Meanwhile, at Army HQ, Stevens tackled the problem of getting a company of his marines to Tabora. The city was far beyond the range of *Centaur*'s helicopters and large fixed-wing transport planes were needed. There was an RAF detachment in Nairobi where British forces were still heavily involved in quelling unrest in the Ugandan and Kenyan armies. Nevertheless they could send down two four-engine Beverley troop-carrying aircraft immediately. These would soon take off for Dar es Salaam, but the flight would last several hours. Meanwhile, there was another possibility: a DC4 transport belonging to the Williamson Diamond Mine Company was serviceable and available for charter. It was promptly hired and warned to be ready for take-off at 3 p.m. with Stevens, his tactical headquarters staff, and 54 men of Y Company. The flight would take about two hours. As soon as they arrived at Dar, the RAF Beverleys would refuel and follow with the remainder of Y company, and a detachment of X Company.

Stevens, who had full operational control of the planned air move, was concerned about the possibility of resistance as his small force landed at Tabora airfield. He had not, at this stage, been told about Jim Bourn, the High Commission's First Secretary in the city – not that it would probably have made much difference if he had been. A few determined men, quickly deployed, could make the landing of one unarmed aircraft very difficult. There could be further loss of life with disastrous political repercussions. He discussed the problem on the radio with Captain Steiner. Steiner in turn called in Commander Kettle and together they examined possible air options. Tabora was beyond the normal range of *Centaur*'s fighter-bomber aircraft, but by reducing fuel consumption, and minimising time over the target, it might be possible to cover the landing of the marines. Kettle had his doubts about the plan: the expensive aircraft in his charge were to be risked over extreme ranges on a mission which did not seem to him vital. However, the Captain was keen to do all that he could to help the land force, and it was soon agreed that *Centaur* would provide a show of force at Tabora. The ship would weigh anchor and go to sea in time to launch the mission. Vixen aircraft were fast, and could not fly in company with the DC4; instead, they would make a brief rendezvous as the marines' aircraft landed at Tabora.

There was still no announcement from the Government or its national broadcasting station. The 1 p.m. news bulletin made no mention whatever of the commandos' operations. This was absurd since there could hardly have been a soul in Dar who did not know at least something of the morning's events. Moreover, Miles had been assured the evening before that Nyerere would

177

make a broadcast speech as soon as the main action at Colito was over. Nyerere eventually broadcast his message at about 4 p.m. on Saturday afternoon. He explained that no popular Government could tolerate an army which disobeyed its instructions. He had therefore decided to ask Britain for help in disarming the troops of the Tanganyika Rifles. He noted that although they had returned to barracks, the troops had already committed the serious offence of mutiny. Then after this grave offence, a number of civilians had committed further offences such as looting. In the work of restoring order some lives were lost. It had later become clear that 'discipline was vanishing among our troops', and no Government could tolerate such a danger to the whole nation. He had therefore decided to disarm all the troops and punish the ringleaders most severely. It had not been easy to disarm an army, and the only force the Government could employ were the Police Field Force, which was depleted because some had been sent to Zanzibar to help maintain law and order there. Therefore, he had had no alternative but to ask for help and, fortunately, Britain had agreed. He added:

I am told that already there is foolish talk that the British have come back to rule Tanganyika again. This is rubbish! I asked the British Government to help in the same way I would have asked our neighbours to help if this had been possible. Any independent country is able to ask for help from any other independent country. I do not want anyone to think that I was happy in making this request. This whole week has been a week of the most grievous shame for our nation. But those who brought this shame upon us are those who tried to intimidate our nation at the point of a gun.

This full, frank and subdued broadcast did much to counter both the immediate unease and the understandable doubts about the wisdom of calling the British back. It was clearly politically desirable for them to leave again as soon as possible, but while there remained urgent problems to solve, they were still needed.

While Stevens was planning the move to Tabora and the President was restoring political control, Brigadier Douglas had organised a show of force through Dar, using Support Company and the Ferret scout cars. They received a great welcome, by no means only from Europeans and Asians. On Sunday, *Centaur*'s Royal Marine band was landed to play in the streets of the city, and this helped to restore confidence that order had finally been restored.

Note

1   PRO: DO185/46 (109) and (110).

14

Operations Inland – The Job Finished

The operation to restore order in Tabora was ordered by Douglas and planned by Stevens less than 12 hours after they had planned the assault on Colito Barracks. Both had been continuously on the go since then. Steiner was not involved, although aircraft from *Centaur* were to make a contribution to the operation. Kawawa's written request had been for Britain to provide military assistance 'to enable us to maintain law and order in the country'. The British force had subsequently been instructed by London 'to intervene to maintain law and order and quell the mutiny in the Tanganyikan army ... under the command of Brigadier Douglas ... and the political direction of the Acting High Commissioner'. After earlier incidents of confusion about the chain of command, the UK had developed a doctrine whereby the political leadership would decide on the military objective, pass it to a military commander to implement and then (at least in theory) stand back until the military reported success or failure.

In Dar, this policy was working well. Douglas was continuing to 'quell the mutiny' by proposing to intervene in Tabora, while keeping the local representative of his political leadership, Miles, closely informed. However, Douglas was in fact acting in two quite different roles: he was still the expatriate Commander of (the temporarily disabled) Tanganyikan forces and therefore still the servant of the Tanganyikan Government; but he was also the (temporary) commander of newly-arrived British land forces.

181

After the reoccupation of Army Headquarters, his operations staff officer, Major Marciandi, was left to bring it back into service by getting the staff back and dealing with the many outstanding problems. In a few short hours, Douglas had established a close professional understanding with Stevens (whom he had never met before) and his commandos, and was confident that they could be trusted to deal with the Tabora mission. Stevens therefore took off from Dar airfield with only his two personal staff officers, the ubiquitous Brutus Holt, and as many marines as could be crammed into the chartered aircraft. The manager of the Williamson Diamond company had insisted on accompanying any flight undertaken by his DC4, so was also found a seat. The remainder of the designated Tabora detachment were to follow once the RAF transport aircraft arrived from Nairobi.

While the marine spearhead flew inland, *Centaur* weighed anchor at 3.36 p.m. and headed offshore to gain sea room to launch her aircraft. 'Flying stations' was piped at 4.10 p.m. after four Sea Vixens had been ranged on deck. The 892 Squadron sortie was led by the squadron commander, Lieutenant Commander Ian Blake. Knowing that Tabora was at extreme range for the Sea Vixens, he planned to minimise fuel consumption by flying at high altitude.[1] However, the aircraft were armed with rockets, which increased their drag and reduced range. They would also gulp fuel when they flew low over Tabora airport and barracks. So they had to arrive at exactly the same time as the DC4 carrying the commando spearhead. The Sea Vixens would then be able to spend only about fifteen minutes over Tabora airfield if all went as planned.

Blake planned the sortie with great care. The aircraft would be catapulted off the carrier, at once turn west, climb at full power, and only gain formation as the flight progressed. Once at their maximum height of 42,000 feet, they would reduce power to low cruising speed to give maximum range. When the power was taken off completely, the aircraft would glide at a rate of two miles for every 1,000 feet of height lost. The engines could therefore be throttled down to idle some 80 miles from Tabora, and the aircraft allowed to glide in to near ground level over the airfield for the 15-minute mission. The return flight would be configured in the same way.

The planning proved accurate. The four aircraft demonstrated their potential over Tabora; and their return was uneventful. As they arrived back over *Centaur*, she was already head to wind and steaming at full operating speed, because the aircraft had only enough fuel for one attempt to land on deck before they would be forced to make an emergency diversion to Dar es Salaam airport. No diversion was needed, as they all landed on their first pass. The pilots' logs recorded a flight time of two and a quarter hours. The Commander (Air) on *Centaur*'s bridge was hugely relieved to see that his squadron commander had got the sums right.

In Tabora, the High Commission's First Secretary, Jim Bourn, had been speaking with his colleagues in Dar. Miles gave him a strong hint that it would be useful for him to be at the airfield in the late afternoon. When he got there, Bourn climbed into the control tower and greeted the expatriate Controller. There was no civilian traffic, but soon two aircraft appeared. Both seemed to be trying to land at once. One was from Nairobi and the other from Dar. This confused situation was then complicated by the arrival of jet fighters flying very low over the airfield. There were sounds of sharp disagreement on the radio control frequency: two competing pilots were claiming priority to land while the views of the airfield Controller were not sought at all. The Nairobi aircraft won the duel convincingly by claiming 'on finals', to signify that it was in the final stage of landing. In his haste, the pilot then – quite improperly – landed downwind.

The British military authorities in Nairobi had been kept informed about the progress of the landing at Dar and the plan to send a force on to Tabora. Sensibly enough, having decided to do what they could to help, they had hit on the idea of seizing Tabora airfield and holding it until the marines arrived from Dar. Their plan was communicated to Aden, but never reached *Centaur*. Unaware of this communications failure, the air staff in Nairobi assembled a small unit of the RAF Regiment, under the immediate command of a senior officer who decided to fly them to Tabora himself in an unarmed, twin-engine aircraft. He planned to arrive shortly before the force coming from Dar did, so that his men could first gain control of the landing ground. But the sortie was delayed. As a result, the RAF pilot found himself arriving at much the same time as the marines' aircraft. He was determined to get there first, however. Using the airfield control frequency, he ordered the pilot of the DC4 to keep clear. True, he was the senior British military officer on the scene, but the marines knew nothing whatever about him or his plans. A man of action, he seized the initiative by short-cutting the circuit, and landing downwind – a dangerous gambit. Stopping immediately in front of the control tower, the well-drilled detachment from the RAF Regiment leapt out to take over the airfield. The irregular landing had the effect of blocking the runway, so the DC4 had no option but to power away for a second approach, carrying some very frustrated marines.

Jim Bourn, making what he could of this, climbed down from the control tower to greet the men from Nairobi. A fit young officer sprinted determinedly past him, a firearm at the ready, followed by a fierce looking squad. Bourn shouted to the officer as he sped past, in language he later admitted was infelicitous: 'Don't panic: there are no mutineers here.' The young officer, bounding into the tower without missing a step, shouted back: 'The RAF never panic, they simply take precautions.' Jim followed to find the British controller being held at gunpoint, the second innocent airport official that day to find himself in such a pickle. Calmer exchanges followed, and the tension evaporated. The race for Tabora airfield had been won by the RAF. But, by landing downwind and far faster than was wise, they had damaged their landing gear. Their aircraft remained out of service until spares had been flown in from Nairobi. The DC4 landed at last and came to a halt. But in the general excitement, the controller had forgotten to order a mobile gangway. The marines, led by their Colonel, had therefore to climb down from the aircraft door swinging from a rope. This inter-British contretemps settled, attention turned to the object of the operation: dealing with the mutiny in the out-of-town barracks.

Stevens was delighted to meet Bourn who had been out to Tabora Barracks the previous evening. He had also spoken recently to the Regional Commissioner, the Commissioner of Police and to Captain Sarakikya, the newly-appointed Commanding Officer of the 2nd Battalion. Stevens was aware that Sarakikya had been the senior African officer at the point when the battalion's British officers had been unceremoniously bundled out of their posts, but did not yet know how far he could be trusted. Once Bourn had briefed him, and assured him that Sarakikya was to be trusted, and while he waited for the rest of his men to arrive, Stevens roughed out planning and briefing notes on the back of a local newspaper. Bourn watched him silently.

Bourn and Sarakikya had already agreed that action needed to be taken quickly against the mutineers. Stevens agreed. The men of the 2nd Battalion had for some time remained in their barracks, some seven miles outside Tabora. They seemed to be unarmed and were at present causing no trouble. On the other hand, they were still under the influence of the ringleaders and their arms were stored in the barracks so were readily available. Any attempt to restore order would not be simple. It might be unwise, even hazardous, to approach them without notice and their consent. But there was still serious tension in town. Most of the Europeans were in hiding, and the Asian community were also keeping their heads well down. The Tabora battalion itself could not be used to restore calm. It must therefore be brought back under the full control of its officers, without being given any opportunity to resist this change of direction. It was on this basis that Stevens drafted his back-of-newspaper briefing notes. Bourn eventually recovered them, and donated them to the Imperial War Museum in London.

At 6.15 p.m. the two RAF Beverleys arrived from Dar es Salaam with X Company and a contingent of Y Company. Stevens now had a force of a 100 of his own men and could act. First he took officers from the two Companies, a section of marines and Captain Sarakikya, to reconnoitre the town. There was an uneasy calm. He then requisitioned a vehicle to drive out to a hill overlooking the barracks, accompanied only by Sarakikya, and by his intelligence and signals officers. Unobserved, the group studied the buildings and their surroundings. Sarakikya asked Stevens if he would like to get a closer look. After a while, lowering his binoculars, Stevens ordered: 'Right, let's go.' Both of his young staff officers, Tony Hazeldine and Pat Howgill, thought that by this he meant 'go back to town'. They were mistaken. To their astonishment, the Colonel drove them straight into the barracks, stopping at the guardroom.[2]

The sentry at the gate saw the officers approaching and called out the guard. It formed up smartly, armed with pickaxe handles in place of rifles. As Stevens acknowledged their salute, a startled junior officer appeared. He invited the visitors into the officer's mess, where they were offered a drink. Everything appeared quite normal. Junior African officers were politely introduced. Howgill, the commando signal officer, remembers it as a surreal situation: wasn't this meant to be an operational reconnaissance? Somewhat to his later regret, Stevens signed the visitors' book. In view of what happened later, it subsequently seemed to him rather a breach of Mess hospitality. While all this was going on, Sarakikya overheard a discussion about whether the visitors should be arrested. It was time to go. The party took their leave, returning to the airfield by about 8 p.m. Stevens then telephoned Douglas in Dar to report and suggest what he thought should be done. As Stevens had discussed matters locally and even ventured inside the barracks, Douglas authorised him to take whatever action he considered necessary.

A case could be made for simply leaving matters in political hands. There was now no trouble in the town and the troops had returned to barracks where Stevens had seen for himself that there were no arms in sight. Sarakikya was, at least nominally, in command, and had been appointed by the proper political authority. Although young and inexperienced, he had been well trained and was obviously a level-headed soldier who had already reached Company command. But, despite Sarakikya's recommendations, there was also a strong case for arresting the leaders of the mutinies, although it was difficult to see how that could safely be done with so few British troops.

As in Dar es Salaam, there was no sign at all of the Provincial Commissioner or his representatives. This may have been a political calculation to avoid association with unpopular measures and let foreign soldiers take the blame if things went wrong. But there was probably also an element of shock; no one in political control in Tabora was experienced, or had ever faced an armed challenge to their authority. The responsibility for restoring order had been accepted by the British Government; and it now lay firmly in the hands of the commanding officer of 45 Commando. He did not shirk it.

Bourn and Sarakikya joined the commando officers in a planning session. Stevens ordered that the barracks, especially its arms and ammunition, should be secured. The mutineers' leaders should then be identified and arrested. His men were to move in the late evening, to surprise the mutineers at night. The marines had no transport but some trucks could quickly and quietly be borrowed from the Public Works Department which was still partially staffed by expatriates. Two more trucks were brought in by willing, but drunken, British civilians (the transport was accepted but not their offer to drive). Some police Land Rovers were also available. Enough transport had been assembled by midnight to move both Companies.

By then, the mutineers must have heard news of the arrival of the British troops in Tabora and had time to think about the implications. The assault on Colito had shown clearly that the

Government was now challenging the mutinies with force. It is difficult to understand why the Tabora mutineers did not react; surely the troops who had overcome their colleagues in Colito were unlikely to remain passively at the airfield? The ringleaders had a number of options. A pre-emptive attack on the marines would have been very hazardous, but if they had moved out into the country, or dispersed to take a brief leave, they would have gained time for negotiation. Whatever they may have discussed, they did nothing. Indeed, most of the soldiers seem to have attended the camp cinema. This surprising indecisiveness greatly weakens any suggestion that there was some guiding hand behind the mutinies.

The marines set off from Tabora airfield just after midnight. They stopped short of the camp, having driven the last two miles without lights. X Company's Commander, Major Mike Banks, took Sarakikya and a small group of his men to secure the guardroom. Driving in quickly but quietly, they overwhelmed the sentries before they had time to raise the alarm. The remainder of X Company followed quickly on foot, securing the weapons store and magazine. Y Company was ordered to the guardroom area. The first objective of the operation had now been achieved: the barracks was secure.

The British marines now had to be careful about any involvement in disciplining the 2nd Battalion. Sarakikya was keen to see the mutiny dealt with at once, and this would probably be his best opportunity. But the British force had reached the limit of its political authority. Stevens's staff found a working telephone, and managed to contact Douglas, who as still the commander of Tanganyikan military forces was able to give Stevens immediate authority to move against the ringleaders.

The commandos were ordered to surround the living quarters. Vehicles were positioned on the corners of the parade ground to be ready to light it up. Then Captain Sarakikya marched on to the parade ground, accompanied by one escort and bugler who sounded the 'general assembly'. The *askaris* fell in without delay, as usual. Once they had done so, the lights of the vehicles were switched on. Sarakikya then took charge, ordering ten ringleaders out from the ranks. They were marched off under marine escort before Sarakikya dismissed the parade.

Marine Binley later recalled that his section surprised a group of mutineers who had stayed off the parade ground. Ordered to keep their hands in the air and keep absolutely still, one was fidgeting uncomfortably. After a while, he explained agitatedly that his cigarette was burning his fingers: could he throw it away? He was told he could.

Captain Hamilton-Meikle and Y Company were instructed to remain behind in the barracks as a 'steadying influence'. Once X Company had finished loading all the arms and ammunition, they returned to Tabora town, depositing their prisoners at Police Headquarters on the way. Stevens then rang Douglas, recommending that one company would be enough to control Tabora, and that his own headquarters and the second company could be released for other duties. Then the exhausted marines turned in to catch up on some well earned sleep. It was 4 a.m., only 22 hours since their initial landing from *Centaur*. Their achievements had been outstanding.

Sarakikya had also come out of these events very well. He had combined an intelligent, responsible and cautiously active approach with an understanding and compassion for his *askaris*. His abilities and attitude were appreciated by his Government, and he was promoted to Brigadier within a few weeks.

After a short rest, Stevens spoke to Brigadier Douglas again at 8 a.m. next morning, Sunday 26 January. They agreed that one company should remain in Tabora for the time being to guard the arms and help restore order in the town. The other company needed to return to Dar as soon as possible because a further operation was planned.

The RAF Argosy was still unserviceable at Tabora airfield, but a small RAF Pembroke aircraft soon arrived from Nairobi carrying spares for the damaged landing gear. Stevens learned that the Argosy's radio had the range to communicate with the RAF command in Nairobi so he spoke to a senior air staff officer to explain the situation. The RAF at once agreed that he could keep both aircraft for further operations. This was typical of the quick and flexible support that the British forces in Tanganyika received throughout the operation.

Finally, Stevens called a brief conference with Bourn and Sarakikya. Both were happy with progress so far, and agreed to the departure of half the commandos. Sarakikya would act in future through Banks until the situation in Tabora was fully stabilised. Stevens and his immediate staff of Hazeldine and Howgill took off at about noon in the relative luxury of the small VIP Pembroke aircraft.

At Dar, the party was met by Major Smith, who had meanwhile been running operations around the city. He reported that the headquarters of the British force was now well established in Tanganyika Army Headquarters. The commandos themselves had moved into the National Sports Stadium, where they had made themselves as comfortable as possible. Patrols had been maintained both in the city and in the countryside around Colito Barracks, where mutineers were still being picked up. The cache of recently-imported Algerian arms and ammunition had been located and checked, but would need a guard for the foreseeable future. It seemed nearly time to hand control back to the civilian authorities. However, there remained a problem to the south.

The company of the 2nd Tanganyika Rifles, detached to the small town of Nachingwea, in Lindi Province, had joined in the mutiny, dismissing their British officers. They were at present causing no trouble, but Douglas's responsibility would not end until all the mutineers had been brought back under control. There was a small airfield there, about 260 miles south of Dar, beyond helicopter range. The only marines available were Y Company, who were on their way back from Tabora so they would have to be flown down in RAF aircraft. Stevens flew out to *Centaur* to confer with Steiner, make his first full report to London, and seek support from naval aircraft for a landing planned for the next day.

A final coordinating conference was held in Army House at 9.00 a.m. on Monday 27 January. It had been reported that the Nachingwea mutineers had handed in their arms to the police when they had heard about the landing on Colito Barracks. In that case, the operation would entail only a flight down followed by some arrests. The news could not be checked, however, and Stevens was uneasy about taking the operation too casually. The situation was much as it had been in Tabora: a mere handful of men, whose identifies might not even be known in Dar, might decide to fight. This could lead to casualties and upset all that had been achieved so far. So it was essential to allow for the possibility of serious resistance.

'H' hour for the operation was set for 1.00 p.m. that same day. Two RAF Beverley aircraft would land Hamilton-Meikle and a Y Company detachment on the Nachingwea airstrip. A British police officer in Nachingwea agreed to make telephone reports up to the last moment before the aircraft landed. The mutineers would be distracted by an order radioed from Dar by Major Marciandi at 12.30, instructing the company to parade in their temporary barracks. This should ensure that they were kept away from the airfield. Finally, *Centaur* would send Vixen jet fighter aircraft to provide cover, as at Tabora – and this time the sortie would be within easy range.

The operation went exactly as planned. Marciandi passed his order at 12.30. By 12.40, a report was received that the company was falling in, the troops mistakenly expecting their Brigadier to land there by helicopter. Five minutes later four *Centaur* Vixens screamed noisily overhead, closely followed by four more. Then the Beverleys landed, the marines disembarked, and made their way to the barracks. This was soon cordoned off, the ringleaders were identified and arrested and the arms and ammunition were

191

secured. The whole British force, together with the mutineers' ringleaders and all the arms from Nachingwea, landed back in Dar before nightfall. It had been a smooth and effective operation which completed the task of restoring order to the Tanganyikan army.

While the marines had been busy ashore, *Centaur* had been engaged in her own programme of activities. Captain Steiner believed he could help reduce tension in the city by demonstrations of peaceful friendliness combined with shows of force. Prominent local figures were offered a day at sea, which included an air display when the jet fighter squadron returned from Nachingwea. *Centaur*'s marine detachment had been sent ashore on the first day of operations. They were accompanied by the 'Seamen's Landing Party', a group which rarely experienced serious employment. Indeed few knew of its existence, how it operated, or even what it could be expected to do.

In the 1960s, it was Royal Navy practice to train a small part of a ship's company (known as the Seaman's Landing Party) in 'aid to civil power'. A platoon of seamen was nominated, and sent on a short course at Portsmouth to learn how to control a street riot in some fictional state. The training lacked focus and fell well short of the imaginative courses later given to soldiers preparing for serious duties in Northern Ireland. There were, nevertheless, occasions (e.g. after civil or natural disasters) when local or national authorities were very glad to have the temporary use of a body of disciplined men.

Tony Drury, from Worthing, was an Able Seaman who had been working aboard *Centaur* on fire patrol and maintenance duties. His most recent challenge had been to help sew up body covers for the dead from the *Lakonia*. He was surprised to hear the piped command for 'Seamen's Landing Party, muster on the quarterdeck', and then to be issued with a rifle and 50 rounds of live ammunition. He soon found himself in a helicopter experiencing his first flight, looking down on a crowd of mostly black faces as it came in to land in the centre of Dar. Assigned to back-up duties with the Royal Marines, Drury lived for several nights in the stadium (most uncomfortable and always too hot, he later recounted). The group carried out some escort and transport duties, and lined the square for an open air concert given by the ship's band. Their main recollection was of the warm welcome they received, and their popularity. There was always a crowd of locals at the stadium gates, and they were pressed to accept gifts of beer, fruit and cakes. Confidence was obviously flowing back to the city after the days of uncertainty and tension.

Centaur's staff were busy dealing with many queries and demands for information from London. An urgent challenge arose when a clandestine Ethiopian radio station charged the British with 'killing thousands of Africans during the landings: some during their ruthless attack on the barracks, and many more by a vicious bombardment by battleships'. It was essential to stop this dangerous story in its tracks. Steiner had tried to reassure London with prompt, succinct signals, but they were perhaps too terse, and London wanted to know more. The team aboard *Centaur* became irritated by what they regarded as London's demand to know every single detail, and this led to one of those communications problems which cause military folk to dread involvement in political matters.

London asked for fuller information about the alleged 'bombardment': just how certain was the British force that nobody had in fact been killed or injured? Captain Steiner drafted a message in response, then 'released' it with his signature. This meant that his Yeoman of Signals could take the message away for encryption and then dispatch by the fixed radio link to the Royal Naval Wireless Station in Mauritius for onward transmission to Whitehall. In the ship's Message Centre, the signal had been dated and given a day and time of origin (DTG). Steiner then had second thoughts and recalled the message. He held it up for about 24 hours, perhaps until he had time to speak to

193

Stevens, by now in Tabora. He then decided that it had been satisfactory in the first place, and gave it back to his yeoman for transmission – but the Message Centre failed to update the original DTG of the message. This lapse led to a furious query from Whitehall about why the urgently needed information had been delayed around 36 hours in transmission.

Tony Laurence. *Steiner was clearly shaken by this implied reprimand. Without consulting me, he replied that the delay had occurred at the Royal Naval Wireless Station in Mauritius. That was quite untrue. There had been delays in signals traffic, but mainly at the Whitehall end rather than in Mauritius. When London questioned Mauritius about their supposed failings, citing 'our' claim, they were understandably outraged. The Flag Officer, Middle East, was drawn into these acerbic exchanges, and his staff hotly defended 'their' radio station. The quarrel rumbled on for months, and it was many years before my opposite number in Mauritius was convinced of my innocence in the matter!*

Back in Tabora, Major Banks was soon satisfied that all was going well. Patrols had covered the area in and around the town, and Banks had visited the barracks every day. The marines now held a large stock of weapons and ammunition. This included not only the small arms they had already removed, but a large quantity of 3 inch mortar ammunition that had been too bulky and heavy to deal with during the operation on the first night. They were ordered to send this down to Dar by train. Wagons were allocated and loading began.

Marine Tom Binley had been detailed to supervise an *askari* working party loading ammunition boxes into the wagons. He had found the whole operation, up to then, 'rather routine' compared with his recent experiences in Aden. He later described what happened when the last box was lifted from the concrete storeroom floor. Under it were two 'bloody great snakes', large

194

and highly coloured. This was anything but routine – and Binley had never been more scared during his whole service with the Commando.

By Monday evening, after the Nachingwea operation had ended, the British force had completed the task given to it. The three senior British officers therefore began to plan how to hand over to civilian control again. The atmosphere in Dar had completely changed and the Australian High Commissioner, Andrew Gilchrist, had even decided that things were now calm enough to go ahead with the first diplomatic reception since the start of the troubles – to celebrate Australia Day. British officers mingled with diplomats and ministers from the Tanganyikan Government. It was clear that the legitimate Government was firmly back in power.

It was time for the British force to take a back seat, acting only when further requested. However, things were still far from settled, so some military force would be needed in the background until the Tanganyika army was reconstituted. For example, one immediate problem was that a dockers' strike was planned. It was also being reported that the police had been intending to strike the very day the British troops landed, but had postponed their action. The next moves needed to be taken by Nyerere and his government, and they lost no time in starting the process.

Notes

1   Blake, Ian: correspondence, 2000.
2   Howgill, Pat: correspondence, 1999.

15

End-game

Julius Nyerere's admirers, of whom there were and remain many, would scarcely describe him as having been essentially a man of action or an outstandingly incisive political leader. His many qualities lay elsewhere and his affectionate nickname of *Mwalimu* epitomises his reputation as a philosopher-king. Yet in the days that followed his return to office he bore a load that might have crushed many a man without his strength of character and solid faith in his own vision. He had to deal with immediate challenges while developing strategies to prevent a recurrence of the problems which had arisen from his Government's weakness. He was surrounded by his own picked team who had proved loyal, but they had shown inexperience and indecisiveness during the crisis.

Nyerere's first priority was to ensure the security of the state. This needed military backing – and he had just lost his army. So he had to confirm with the British that their force would remain in Dar es Salaam until they could hand over to African troops or until his own army could be reorganised. At the same time he had to decide how to deal with the mutineers, shore up his position at home, limit the damage done abroad to his credentials as a leader of the pan-African movement, and get help to retrain and restructure his army. It was a formidable task, but Nyerere manoeuvred adroitly.

British forces around the world were themselves stretched, but

London recognised Tanganyika's plight. So while 45 Commando was urgently needed back in Aden, it was quickly decided that 41 Commando, which had only recently arrived in Nairobi from Britain, would be sent down to take over from them – though only for a short period. Nyerere confirmed at once that although Sarakikya would remain Commander of the Tanganyikan Army, he wanted Douglas to stay on for the time being as his military adviser as well as being temporarily in command of all British troops in Tanganyika. Douglas remained in Dar until early March.

On Tuesday 28 January, Miles and Douglas called on Kawawa and Kambona to work out the terms under which the British troops should operate in support of the civil power.

> Christopher MacRae. *I was told to come along to take the record. The meeting was extremely cordial and businesslike and general agreement was quickly reached. It was left to me to draft the text of the memorandum of understanding – the first time I had played any part in an international negotiation.*

In answer to a question from Douglas, Kambona said that the British troops would be needed for more than a month. He also suggested that Douglas and Sarakikya might together work out specific proposals for a training team for the new army. Asked by Miles whether they had any comments on the public relations aspects of the British army assistance, Kawawa and Kambona replied that everything was going well and the conduct of the British troops had been admirable.[1]

Indeed, in the immediate aftermath of the restoring of order by the British troops, relations could scarcely have been warmer. Not only did Nyerere at once express his thanks publicly in his broadcast on Saturday 26 January, but with instinctive generosity of spirit, he expressed his deep gratitude more formally in a letter to Duncan Sandys sent later that day. 'The success of the operation had,' he said, left 'his people much indebted,' and he added how glad he was that there had been no injury or loss of life among the British soldiers or sailors involved.[2] Miles described this as 'most generous in view of the great humiliation the Tanganyikan Government has suffered'. The letter went much further than any thanks expressed publicly by his fellow East African leaders, and cynics might have advised Nyerere to keep his feelings to himself.

Locally, however, he was more circumspect. Captain Steiner had invited members of the Government to a flying display at sea on Monday 27 January. Nyerere had initially agreed to fly out to *Centaur* for this, but at the last minute sent Kawawa in his place with Lusinde and some more junior Ministers. There was little publicity for the visit which rated only a brief paragraph in the *Tanganyika Standard*. The British troops were requested to stay off the streets, at least by day, and to keep their training and administrative activities as inconspicuous as possible. They remained modestly (and uncomfortably) quartered in the Sports Stadium.

Lieutenant-Colonel Stevens had been busy coping with political and administrative problems. His original operational terms of reference had been very limited; and after the marines had settled into the Stadium, he found his men could not even enter buildings unless invited, or requisition stores or transport. There were delays in obtaining even the simplest of facilities. However, he put this down to bureaucracy rather than malice, and worked quietly with Douglas's small team to set up a temporary administration. The exposed conditions in the Stadium could have made the marines' stay there very difficult, but they were treated most cordially by the general public ('embarrassingly so by the Europeans', Stevens later reported). To clarify his Commando's future, he flew to Nairobi in one of *Centaur*'s Gannet aircraft for discussions with Lieutenant-General Freeland, the Commander of British land forces, Kenya. There he learned of the plan for 41 Commando to take over from his force, releasing his men to stand by if needed in Zanzibar.

199

Meanwhile, it had been decided in London that *Centaur* must continue at once on her postponed voyage to Singapore and that she should be replaced off the East African coast by another aircraft carrier, HMS *Victorious*. *Centaur* left Dar es Salaam harbour at 4 p.m. on 29 January. It was just nine days since she had entered Aden harbour and embarked 45 Commando and less that five days since she had been ordered to put an end to the mutiny. It had been a dramatic period which had shaken down the ship's organisation far more thoroughly than any formal 'work-up' exercises or the expected operational readiness inspection could possibly have done. The ship had a new-found confidence and sense of purpose which lasted the whole of the busy commission which followed.

The arrival of *Victorious* was timed to coincide with the rotation of troops. So on Thursday 30 January, 41 Commando were flown in to Dar under the command of Lieutenant-Colonel Nick Carter, while 45 Commando started to embark in *Victorious*, Z Company being lifted straight from Colito Barracks by naval helicopters. Once the handover to 41 Commando was complete, the rest followed, including the Belvederes themselves. *Victorious* then sailed to stand by off Zanzibar in case she was needed there – which she turned out not to be.

On Tuesday evening, Nyerere had invited Captain Steiner, Lt. Col. Stevens, Douglas and Miles round to State House for a farewell drink. To their surprise, they found not only Kawawa and Kambona there, but also the entire Cabinet. Miles reported that, 'All had come to express their appreciation of the British military intervention. The President presented us with gifts (ebony and ivory fruit bowls) and signed photographs.' 'Despite this,' Miles went on, 'I am sure we must be extremely sensitive to the feelings of the Tanganyikans who have undergone the humiliation of admitting failure and calling in the former colonial power to clear up the mess.'[3] He added that he had told leading members of the British community to pass the word around that there must be no 'victory celebrations'; and that so far, 'everyone has behaved very properly'. To Sandys, he reported that now the issue was not when British troops were going to be withdrawn but how long they could stay.[4]

Once Nyerere had secured his short-term aim of having suitably low profile British troops stay on for the time being to guarantee basic security, he was able to focus on how to start repairing the political damage both at home and elsewhere in Africa. He had railed bitterly against the mutineers in his broadcast of 25 January: they shared nothing of his devotion of African values, and he had no hesitation in bringing the full force of the law against 'those who [had] brought shame upon us [and] tried to intimidate us at the point of a gun'. A prosecution was swiftly launched against 19 of the ringleaders, from both battalions. But there was a snag: existing laws left over from the colonial period did not cover the mutineers' actions. So the National Assembly was at once set to work to pass amending legislation to the Military Courts Bill 1964, to make sure that the ringleaders were severely punished. The Chief Justice, Sir Ralph Windham, concurred – perhaps reluctantly – with these retrospective amendments, drafted by a compatriot. Soon it was announced that the ringleaders would be tried by a tribunal set up by the High Court and consisting of a High Court Judge with two military assessors; decisions would be by majority vote. On 1 February, the government also announced the discharge of all soldiers from the Tanganyika Rifles' 1st battalion with effect from 28 January.

Meanwhile, public support was being mobilised. On Sunday 26 January, only a day after the British troops had landed, the TANU Youth League paraded through the streets of Dar to express support for the government. Nyerere used the occasion to call on them to enrol as soldiers: 'From this group we shall try to build the nucleus of a new army for Tanganyika'. Three days later, he addressed a delegation of TANU women led by the formidable Bibi Titi Mohammed, who had also called to show support. The Government's Tanganyika Information Service (TIS) issued a press release next day, clearly at Nyerere's demand, to straighten out any misconceptions:

> It is apparently also necessary to repeat that the British troops entered Tanganyika at the request of the Tanganyika Government, with the purpose of disarming with a minimum of bloodshed the troops who were terrorising the towns of Dar es Salaam, Tabora and Nachingwea. Far from violating the sovereignty of Tanganyika, the British troops upheld the sovereignty of the people at the request of the people. They will leave as soon as satisfactory alternative arrangements can be made.[5]

That last sentence hinted at how Nyerere's mind was now working over how to find replacements for the British troops. Only two days after the mutiny had been ended, he had launched an appeal to the Foreign and Defence Ministers of the Organisation of African Unity (OAU) to attend a meeting to discuss the crisis: 'The situation in East Africa is critical,' he said. 'Within the last week army revolts have suddenly spread throughout East Africa. This constitutes a grave danger, not only for our area but for the whole of our continent. African unity is at stake.'[6] Having first refused to come, President Nkrumah, who regarded himself as Black Africa's undisputed leader and resented Nyerere's pan-African credentials, made a vain attempt to hijack the meeting. Indeed, Kambona admitted to Miles on 30 January that the primary reason for holding the meeting was to 'shut Nkrumah up'. He had, said Kambona, tried to undermine plans for East African federation, and now he wanted to try to demonstrate that the East African leaders were in the pocket of the British. So Nyerere needed approval from his peers in Africa for what he had done.

The OAU meeting duly took place in Dar on 12 February. In his opening speech, Nyerere described what had happened quite candidly: 'Our national humiliation arises from the necessity of

202

having non-Tanganyikan troops to do our work for us; it is not much affected by their nationality.' But 'the presence of British troops ... is a fact which is too easily exploited by those who wish to divide Africa ... Although from [our] point of view, we could ask the British troops to remain here until the new Tanganyikan army is ready, our frontier position as host to the Liberation Movement demands that Africa as a whole should have an opportunity to consider the matter'.[7]

> Christopher MacRae. *I was sitting in the gallery as Nyerere delivered his speech, having been sent to report on the meeting. What happened next was that the ministers went into closed session; so the observers and journalists were left to hang around. We later learned that as expected, Nyerere had put forward a proposal that the British force should be replaced by African peacekeeping troops from countries of Tanganyika's own choice. This had been agreed, and Nigeria had undertaken to provide a ground force while Ethiopia would send some aircraft.*

Things were now beginning to fall in place for Nyerere. Short term security was secured, African replacements for the British troops should soon arrive and the trial of the mutineers was in hand. There remained the thorny problems of how to restructure and retrain the army, and how to deal with any political opponents.

Immediately after the end of the mutiny, Miles had advised the CRO that he believed that 'British troops should remain for a long time'. At this point he favoured the idea of some sort of 'mobile fire brigade' for the whole of East Africa for up to five years, although he recognised that 'politics and the indignity of having to rely on the ex-colonial power might make this impossible'.[8] Whitehall was unenthusiastic. The MOD and CRO were fully aware of the resentment which might all too easily build up against the British troops if they outstayed their welcome[9] and felt that from the point of view of international politics, there would be great advantage in withdrawing the troops as quickly as possible. In any case, the MOD felt that if a request were to come for a military training team, it should be met mainly from existing resources in Kenya. Nevertheless, in his immediate response to Kambona's early message of thanks, Sandys offered to visit East Africa if it would help, and this had at once been warmly welcomed by Kambona on 30 January, who had added that in his view, British troops would be needed in Tanganyika for a long time.[10] By the time Sandys eventually arrived in Dar on 6 March, however, things had moved on. London had been aware as early as the beginning of February that the Tanganyikans had lost no time in approaching the West German government for a military training team, saying that they would wait for a response before going on to try Yugoslavia (the Germans at once sought British advice).[11] This was in line with Tanganyika's previous reputation for shopping around, not only to get the cheapest deal but also to demonstrate political neutrality. Nevertheless, Sandys arrived with an offer in his pocket to provide training for the new Tanganyikan army, but based mainly on courses to be run out of Kenya plus extra officer training places at Sandhurst and Mons. Nyerere politely declined. Sandys had his nose put temporarily out of joint, but by that time, the steam had gone out of the situation. Eventually, it was Canada that provided the first army training team – after Britain had pressed them strongly to do so.

In the background, action against the mutineers was continuing. The tribunal which judged the ringleaders consisted of the (British) Chief Justice himself, assisted by Captains Twalipo and Shataeli.[12] Herbert Chitepo, Director of Public Prosecutions, called for the death penalty for all (though looking unhappy as he did so), while the defence was ably handled by an Australian lawyer, Adrian Roden. In early May, the tribunal acquitted 5 of the 19 accused from lack of evidence, and sentenced the rest to terms of five or ten years in prison, depending on their degree of involvement. Ilogi alone was given 15 years. Nyerere publicly deplored the leniency of the sentences.[13] Kambona had contrived to be abroad during the trial so did not appear. But that was not the end of the affair. Kavana was arrested as late as September 1964 along with Capt. Jumbe, 16 NCOs and ten *askaris*, charged with having been 'in a position to stop the mutiny of which they had knowledge but failed to report to higher authority'.[14]

It was not only the army which was being purged, but also the police force – and above all the trade unions. Some 60–70 policemen were detained in Dar, and up to 600 throughout the country,[15] although few convictions stuck. A large number of union leaders had been arrested on the evening of Sunday 27 January, the day after the British intervention.[16] The speed and scale of this reaction shows how badly rattled the government had been. Even several 'freedom fighters', including two black South Africans, had been picked up during the initial mopping up.[17] Nyerere seemed particularly determined to punish the 'Morogoro plotters'. After screening, those able to demonstrate their innocence were released, but others were given long prison sentences.

More generally, Nyerere seems to have used the sense of national emergency to establish once and for all the dominance of TANU over the TFL from which it had sprung. The 'Morogoro plotters' apart, no convincing evidence of serious collusion between the mutineers and the TFL was ever established. In early February, the TFL leadership was released after a week behind bars and called in to meet the President. There they learned that the TFL had been disbanded, together with all associated unions. In its place was a new Government-controlled union, the National Union of Tanganyika Workers whose General Secretary and his deputy were both appointed by the Government. Disappointed socialists felt that TANU, nurtured from the start by the TFL, had used the crisis to devour it. Nyerere's grip on the state had certainly been strengthened.

While all this was going on, 41 Commando were maintaining a low profile as they carried out their temporary peacekeeping duties. Their stay lasted a little over two months and was largely uneventful. For most of the young marines, the experience was all very new. With no armoured cars or helicopters, and with little alternative transport available, there was not much the unit could achieve other than act as a backstop to the police and try to keep fit. One company was sent up-country for some basic training. Another small detachment, commanded by Lieutenant Matthew White, took control of the almost deserted barracks at Colito.

As a troop commander in G Company, White was delighted to find himself left unsupervised for a change. He shared accommodation with some Tanganyika Rifles officers left over from the 1st Battalion. Nothing much happened. There was no patrolling or guarding to do. He was able to see a little of the country and even had time towards the end to join a rugby tour. His only serious emergency happened when cruise ships began to visit Dar again. Out of the blue arrived his Aunt Phoebe, a very powerful lady indeed, who had come to take tea with her nephew in the officers' mess. From being a proudly independent detachment commander, Matthew quickly reverted to his role of scruffy nephew as Aunt Phoebe reviewed his haircut.

Others who should have known better misunderstood the role of the marines. On 5 February arrived a signal from the Commander in Chief Middle East, instructing 41 Commando, by now guarding the Algerian arms cache, simply to dump the lot in the sea. Stephen Miles, hearing about this order, sent a robust objection pointing out that whatever their history and usefulness, these arms belonged not to the British but to the Tanganyikan Government. The arms were duly turned over intact to the Tanganyikans after 41 Commando left.[18]

Towards the end of 41 Commando's stay, the first troops of the new TANU-sponsored army began to appear. The British troops found them ill trained, undisciplined and difficult to work with. Nevertheless, when they left, 41 Commando found that their efforts had been appreciated. In his speech at a formal farewell parade on 5 April, President Nyerere, accompanied by Kawawa and Kambona, said that Tanganyika was grateful to the marines 'for the cheerful and willing manner in which they had performed their duties here'. The President was described as being 'relaxed and on top form'.[19]

The Nigerian peacekeeping force arrived to take over from the Royal Marines in early April. The officers of 41 Commando joined British High Commission staff at the airport to greet the 3rd Nigerian Infantry Battalion who arrived in three transport aircraft.

> Christopher MacRae. *We watched as the first plane drew up opposite the formal welcoming party in front of the control tower. The stairs were quickly positioned; and the aircraft's door was flung open. It was a solemn moment — which soon dissolved into bathos! Instead of the Commanding Officer, there stood the uncertain figure of a small, elderly Nigerian in flowing robes. He turned out to be the civilian caterer. The Nigerians had heeded Napoleon's maxim about an army 'marching on its stomach' and the aircraft was filled with food from Nigeria, much of it fresh, including yams and meat. Out of the third, most distant, aircraft emerged Colonel Pam, Commander of the Battalion. He shook hands cordially with the various official greeters.*

Later in the day, Colonel Pam reacted sharply when shown the National Stadium allocated for his men, and where the British troops had been quartered. That wouldn't do, he said: his men could not put up with such rough conditions. It was hastily agreed that the Nigerians would be accommodated in Colito Barracks, while the new Tanganyikan force under training would find somewhere else for the time being. Two good houses for senior government staff were also allocated, one as the officers' mess and the other for the Commanding Officer himself (whereas Colonel Carter had roughed it with his men). Once this paradoxical little post-colonial problem had been sorted out, 41 Commando tidied up the Stadium and flew home.

The Nigerian troops (for whom Tanganyika had to pay) stayed until August and were not replaced. Two or three Ethiopian fighter aircraft had been sent to Dar and had flown over the city a few times, but they too had soon returned home. By the summer, the mutiny seemed already well in the past. Responsibility for security was devolved to the police and the fledgling new military forces of the United Republic of Tanganyika and Zanzibar (URMF) as it was by then called.

This last title points to what by now was uppermost in most people's minds: union with Zanzibar. This was perhaps the most important side effect of the Dar mutiny and the revolution in Zanzibar which preceded and partly triggered it. The chaotic situation so close over the water greatly worried people in Dar, once their immediate concerns over the mutiny faded. By early February, the Soviet Union, East Germany and China were all pushing hard to provide aid and advisers. Paul Bomani, the level-headed Tanganyikan Minister of Finance, described Zanzibar as 'an African Cuba'.[20] Stephen Miles pressed the British Government to recognise the new regime swiftly before Zanzibar 'went red' and to encourage badly-needed British experts to stay on. The East African leaders, concerned about the fragile security situation there, agreed that the islands should come under Tanganyika's protection. Nyerere moved quickly to offer, then negotiate, a union between the two nations and within three months of the mutiny, that had come about. The effects of this decision have been considerable and are still with Tanzania today; but that lies well outside the scope of our story.

Notes

1   PRO: DO 185/46 (163 and 166).
2   PRO: DO 185/46 (127 and 128).
3   PRO: DO 185/46 (163 and 161B).
4   PRO: DO 185/46 (166A).
5   PRO: DO 185/46 (170B).
6   PRP: DO 185/46 (169A).
7   PRO: DO 185/47 (224).
8   PRO: DO 185/46 (166A).
9   PRO: DO 185/46 (159).
10   PRO: DO 185/46 (169B).
11   PRO; DO 185/47 (186).
12   PRO; DO 185/47 (250).
13   PRO: DO 185/47 (255).
14   PRO: DO 185/47 (283).
15   PRO: DO 185/47 (247).
16   PRO: DO 185/46 (164).
17   PRO: DO 185/47 (211).
18   Later a report gained acceptance that a team from *Centaur* had sunk the arms and ammunition in the harbour (after asking the harbourmaster if he minded, perhaps!). The story was completely false: when they left, 41 Commando handed over the keys of the intact arms stores to the Nigerian force which replaced them.
19   *Tanganyika Standard*, 6 April 1964.
20   PRO: DO 185/47 (237).

16

Reflections

The mutiny and its aftermath were of lasting significance to Nyerere and the Tanganyika Government, as their subsequent actions showed. It was of less moment to the British, but they too had political and military lessons to learn. Forty years on, and with the benefit of hindsight, it is worth revisiting some of the issues.

The first question to ask is exactly why the mutiny occurred in the first place. The account above points to most of the answers. Factors that led to the mutiny include: the growing inappropriateness of using British officers to run (rather than just train) what was, with hindsight, probably bound to become a politicised army in a newly-independent state; the resulting disappointment of the *askaris*, and more particularly the NCOs and Warrant Officers, at the slow rate of Africanisation among the officers, compounded by the failure to develop a timetable for this process and explain it clearly; Kambona's lack of support for his officers, British or African, and some of his ill-judged initiatives; the Government's failure to maintain the *askaris'* real pay levels; the lesson quickly learned from the Zanzibar revolution next door that armed uprisings could easily succeed if the insurgents could at once seize the armouries; and the disbanding of the old Special Branch intelligence machine combined with a failure to devise an effective substitute. Nyerere's speech of 7 January 1964 warning against excessive speed over Africanisation, which ran directly counter to the ambitions of many as yet unqualified and inexperienced Tanganyikans, hardly helped.

Anti-colonial commentators have found it easy to argue that, by 1964, seconded British officers and NCOs should never have been present in the Tanganyika Rifles at all. Yet a transitional period in which British officers were used to train the army of a newly-independent former colony had been a feature of the way the British had dismantled their empire. This process had worked well, for example, in India, Pakistan, and Ghana. Indeed, the Commanding Officer of the Nigerian army who took over responsibility from the British marines as peacekeepers in March 1964 was a British General – an irony lost on the Tanganyikan radicals of the time. The system was thus tried and tested elsewhere and there is no reason why it should not have worked in Tanganyika.

Both sides made mistakes, however. In the first place, British colonial and military administrators, trying to train up enough Tanganyikans as senior officers, were caught short (as were Nyerere and most of his fellow nationalists) by the speed with which independence was granted – a situation mirrored, though less acutely, in the civilian administration. That was why Nyerere had asked for a limited number of British officers and NCOs to train the new army for the time being. The British Government might have recognised earlier the dangers of leaving their soldiers embedded in the command structure, and have suggested earlier the creation of a British Army training team – a solution which later became standard elsewhere. Moreover, the British would have been wise to set a limit to the time they were prepared to lend (and pay for) officers working outside their command for Tanganyika. Had it been clearly stated from the outset that the British officers and NCOs were going to stay only until the end of 1964 (which was in fact the case by January 1964) or even a year or two more, the trouble might never have arisen at all.

This problem was compounded by a difference of political perception. A smooth and rapid transfer to an all-African officer

212

corps would not in itself have guaranteed protection against mutinies or coups to remove the Government: many such events occurred in Africa and elsewhere after the colonial officers had left. The new state was bound to take steps to ensure the loyalty of the army. In developing countries still lacking effective systems of democratic checks and balances, close political integration of the defence forces into the ruling party may sometimes have been the best solution. Yet this ran counter to British political and military philosophy which insisted on the political neutrality of its armed forces. That led to misunderstandings.

Did the attitudes and actions of the seconded British officers and NCOs contribute to the malaise in the Tanganyika Rifles and the failure to foresee the mutiny? Brigadier Douglas himself was a decent man and an effective leader who was very sympathetic to the aspirations of the new Tanganyikan leaders to whom he answered, even if he found Kambona's management style hard to fathom and was sometimes suspicious of his motives. Both Marston and Mans had only just taken command of their battalions – and in the latter's case, his World War II experience with East African troops elsewhere may not have been much help to him in interpreting current post-independence realities. It has been implied[1] that the British NCOs contributed to the lack of communication between the *askaris* and the officers. But most were specialists who were training their Tanganyikan counter-parts in some particular skill. They had separate messing arrangements, but there is no evidence that they mistreated their counterparts or the *askaris* in any way.

By mid-December 1963, both Douglas and Mans realised that something was afoot. But they read the signs as perhaps signalling an attempted coup to overthrow the Government, so started to prepare against that threat. There is no evidence that any of the potential mutineers or their contacts hinted beforehand to any of the British officers that trouble was brewing – what vague warnings there were came from Kambona and his ministry. The mysterious 'warning letter' mentioned in some accounts, if it ever existed, clearly never reached Douglas or Mans. It has been argued that British intelligence should have picked up the signs that a mutiny was being planned.[2] The truth is that the British intelligence services had no interest whatsoever in the Tanganyikan forces, which in the East African context would have seemed an insignificant target. With the Cold War in full swing, it would have ranked very low on the list of priorities. There was an intelligence failure, however, on the part of the Tanganyikan Government. During the colonial period, internal intelligence had been the responsibility of the police Special Branch. But this had been disbanded and there was no effective replacement. Moreover, Douglas, although Commanding Officer of the army, had been deliberately excluded from the National Intelligence Committee in September 1963.

After the mutiny, the Chief of the UK Defence Staff, Admiral Louis Mountbatten, followed tradition in holding culpable the Commanding Officers of the two units which had mutinied – even though the Tanganyikan armed forces were not under his command. Mans and Marston had been serving the Tanganyikan Government on secondment at the time. In a short and difficult interview in Whitehall, he reprimanded Marston along the lines: 'there are no bad troops, only bad officers; you should not have been caught out by an unexpected mutiny'.[3] He may have made similar comments to Mans. The army authorities must have thought otherwise since both men were later promoted and appointed to further commands.

The British failures were thus mainly of omission rather than commission – things they might have done but did not. As for the Tanganyikan side, its Government can certainly be excused for not having put defence higher on their agenda for the first two years after independence. There were no obvious threats to internal or external security, so it was far more important to address the pressing needs of education, health and rural development. The key question is whether Nyerere's decision to allow the impetuous, inexperienced Kambona to hold simultaneously the portfolios of Foreign Affairs and Defence contributed to the confusion and resentment which had built up in the army by late 1963. There is no evidence whatever to confirm the claims made at the time that Kambona was acting under the influence of Communist countries or sought to take over power himself. On the contrary, he emerged from the mutiny with his stature enhanced, as the only Minister to have shown real leadership in a crisis. He may have made errors of judgement during those first three critical days, but had he not acted so decisively, disaster might well have followed. In the preceding year, however, he had shown only spasmodic interest in the defence aspects of his job, never really understood the problems or how to solve them and too often tended to 'fire from the hip' without thinking through the consequences. Critically, he made little effort to work constructively with the commander of the army, Douglas, to work out the best and quickest way to replace the British officers without damaging the army's effectiveness. Worse, he contributed directly to the chain of events leading to the mutiny by sending off unqualified TANU members for military training in Israel, and insisted on their being commissioned despite most of them being unsuitable. He did this behind the back of not only Douglas but also most of his ministerial colleagues.

The mutineers' conviction that they were ill-paid (a belief not necessarily shared by many civilians), was probably justified. Tanganyikan Ministers later accepted that they had made a mistake not to raise the wages of the *askaris* in line with a national settlement for civilian workers in 1962.[4]

As to the almost simultaneous outbreaks of indiscipline in the armies of Uganda and Kenya as well as Tanganyika, no evidence has come to light of any coordination between the soldiers of the three mainland armies. They all had broadly similar complaints about pay and the speed of Africanisation, but communications in East Africa were much less rapid then – these events happened three decades before the advent of the internet. Neither is there any proof that Okello, who had led the Zanzibar revolution two

215

weeks earlier, ever met the Dar mutineers. As Nyerere ruefully admitted to Miles, it was in fact his Government that had invited Okello over to the mainland for a short break, partly to help Karume consolidate his position, and partly because Okello's behaviour had become so erratic. However, the ease with which the Zanzibari revolutionaries toppled the Arab dominated Government is bound to have influenced the plotters in Tanganyika. It provided a lesson – from right next door – on how to seize power.

The next cluster of questions revolves around whether Nyerere was justified in asking for help from the British and whether the British were right to respond. On the first, two points arise. Nyerere's claim, many years later,[5] that the British had forced him to take this decision because otherwise they would have acted unilaterally, is simply not true. Most people's memories play tricks with them and this lapse is understandable since it was a choice which had been difficult for Nyerere at the time since for several reasons it did not sit easily with his reputation as an exemplary African nationalist leader. But the argument that Miles put unreasonable pressure on him does not stand up to serious scrutiny of the evidence. In any case, he had quite recently caused Miles's predecessor whom he had suspected (rightly or wrongly) of using bullying tactics, to be withdrawn, so he was well able to stand up to any undue outside influence.

Rather, on Friday 24 January, he had run out of options. By then he realised that that the mutiny was more than a mere labour dispute over pay and conditions. As Cyril Adoula, the Congolese Prime Minister – who had direct experience of this problem – commented at the time, soldiers who have once mutinied can never again be trusted.[6] Moreover, evidence had accumulated the day before that some of Nyerere's political rivals and some trade unionists were aiming to profit from his vulnerability. There was no available counterweight at home since the police were not well enough armed to take on the mutineers. Recourse to regional help was ruled out by the simultaneous troubles in the neighbouring

216

countries, UN peacekeeping forces, still in their early days, would have taken weeks or months to deploy and as Tanganyika was decidedly non-aligned in the Cold War, there was no question of turning to the Americans. That left the British as the only available source of timely support. The logic of this was rapidly accepted by most of his fellow countrymen, once it became clear that the British had no plans whatever to stay, and even the Algerian Government, one of the staunchest in the anti-colonial camp at that time, promptly congratulated Nyerere.[7]

The motives of the British government for getting involved in the crisis have been interpreted by some[8] as 'clipping Tanganyika's wings and cutting her down to size'. The contemporary records give the lie to this revisionist view of history. The first – overriding and legitimate – concern of the British Government had been to protect the British expatriates living in Zanzibar and Tanganyika. It also had responsibilities to other British passport holders, mostly Asians. The numbers were too great, and the individuals too scattered, for them all to be evacuated. The British Government therefore had a strong interest, if asked, to help restore order and thus improve security. Secondly, Britain considered it had a moral obligation to help fellow Commonwealth countries in trouble. It is easy now, in a more cynical age, to scoff at any such altruistic notion. There may indeed have been an element of wanting to see the newly-independent Commonwealth countries stable and successful because that would reflect well on the former colonial power, and a hope that the effort and financial suppport involved in bringing the country to independence would not be wasted. But a feeling of responsibility for helping East African leaders maintain stability certainly existed. Finally, at that particular moment in history, Britain happened to have (somewhat by chance) the military assets close at hand to be able to respond quickly.

Lessons can be learned from the way in which the military intervention was carried out, and also from the handling of its aftermath both by the British and also by Nyerere.

The success of the military operation with minimal casualties was a triumph of improvisation. The obvious precondition was that the intervention had been requested by the Tanganyikan Government who collaborated as much as they could (down to Kambona's preparation of the message in Swahili that Douglas was to shout to the mutineers). Detailed local knowledge was an essential ingredient: Douglas and Marciandi were able to tell the marines exactly where to land and how best to carry out their attack to surprise the mutineers. The speed of the response was possible only because the local commanders from three services were allowed to take all their own decisions and were prepared to devise a rapid action plan. Although the relevant Minister, Sandys, was directly involved in defining policy and the Chief of Defence Staff, Mountbatten, also took a close personal interest, London did not interfere in the execution of their decisions but left things entirely to the men on the ground or at sea. In this amphibious operation, the coordination between the naval forces, the marines and the RAF, although not without hiccups, worked well overall. So did the cooperation with the diplomats ashore, once contact had been established. Perhaps most important of all was that everyone involved was as disciplined in the use of arms as they would have been in the UK, and was under the closest supervision. The order that casualties must be kept to a minimum was no mere formality and absolutely no disrespect was shown to the local people, still less triumphalism.

Miles set the tone for the British handling of the aftermath to the intervention by his immediate and prescient reporting that although the Tanganyikan Government's initial response to the success of the operation was euphoric, the British side had to understand that the Tanganyikans had suffered a humiliating experience and must be treated with great sensitivity. After the initial operation, the British troops kept an extremely low profile, just staying at hand in the background in case the Tanganyikan Government needed them while it recovered from its setback. (Some of this basic understanding of local sensibilities might have stood American decision-makers in good stead in Iraq in 2003.) The British also made it clear from the outset that they were not prepared to leave peacekeepers in place for more than a brief period and were more than happy to hand over to the Nigerians. Although Sandys was initially disappointed by Nyerere's rejection of his offer of a military training package, the British Prime Minister was soon encouraging his Canadian counterpart to take on this task instead. Meanwhile, to meet Tanganyika's immediate needs, officer training in Britain at both Sandhurst and Mons, was stepped up. Respect for Tanganyika's position, and tact and flexibility in responding to its changing requests, were the key.

With his initial flight into hiding immediately after the mutiny behind him, Nyerere's handling of the post-intervention situation proved highly effective. He secured his immediate aim of quickly shoring up his political position at home, and by actively involving the OAU, deflected any possible criticism from other African leaders for having asked the former colonial power for help. Moreover, he soon secured support from a fellow African Commonwealth country to take over the security backstop role from the British. Even the longer-term problem of how to retrain the army was eventually settled. The fact that the national and international ripples from this incident had virtually disappeared six months later is a testament to the good sense of both the Tanganyikans and the British.

Notes

1 Tanzania People's Defence Force (TPDF): *The Tanganyika Rifl es Mutiny*, p. 28.
2 e.g. TPDF: ibid., p. 64.
3 Marston, Miles: interview with author, 2000.
4 It was Paul Bomani (Minister of Finance) who said this.
5 Parsons, Timothy: *The 1964 Army Mutinies and the Making of Modern East Africa.*

6   PRO: DO 185/46 (168C).
7   PRO: DO 185/46 (115A).
8   TPDF, *op. cit.* Indeed this account goes further by claiming somewhat incongruously that the British instigated the mutiny themselves!

Epilogue

This has not been a fairy story, so not everything ended happily ever after. But here is what happened to the main actors in this curious drama in which the main parts might be said to have been played by the Tanganyikan Government and by the Tanganyikan and British armed forces involved.

The history of Tanganyika/Tanzania over the last four decades can be found elsewhere. Whatever criticisms can fairly be made of the socioeconomic policies introduced by Julius Nyerere and followed by his Government until he finally stepped down after 23 years in office, Tanzania remained a beacon of stability in a continent wracked by civil wars, famine, ethnic tensions and systemic failure. It also remained resolutely non-aligned, although a member of the Commonwealth, and a leader of the struggle to end white domination in southern Africa. Nyerere's reputation as one of the rare African leaders free from any taint of personal corruption followed him to the grave. Nevertheless, as he surveyed his life and legacy the year he stepped down (one of the few African leaders to have done so voluntarily), the Dar mutiny incident must still have bothered him: for it was at an opening ceremony for an Armed Forces Conference that year (1985), that he challenged the Tanzania People's Defence Force (TPDF) to write a detailed account of what had happened, something which had until then been glossed over in Tanzanian history books.Nyerere continued to act as a respected elder statesman as late as1996 when he was the chief regional mediator in the Burundi conflict. He died in London of leukaemia in 1999, having retired from active politics in 1985.

Oscar Kambona also died in London, two years earlier than Nyerere, but in relative obscurity. He was blamed for the fiasco of the 'western plot' described below, and within a year of the mutiny had fallen out seriously with Nyerere over the Ujama policy of dispossessing small farmers in favour of collective villages. Soon he began to criticise the one-party state as leading to dictatorship. In 1967, fearing for his life, he went into exile in Britain where, lacking any financial support, he took a series of low paid jobs with London Transport while continuing to act with dignity and humour as a friend of exiles more fortunate than he. He returned to Tanzania in 1992 but found the country's progress towards true democracy disappointingly slow.

The Tanganyika Rifles was eventually transformed into the Tanzania People's Defence Force in September 1964. Within two years, it had been expanded to four battalions, one commanded by Bill Chacha, the former *effendi* whom some had suspected of having been involved in the mutiny, a charge never proved.[1] The Canadian training team worked well with their local counterparts. Captain Sam Sarakikya, who had acted so decisively in Tabora and had been rewarded with promotion from Captain to Brigadier, soon became a General. He led the army for 10 years, and later became High Commissioner to Ghana. Captain Alex Nyirenda, who had cooperated so closely with the British, was dismissed later in 1964 (perhaps partly because of his Nyasa origins, partly because he had been sharply criticised by Lieutenant Kavana – who was himself arrested later in the year). But he became a successful businessman, as did Captain Kashmiri. Sergeant Hingo Ilogi served out his sentence, and by 1987 was giving his version of the events he had initiated to the authors of the TPDF history of the mutinies.

Relations between Tanzania and Britain had their ups and downs. There were some tranquil months following the mutiny, with

222

warm thanks and compliments handed out by Nyerere and his Ministers to both 45 and 41 Royal Marine Commandos when they left Dar. But in October 1964 the British suddenly found themselves in the dock alongside the Americans, accused with having tried to overthrow the Tanzanian regime in a 'western plot'. Relations suddenly became tense. The letter that caused this flurry, which originated in Kinshasa, was soon shown to be a clumsy fake, probably planted by an East European security service at the behest of the Soviets.[2] But the damage had been done: several British farmers in the Moshi/Arusha area, for example, were summarily expelled – despite the dubious logic of this reaction. Generally, however, bilateral relations remained reasonably good over the next four decades; and the UK remained a major source of development aid for Tanzania.

HMS *Centaur* was the star of the British armed forces' response to this unusual task. She continued on her way to Singapore and an eventful commission.

Otto Steiner was promoted to Rear Admiral after leaving *Centaur*, and went to London as an Assistant Head of Defence Staff for one appointment before retirement. A passionate and skilful sailor, he was much involved in trans-globe sailing expeditions and continued to go to sea in merchant ships, as bridge watchkeeper or Master, into old age.

His able deputy, Derek Bazalgette, was also promoted. He later commanded HMS *Bulwark*, a sister ship of *Centaur*, which had by then been transformed into a commando carrier. Later he too became a Rear Admiral; and after retirement was actively involved in many charities.

Paddy Stevens brought 45 Commando back to Aden to conduct a demanding and dangerous but highly successful operation in the South Arabian Federation. Promoted to Colonel, he served in several staff appointments and at the Imperial Defence College before a final tour at NATO headquarters in Brussels. Retiring as a relatively young man (because of his early wartime promotions), he pursued a second career in the Home Civil Service, retiring as an Assistant Undersecretary. He died in 1998, aged 76.

David Hankinson, who had commanded HMS *Cambrian*, soon retired and became a successful portrait painter.

Petty Officer Don MacDonald, Cambrian's gunner, who overcame so many mishaps to keep the diversionary bombardment going, had interesting jobs in the navy for the next nine years (including a spell in Libya), before retiring to a second career in the design of weapons control systems.

Finally, Stephen Miles, who was awarded a CMG for his role in the mutiny crisis, went on to serve in Ghana, St Louis (USA), Calcutta and then in both Zambia and Bangladesh as full High Commissioner. Retiring in 1980, he has since been a local councillor in Surrey.

Colito Barracks still stands; and remains one of the battalion headquarters of the TPDF. But it has been renamed Lugalo Barracks after an African hero from a battle against the Germans near Iringa. Dar es Salaam has grown hugely in size since those days and almost laps at the boundary fence of the barracks.

Notes

1   PRO: DO 185/50.
2   PRO: DO 185/8 (file: alleged western plot)

Appendix 1: Minutes of Preparatory Meeting in HMS Centaur

45 Commando, Royal Marines
HMS CENTAUR
at Sea
January, 1964

ASSAULT LANDING ORGANISATION AND PROCEDURE

The process outlined below is designed to ensure that the commando is landed so that it can carry out its operational role. It is based where possible on the procedure adopted by HMS ALBION. The process can be subdivided into the following stages:

a. Planning
b. Orders
c. Documentation
d. Assault organisation

a) *Planning*
To facilitate preliminary planning the following teams have been set up:

Team	Ship's Staff	Commando Staff	RAF
a. Intelligence	Lt Cdr Ops 815 Sq. (Snr Observer) Maj ANDERSON (CBGLO)	Intelligence	
b. Assault	Lt Cdr Ops CO 815 Sq Lt Cdr (F) Flight Deck Off Dep. Supply Off SATCO	2I/C OCR HQ Coy QM	CO 26 Sq
c. Communications	SCO	Signals Officer	

1 The outline plan will be drawn up as a result of a conference between the Captain of the Ship and the CO 45 Commando, advised by the Commander (Air) and where necessary members of the above planning teams. The detailed plan will then be worked out in conference by the planning team as a result of which heads of departments will have sufficient knowledge to be able to produce their own plans.

b) *Orders*
The military, ship and air departments will issue their own separate Orders. Representatives of the Commando should attend Ship's and Air Department's briefings who in turn should attend the Commando's Orders group.

c) *Documentation*
In order to ensure that the maximum and most efficient use is made of the available transport lift the following documents will be produced.

226

a. *Helicopter availability and outline landing table*

b. *White card.* Produced by individual Commando Sub unit Commanders as a result of the Commando O Gp from the information contained in 'a' above on the basis of one per aircraft lift. The Card contains all the information regarding the personnel and/or stores to be carried in the helicopter to enable a state to be maintained of what has gone ashore.

c. *Helicopter detailed landing table (Stickorbat)* Produced by Commando Adjutant in concert with Lt Cdr Ops from 'a' above and the white cards handed in by sub unit commanders. It contains all the information relevant to the landing. On completion the White Cards are returned to sub unit commanders for retention by stick leaders.

d. *Complan.* Produced by ship's SCO and the Commando Sigs Officer – containing all the Signals arrangements for the operation.

2 *Landing procedure*

Personnel. At an appropriate time before F hr (the time the first aircraft takes off) the first sticks will be called forward from the assault stations (C Hangar) by Lt Cdr (F) to the after lift. At the top of the lift they will be guided by Deck Marshalls (IC Lt Cdr Burton, Lt George, and Lt Moverley) to the helicopter waiting spots. The two Belvedere spots will be on the after end of the flight deck and the two for the Wessex at the forward end. Stick leaders will hand their white cards to the Marshalls immediately prior to emplaning who will in turn hand them into Flying Control on take off where the Commando Instructor Officer will keep a tally of the landing programme.

3 *Stores.* Company and Department F and A Ech stores dumps will be positioned on the flight deck on D-1 in accordance with priorities in the helicopter detailed landing table. Stores sticks will be in units of 1000lb. The remainder of the stores will be centralised under the Commando QM and the Coy CQMs and phased ashore in accordance with the priorities in the DETAILED

227

LANDING Table or such other means as may be available. The Assault supply officer will coordinate the logistic build up as required by the Military Force Commander.

d) *Assault organisation.* Control of the unit landing and subsequent build up will be exercised from the Ops Room through flying control. The following agencies will operate.

	Ship	*Unit*
a. Ops room	Lt Cdr Ops (2) Assault Ops Off (Maj Anderson)	A/Adj
b. Flying control	Lt Cdr (F)	2IC
c. Aircraft control room	ACRO (Lt Martlew)	Assault Supply Off (ASO) (2/Lt Aird)
d. Assault Stas/Lift Waiting Spots	Deck Marshallers IC FDO (Lt Cdr Burton) Lts Moverley, George	CSM HQ Coy (in hangar)

4 *HCT.* A helicopter control team will be flown ashore with the leading wave and will establish itself at one of the LS with the HLSCT (see para 5) to control and direct subsequent helicopter movement. It will comprise Lt Cdr Holt and S/Lt Hawsley who will be equipped with one SRA43 supplied by 45 Commando.

5 *HLSCT.* The Commando is responsible for providing a helicopter landing site control team which will land with the first company. It will mark out the LS, ensure its security and will control the deplaning and dispersal of troops and stores as they are landed.

6 *HLO*. Should helicopters be required to operate ashore on TACON under the Military Force Commander, Lieut MacGregor (815 Sq) will act as the helicopter liaison officer.

7 *Preparations for landing.* The following preparations will be made on D-1.

a. Rehearsal of the calling forward of sticks from C hangar to waiting spots on the flight deck.
b. Bringing up all operational ammunition from magazine issuing what each man in the unit should carry ashore and centralise the balance in the view to its subsequent movement ashore (RSM, Gunnery Off, FDO, ASO).
c. Filling jerricans (unit QM).
d. Prepositioning stick loads of stores on the flight deck (FDO, unit QM, ASO).

Appendix 2: Agreement on the Use of British Forces

28 January 1964

1 The general role of British forces in Tanganyika: The British forces had been called in by the Tanganyika Government for the purpose of restoring law and order. Now that the mutiny had been crushed, the question of their future role needed to be settled.

IT WAS AGREED that the general role of British troops in Tanganyika should be to come to the aid of the police force only after the police force was found unable to cope with any situation in which security was endangered.

2 The likely duration of the task for the British forces: IT WAS AGREED that the precise duration of the task for the British forces could not be determined at this stage. For administrative purposes, the British authorities could proceed safely on the assumption that the Tanganyikan Government would require the presence of British troops for more than a month.

3 Patrol duties: IT WAS AGREED that British troops would continue on patrol duties until further notice; but patrols should take place only in the early morning, in the evening and at night.

4 Disposition of British troops: IT WAS AGREED that the British troops should be allowed to use the National Stadium as their base for the present. All arms and ammunition from Colito, Tabora and Nachingwea should be centralised there until further notice, and kept under guard of British troops. A military guard should be posted at the Government Stores at Pugu Road.

5 Transport: IT WAS AGREED that British troops should continue to use Tanganyika Rifles transport for the time being until recruitment for the new army starts, when new arrangements for transport will be made with the Public Works Division.

6 Intelligence: IT WAS AGREED that the closest liaison between the Tanganyika Intelligence authorities and the British forces was essential. The Director of Intelligence should be asked to maintain regular and close contacts with the Commander of the British Forces.

7 Military Adviser: the Tanganyika Government has asked the British Government to retain Brigadier Douglas as Military Adviser to the Tanganyika Government.

Appendix 3: President Nyerere's Speeches

Speech of 23 January 1964

The President seeks to re-establish confidence. This was the TIS's translation of the speech, which was made in Swahili.

On Monday twentieth we learned a lesson. This lesson was that the end does not justify the means. A perfectly reasonable objective can be marred by the method used to achieve it. We learned in particular that people whose responsibility it is to look after lives should not themselves engage in activities which might endanger lives.

The soldiers of the Tanganyika Rifles had grievances. Early on Monday morning those of the 1st Battalion staged a protest, or a revolt. By about midday this revolt was over and the soldiers had returned to their barracks. But the harm had been done. Some civilians began looting shops. Then we asked the soldiers to come back and help to maintain law and order; this both the soldiers and the police did. And it was while they were doing their duty of maintaining law and order that lives were lost.

It would be foolish to pretend that these events are unimportant, or that they have not damaged Tanganyika's reputation overseas. Because in addition to the incidents themselves, the rumours which were spread have raised all sorts of doubts about the stability of our country and our Government.

We recognise that some of these problems were exacerbated by the Government's failure to keep the people fully informed from hour to hour. This was a mistake which I fully acknowledge. But it will be realised that it in conditions like those it is not always possible to answer immediately all the questions which might occur to fearful minds; and it is never possible for the Government to stop all rumours – only the people themselves can do that.

The important thing now is that we should get on with the big job we have to do. We have to restore confidence in our country, and win back the reputation we had as a peaceful and mature country. This is especially urgent because the Five Year Development Plan must come into operation before the end of this year; it is an ambitious Plan which calls for the whole-hearted efforts from all Tanganyikans, and also for much financial and technical help from outside. We must make this Plan a success, but our task is more difficult now. It will take months and even years to erase from the mind of the world what they heard about the events of this week. But I know that we can do it, and I am confident that every Tanganyikan – whether he is in the army, the police, or is a civilian – will play his or her part. And that our reputation as a friendly, peaceful, country will be restored by our united efforts.

Speech of 25 January 1964

Speaking at 4 p.m. on the day the British landed, Nyerere seeks to explain why the Tanganyikan Government had to call for help.

My fellow countrymen, I wish to speak to all of you. As I said last Tuesday there was trouble in Dar es Salaam on Monday which arose out of some grievances of the 1st Battalion of the Tanganyikan Rifles. We promised the army that the Government would consider their justified claims and the troops appeared to be satisfied. On the same day they went back to their barracks. But they had already committed a most serious offence. The offence of mutiny. After this grave offence had been committed by our troops a number of civilians committed offences such as looting, and in the work of restoring order after this some lives were lost. I had hoped that after this most of the soldiers and certainly their leaders would regret the error of their ways. I have no doubt that many of the soldiers did repent and no doubt some of their leaders did the same, but some of them would not admit that they had done anything wrong, and when we asked the leaders to ask their soldiers not to wear battledress but to go back to ceremonial uniform some of the leaders of the mutiny refused. Nothing was more evident than that discipline was vanishing among our troops and indiscipline mounting up.

No popular Government can tolerate an army which disobeys its orders. An army which does not obey the laws and orders of the people's Government is not an Army of that country and it is a danger to its own nation. It was therefore necessary to consider what to do. Finally I decided that there was only one thing which could be done and that was to disarm all the troops and punish the ringleaders most severely. But obviously it is not easy to disarm an army especially when it is already intoxicated with the poison of disloyalty and disobedience. The only force which we could deploy in this task of disarming the army was the Field Force of the police. But this force was already depleted because we had previously sent some of them to Zanzibar to help maintain law and order there. I had therefore no alternative but to ask for help. The countries which would have been able to help us quickly are our neighbours, Kenya and Uganda. But as you may already have heard they are having this problem with their own military forces. Therefore yesterday evening I decided to ask Britain for help. Fortunately Britain agreed. This morning therefore the 1st Battalion of the Tanganyika Rifles here in Dar es Salaam were disarmed in their barracks. Those troops in the city handed over their arms to the police force. It is possible that there are some soldiers who have not yet handed in their arms. If so they

235

must go at once to the nearest police station and give up their weapons.

All is now calm and no one should be frightened by the British troops in the city or the planes and helicopters flying around.

Clearly it is essential that we should build up the Republic's army once again. I call upon all members of the TANU Youth League wherever they are to go to the local TANU office and enrol themselves. From this group we shall try to build a nucleus of the new army of the Republic of Tanganyika.

I am told that already there is foolish talk that the British have come back to rule Tanganyika again. This is rubbish. I asked the British Government to help us in the same way as I would have asked our neighbours to help us if this had been possible. Any independent country is able to ask for the help of another independent country. Asking for help in this way is not something to be proud of. I do not want any person to think that I was happy in making this request. This whole week has been a week of most grievous shame for our nation. But those who brought this shame upon us are those who tried to intimidate our nation at the point of a gun.

The torch of freedom will still burn on the top of Mount Kilimanjaro.

Uhuru na Amani.

Bibliography, Unpublished and Oral Sources

UK Public Records

Records at the Public Records Office, National Archives, Kew, London
The many relevant contemporary files from the British High Commission (BHC) in Dar es Salaam, the CRO in London, and other government departments, include:

British High Commission, Dar es Salaam
DO 185/4. Tanganyika: economic affairs generally.
DO 185/8. Alleged 'western plot' against Tanzania of October 1964.
DO 185/42. Integration, training and deployment of the TPDF.
DO 185/45. Possible unification of defence and external affairs between Tanganyika and Uganda.
DO 185/46 and 47. Mutiny of the Tanganyika Rifles, part 1 and 2.
DO 185/48. Expansion policy for Tanganyika military forces, and gift of military equipment by Algeria.
DO 185/49. Cooperation between Kenya, Uganda, and Tanganyika on security and intelligence matters.
DO 185/50. Lt. William Chacha's possible involvement in the mutiny.

DO 185/51. Internal security and the possibility of military intervention in Zanzibar.

DO 185/65. Union of Tanganyika and Zanzibar.

British High Commission, Nairobi
DO 226/10. The Tanganyika Mutiny.

CRO, East African Department files (after Independence)
DO 213/1 and 2. British Forces in East Africa including seconded personnel.

DO 213/3–5. Disposal of East African military assets.

DO 213/13 and 14. Tanganyika armed forces.

DO 213/15. Movement of troops.

DO 213/17. Relations between British High Commission and freedom movements.

DO 213/40. Expulsions from Tanzania.

DO 213/238. *History of Tanganyika* by Countess Listowel.

MoD, War Office and Admiralty files
ADM 1/29063. Post-action reports of the Commanding Officers of HMS *Centaur*, *Rhyl*, *Cambrian*, and *Owen*; and 45 Royal Marine Commando (enclosures to Flag Officer Middle East's letter of 29 Feb 1964).

ADM 53/161436. Ship's log January, HMS *Centaur*.

ADM 202/509. 45 Commando internal security operations in Tanganyika after mutiny.

ADM 202/510. Succession to 41 Commando after mutiny.

Cabinet Office
PREM 11/4082. Visit of Milton Obote and Rashid Kawawa to UK (January 1963).

PREM 11/5136. Main file of Prime Minister's office covering mutiny.

Treasury:
T 213/1018. Secondment of UK service personnel to Tanganyika: policy (1963–4).
T 317/583. Tanganyika: cost of military forces after Independence.

Foreign Office
FO 371/176569. Military Assistance to Tanganyika, 1964.

Miscellaneous
45 Commando, Royal Marines. *Preliminary Report on Operations in Tanganyika*, dated 8 February 1964. (Draft supplied by David Smith, 2 i/c 45 Commando.)
HMS *Centaur. The Fourth Commission of HMS Centaur.* Ship's company publication, 1965.
Fleet Air Arm. Royal Navy Air Logs 892 and 815 Squadrons, and 849B flight: reports for January 1964. Fleet Air Arm Museum, Yeovilton.
Admiralty Chart 674. *Approaches to Dar es Salaam*, dated 4 March 1954, with some later corrections.

Private Papers, Personal Correspondence and Interviews with People Playing Some Role in These Events

Private collections of papers
The authors have had access to collections of private papers belonging to the following (titles in brackets indicate the position of the person at the time of the mutiny):

Callaghan, Michael (Company Commander, 1st Battalion. Tanganyika Rifles), including manuscript personal account of events, c.1999.
Douglas, Patrick (Commander, Tanganyika Defence Force), including unpublished account of the mutiny, c. 1980.
Laurence, Anthony. (Signal Communications Officer, HMS *Centaur*). Diaries and letters.

Mans, Rowley. (Commanding Officer 1st Battalion Tanganyika Rifles). *Summary of Events in Tanganyika*, 4 March 1964. Royal Marines Museum, Southsea, UK.

Marciandi, Brian (Staff Officer, Tanganyika Defence Force), including notes made during the mutiny, and later notes for lecture to Joint Service Staff College, 1965–6.

Miles, Stephen and Joy, including manuscript notes during the mutiny and the original of Vice President Kawawa's crucial letter of 25 January 1964.

Personal correspondence and/or interviews

Among others, the authors corresponded with or interviewed:

Ainley, John (Regional Agricultural Officer)

Ames, Peter (HMS *Centaur*)

Banks, Mike (Commanding Officer, X Company, 45 Commando)

Baxter, Colin (Technical Instructor, Dar)

Bazalgette, Derek (Commander, HMS *Centaur*)

Binley, Tom (X Company, 45 Commando)

Blake, Ian (Commanding Officer, 892 Squadron, HMS *Centaur*)

Bourn, James (First Secretary, British High Commission, Dar es Salaam)

Brettell, Keith (X Company, 45 Commando)

Bridgman, John (insurance company manager, Dar es Salaam)

Brind, Roger (Adjutant 45 Commando)

Brooke, Michael (Commander, Ferret armoured car detachment 16/5th Lancers)

Brown, Roland (Attorney General, Tanganyika)

Brumage, Bill (Director British-American Tobacco, Dar)

Bullivant, Robert (Communications Officer, British High Commission, Dar)

Burns, William (marine, 45 Commando)

Callaghan, Michael (see above)

Carter, Nick (Commanding Officer, 41 Commando)

Clifford, Richard (lived in Dar es Salaam as a civilian 1953–63)

Colley, William (Post and Telegraph Engineer)

Cook, J.L. (driver, 45 Commando)

Coxon, Arthur (First Lieutenant, HMS *Centaur*).

Cunningham, John (Second Navigation Officer, HMS *Centaur*).

Dingle, Tony (First Secretary, Australian High Commission, Dar es Salaam)

Dinwiddy, Bruce (British High Commissioner, Tanzania, 2002–3)

Drury, Tony (Seaman, HMS *Centaur*)

Ealand, Tim (Commanding Officer Training Wing, 1st Battalion Tanganyika Rifles)

Eberlie, Richard (former Civil Servant, Tanganyika)

Freeman, Mike (Communications Officer, HMS *Centaur*, 3rd commission 1962–3)

Gabb, Geoffrey (Ministry of Agriculture)

Goddard, Ted (45 Commando, Aden rear link)

Gurdon, Alan (King's African Rifles at Independence)

Hankinson, David (Commanding Officer, HMS *Cambrian*)

Hannington, Richard (Commander, Police Field Force)

Hazeldine, Tony (Intelligence Officer, 45 Commando RM)

Heathcote, Willie (Operations Officer, HMS *Centaur*)

Holt, G.J. (Senior Air Traffic Control Officer, HMS *Centaur*)

Howgill, Pat (Signal Officer, 45 Commando)

Kettle, Randal (Commander Air, HMS *Centaur*)

Lamond, Joe (Adjutant, 1st Battalion Tanganyika Rifles)

Laurie, Douglas (NCO in the 6th KAR/1stTanganyika Rifles before mutiny)

Lavery, Ray (Cook, 45 Commando)

LeMesurier, Charles (Navigation Officer, HMS *Centaur*)

Lethbridge, Christopher (CDC Official in Dar es Salaam)

Macdonald, Don (Gunnery Instructor, HMS *Cambrian*)

Mans, Rowley (see above)

Marciandi, Brian (see above)

Marston, Miles and Mrs (Commanding Officer, 2nd Battalion, Tanganyika Rifles)

Miles, Stephen and Joy (see above)

Parton, Barry (Brooke Bond representative in Tanganyika)
Paul, A.C. (X company, 45 Commando)
Pennington, Ivor (Y company, 45 Commando)
Rollinson, John (Tanganyikan Civil Service)
Russell, Gillean (Physiotherapist, Dar es Salaam)
Sale, Ewan (Assistant Adjutant, 45 Commando)
Skinner, Joy (living in Dar, wife of journalist)
Sloan, Gil (Petty Officer Electrical (Air), HMS *Centaur*)
Smith, David (2 i/c, 45 Commando)
Sparrow, Denis (Z company, 45 Commando)
Steiner, Anthony and Mrs Eleanor (son and second wife of Captain Steiner)
Tice, Trevor (British-American Tobacco, Dar es Salaam)
Unwin, Tom (Tanganyikan Civil Service)
Weall, Stephen (Troop Commander, 45 Commando)
White, Matthew (Troop Commander, 41 Commando)

Published Secondary Sources Include

Listowel, Judith: *The Making of Tanganyika* (Chatto and Windus, London, 1965).
McCart, Neil: *HMS* Centaur, *1943–72* (Fan Publications, Cheltenham, 1997).
Nye, Joseph S.: *Pan-Africanism and East African Integration.* (Harvard University Press, Cambridge, MA, 1965).
Nestor N. Luanda, E. Mwanjabala, and Mwesiga Baregu. Tanzania People's Defence Force: *Tanganyika Rifl es Mutiny January 1964* (Dar es Salaam University Press, Dar es Salaam 1993).
Parsons, Timothy H.: *The 1964 Army Mutinies and the Making of Modern East Africa* (Greenwood publishers, USA, 2003).
Petterson, Don: *Revolution in Zanzibar: An American's Cold War Tale* (Westview Press, Boulder, CO, 2002).
Stevens, T.M.P.: 'A Joint Operation in Tanganyika', article in the

Journal of the Royal United Service Institute (RUSI) on the
mutiny, June 1964 – see doc 275 in DO 213/46.
Young, David: *Four Five – the story of 45 Commando, Royal
Marines* (Leo Cooper, London, 1972).

246

248

Lightning Source UK Ltd.
Milton Keynes UK
UKOW050638091211

183453UK00003B/15/P